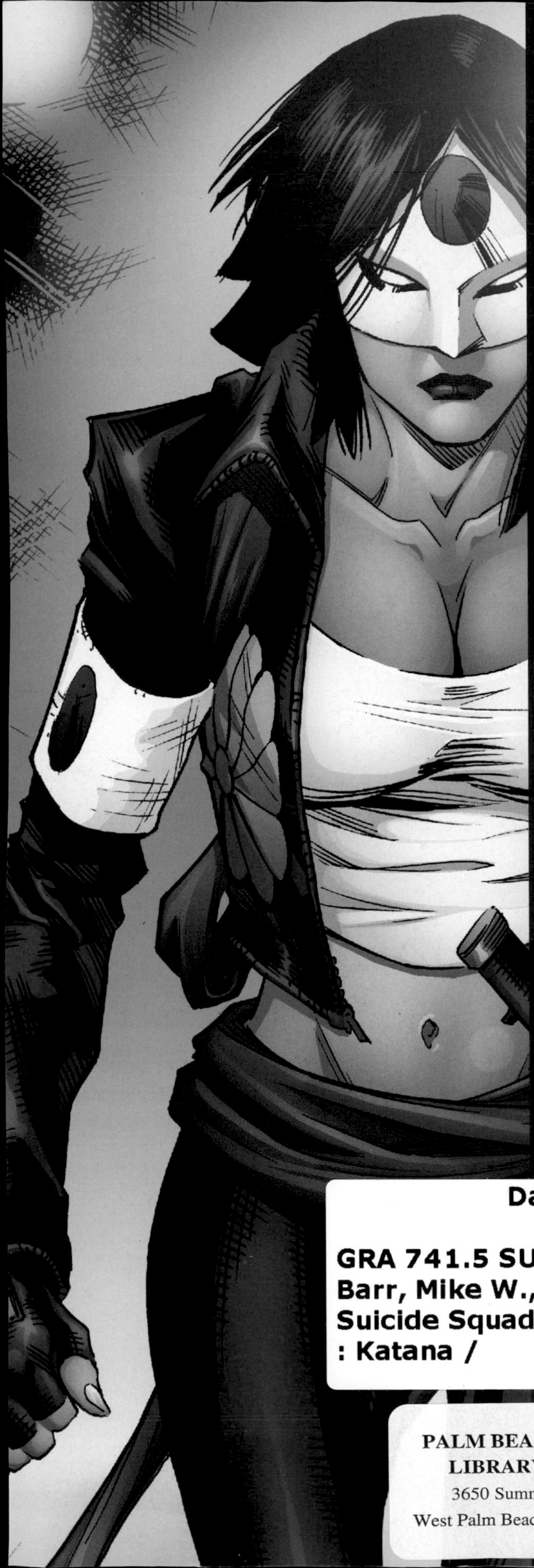

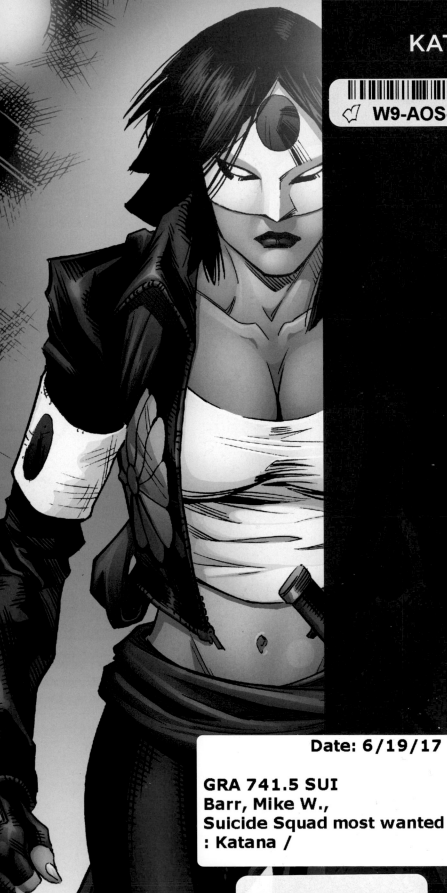

KATANA

SUICIDE SQUAD MOST WANTED

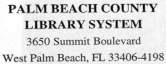

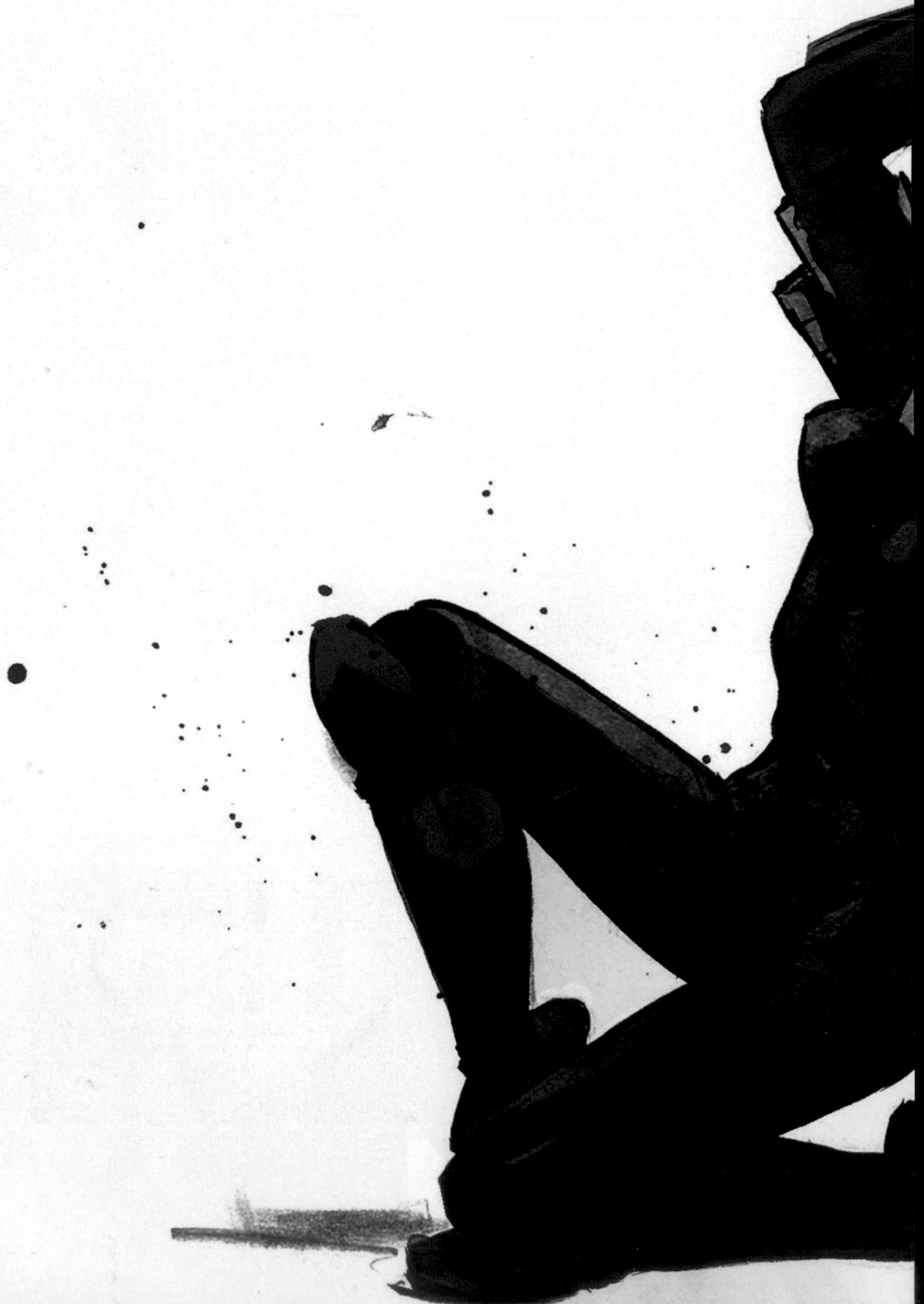

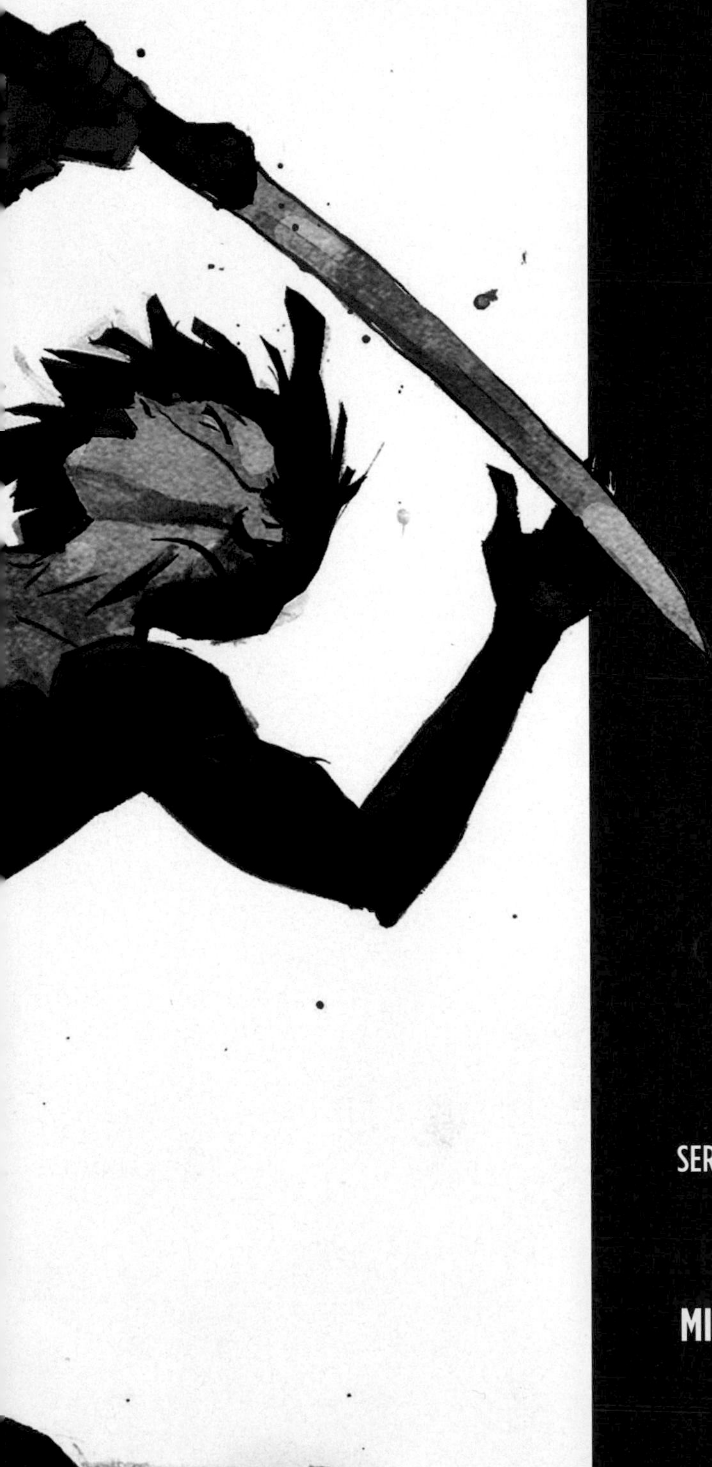

SUICIDE SQUAD MOST WANTED

KATANA

WRITTEN BY
MIKE W. BARR

ART BY
DIOGENES NEVES

INKS BY
RUY JOSÉ
JUAN ALBARRAN

ADDITIONAL PENCILS & INKS BY
RONAN CLIQUET

COLOR BY
CARRIE STRACHAN
WENDY BROOME

LETTERS BY
SAIDA TEMOFONTE

SERIES & COLLECTION COVER ART BY
CARY NORD

KATANA CREATED BY
MIKE W. BARR & JIM APARO

TO JIM APARO,
WHO FIRST DREW THE SWORD.
— MWB

KRISTY QUINN Editor - Original Series
JESSICA CHEN Associate Editor - Original Series
JEB WOODARD Group Editor - Collected Editions
PAUL SANTOS Editor - Collected Edition
STEVE COOK Design Director - Books
DAMIAN RYLAND Publication Design

BOB HARRAS Senior VP - Editor-in-Chief, DC Comics

DIANE NELSON President
DAN DIDIO and JIM LEE Co-Publishers
GEOFF JOHNS Chief Creative Officer
AMIT DESAI Senior VP - Marketing & Global Franchise Management
NAIRI GARDINER Senior VP - Finance
SAM ADES VP - Digital Marketing
BOBBIE CHASE VP - Talent Development
MARK CHIARELLO Senior VP - Art, Design & Collected Editions
JOHN CUNNINGHAM VP - Content Strategy
ANNE DEPIES VP - Strategy Planning & Reporting
DON FALLETTI VP - Manufacturing Operations
LAWRENCE GANEM VP - Editorial Administration & Talent Relations
ALISON GILL Senior VP - Manufacturing & Operations
HANK KANALZ Senior VP - Editorial Strategy & Administration
JAY KOGAN VP - Legal Affairs
DEREK MADDALENA Senior VP - Sales & Business Development
JACK MAHAN VP - Business Affairs
DAN MIRON VP - Sales Planning & Trade Development
NICK NAPOLITANO VP - Manufacturing Administration
CAROL ROEDER VP - Marketing
EDDIE SCANNELL VP - Mass Account & Digital Sales
COURTNEY SIMMONS Senior VP - Publicity & Communications
JIM (SKI) SOKOLOWSKI VP - Comic Book Specialty & Newsstand Sales
SANDY YI Senior VP - Global Franchise Management

SUICIDE SQUAD MOST WANTED: KATANA

DC Comics, 2900 West Alameda Ave., Burbank, CA 91505
Printed by RR Donnelley, Salem, VA, USA. 8/12/16. First Printing.
ISBN: 978-1-4012-6464-2

Library of Congress Cataloging-in-Publication Data is available.

PEFC Certified
Printed on paper from sustainably managed forests and controlled sources
PEFC
PEFC/29-31-75
www.pefc.org

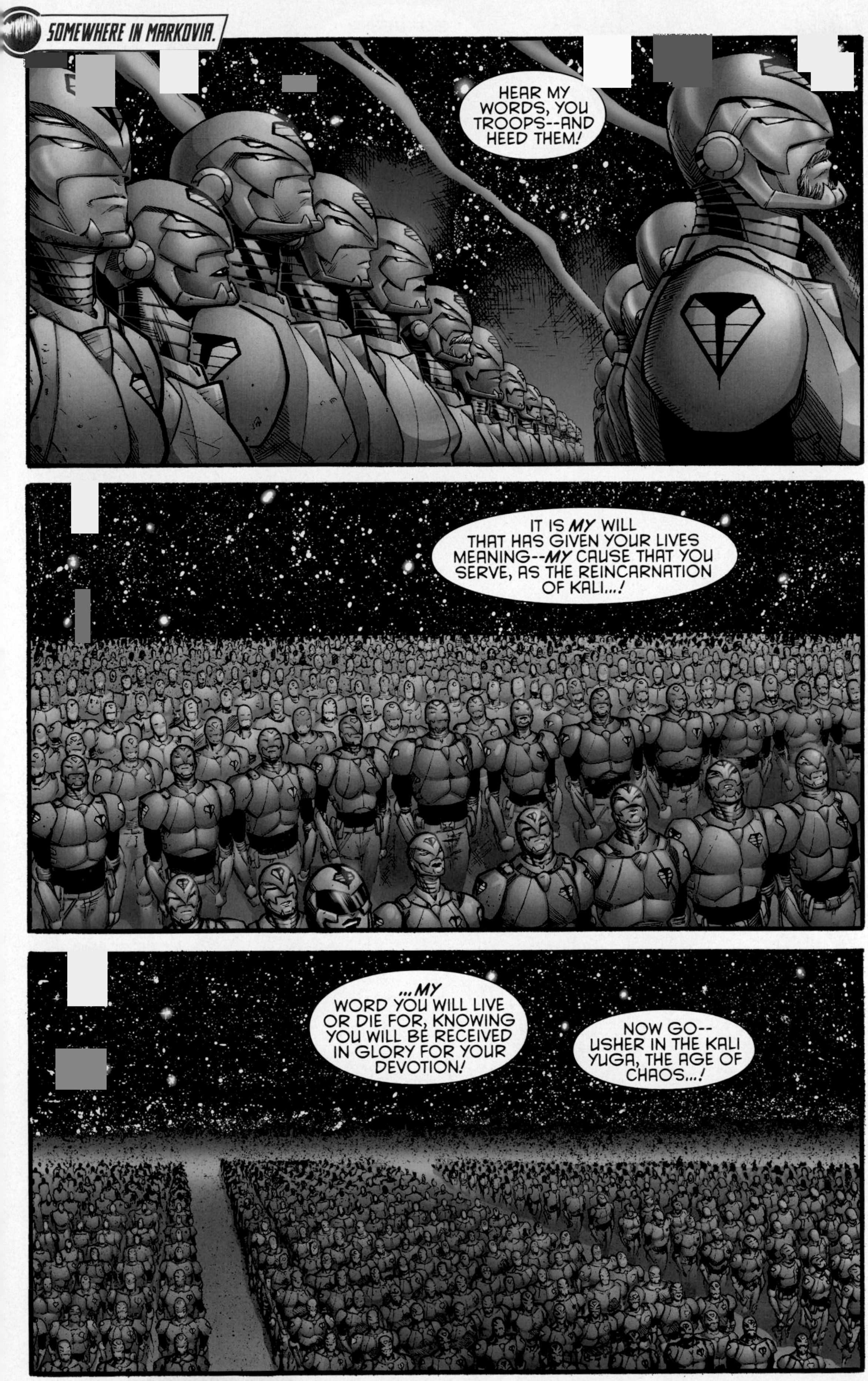
SOMEWHERE IN MARKOVIA.
HEAR MY WORDS, YOU TROOPS--AND HEED THEM!
IT IS MY WILL THAT HAS GIVEN YOUR LIVES MEANING--MY CAUSE THAT YOU SERVE, AS THE REINCARNATION OF KALI...!
...MY WORD YOU WILL LIVE OR DIE FOR, KNOWING YOU WILL BE RECEIVED IN GLORY FOR YOUR DEVOTION!
NOW GO-- USHER IN THE KALI YUGA, THE AGE OF CHAOS...!

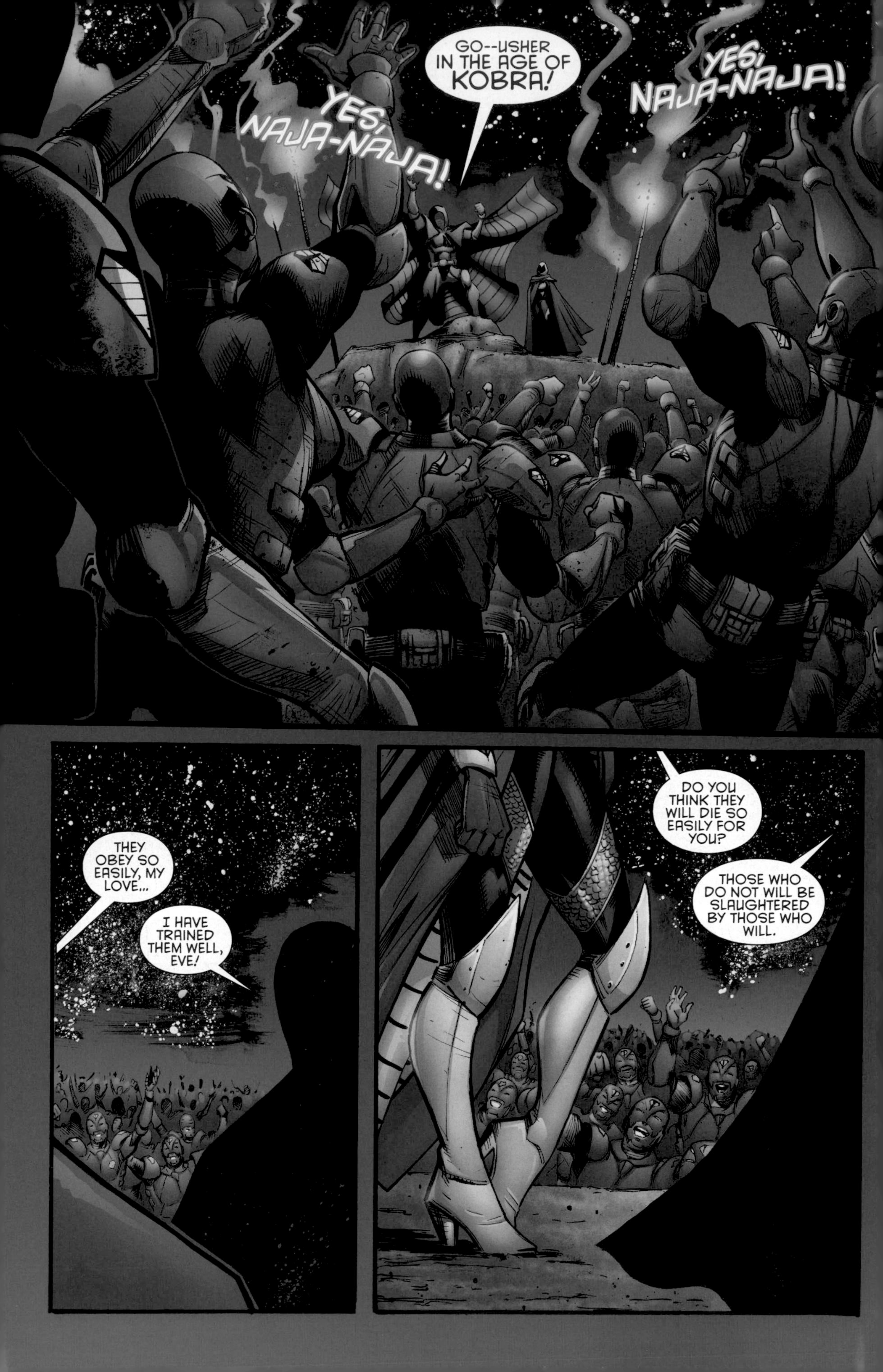
GO--USHER IN THE AGE OF KOBRA!
YES, NAJA-NAJA!
YES, NAJA-NAJA!
THEY OBEY SO EASILY, MY LOVE...
I HAVE TRAINED THEM WELL, EVE!
DO YOU THINK THEY WILL DIE SO EASILY FOR YOU?
THOSE WHO DO NOT WILL BE SLAUGHTERED BY THOSE WHO WILL.

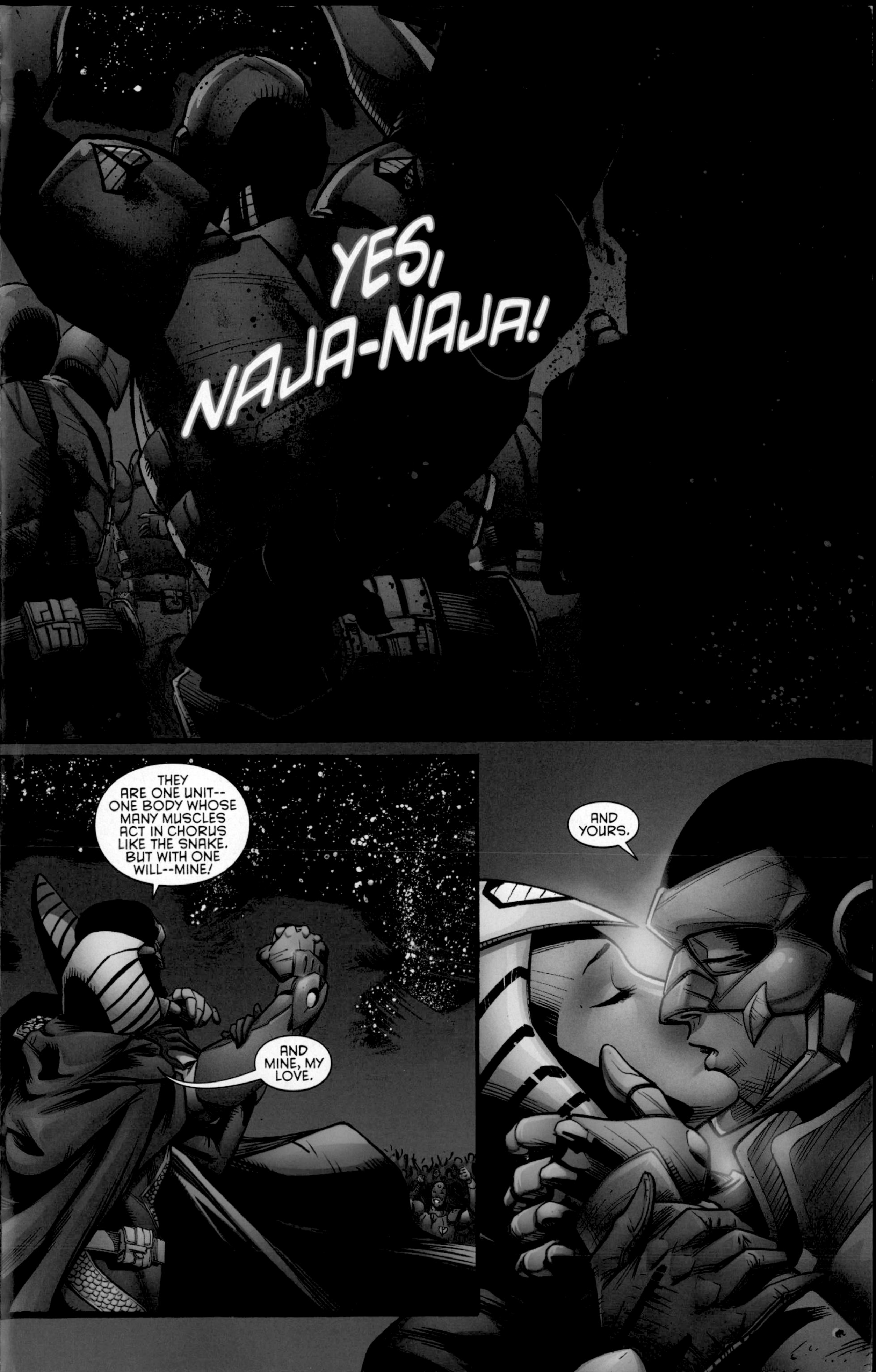
YES, NAJA-NAJA!
THEY ARE ONE UNIT-- ONE BODY WHOSE MANY MUSCLES ACT IN CHORUS LIKE THE SNAKE. BUT WITH ONE WILL--MINE!
AND MINE, MY LOVE.
AND YOURS.

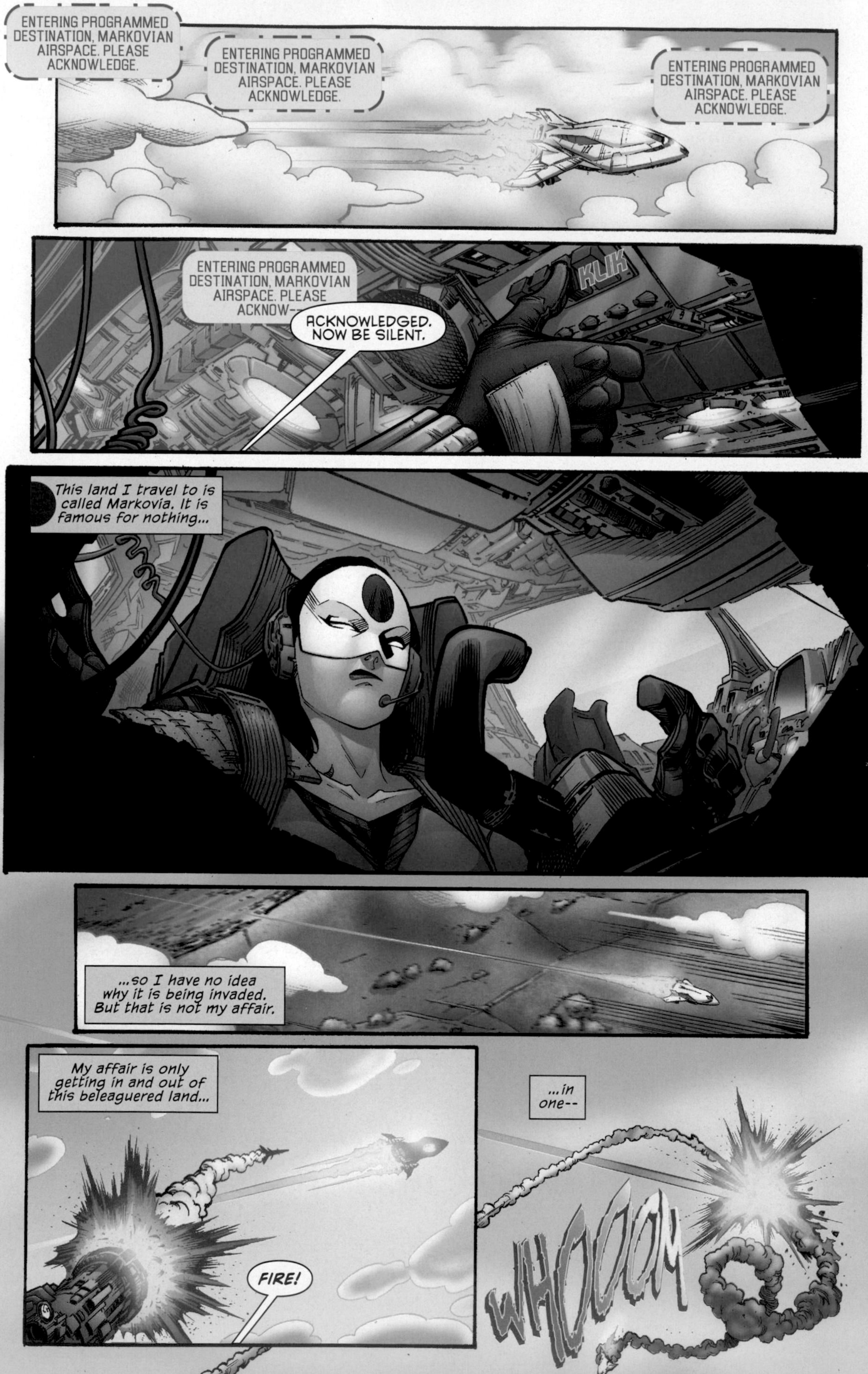
ENTERING PROGRAMMED DESTINATION, MARKOVIAN AIRSPACE. PLEASE ACKNOWLEDGE.
ENTERING PROGRAMMED DESTINATION, MARKOVIAN AIRSPACE. PLEASE ACKNOWLEDGE.
ENTERING PROGRAMMED DESTINATION, MARKOVIAN AIRSPACE. PLEASE ACKNOWLEDGE.
ENTERING PROGRAMMED DESTINATION, MARKOVIAN AIRSPACE. PLEASE ACKNOW--
KLIK
ACKNOWLEDGED. NOW BE SILENT.
This land I travel to is called Markovia. It is famous for nothing...
...so I have no idea why it is being invaded. But that is not my affair.
My affair is only getting in and out of this beleaguered land...
FIRE!
...in one--
WHOOOM

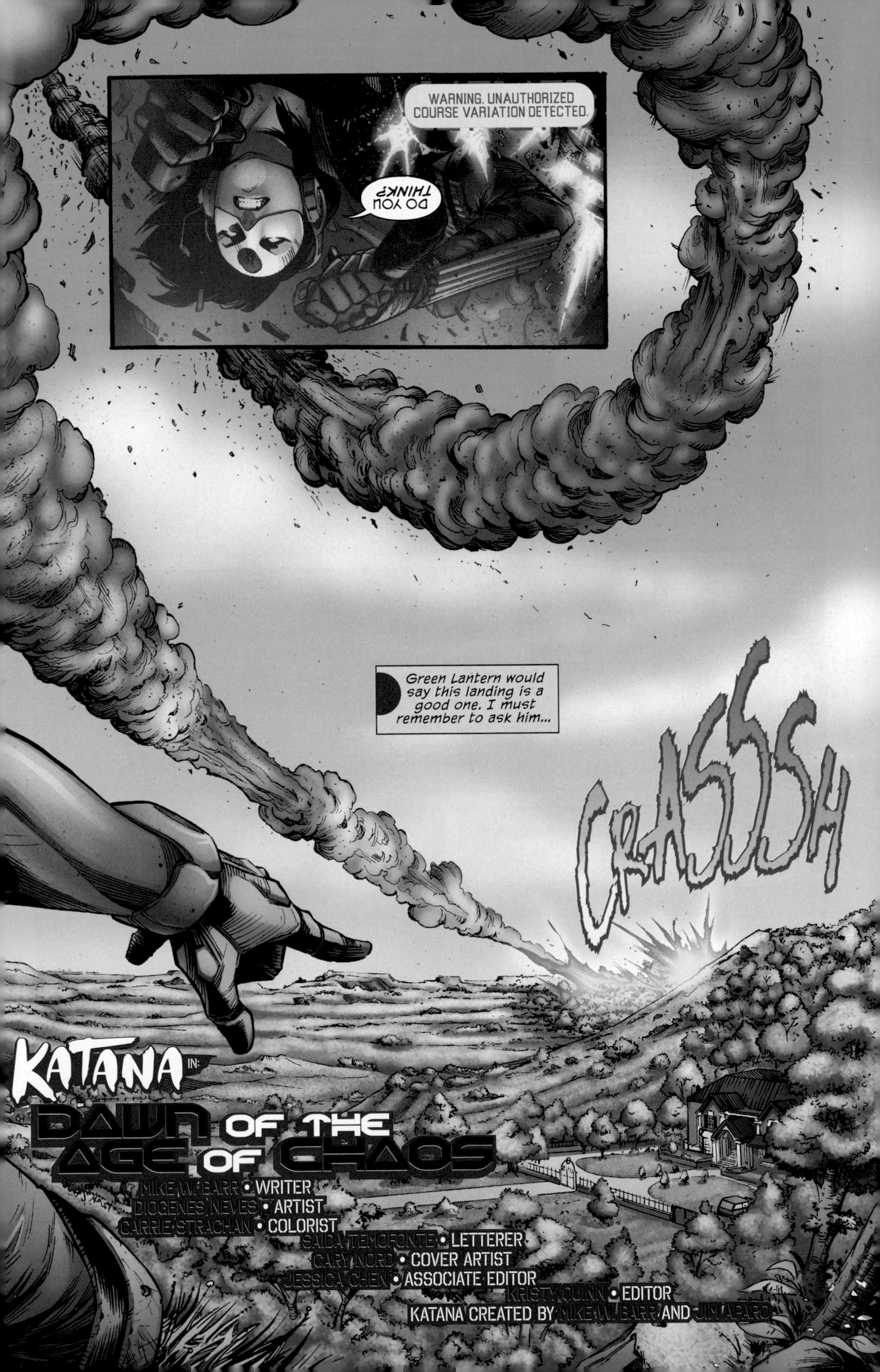
WARNING. UNAUTHORIZED COURSE VARIATION DETECTED.
DO YOU THINK?
Green Lantern would say this landing is a good one. I must remember to ask him...
CRASSSH
KATANA IN:
DAWN OF THE AGE OF CHAOS
MIKE W. BARR • WRITER
DIOGENES NEVES • ARTIST
CARRIE STRACHAN • COLORIST
SAIDA TEMOFONTE • LETTERER
CARY NORD • COVER ARTIST
JESSICA CHEN • ASSOCIATE EDITOR
KRISTY QUINN • EDITOR
KATANA CREATED BY MIKE W. BARR AND JIM APARO

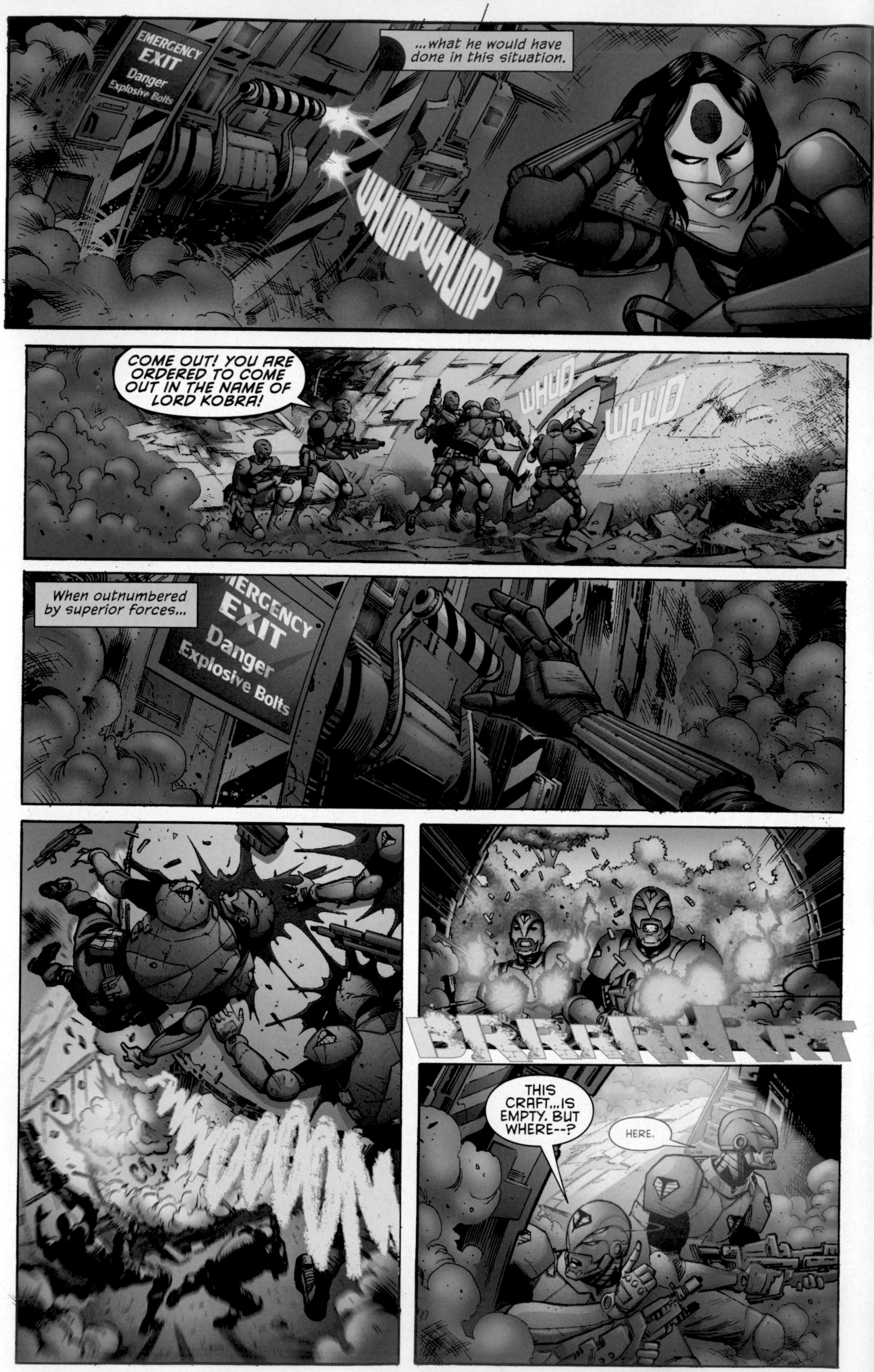

...what he would have done in this situation.
EMERGENCY EXIT
Danger
Explosive Bolts
WHUMPWHUMP
COME OUT! YOU ARE ORDERED TO COME OUT IN THE NAME OF LORD KOBRA!
WHUD
WHUD
When outnumbered by superior forces...
EMERGENCY EXIT
Danger
Explosive Bolts
THIS CRAFT...IS EMPTY. BUT WHERE--?
HERE.

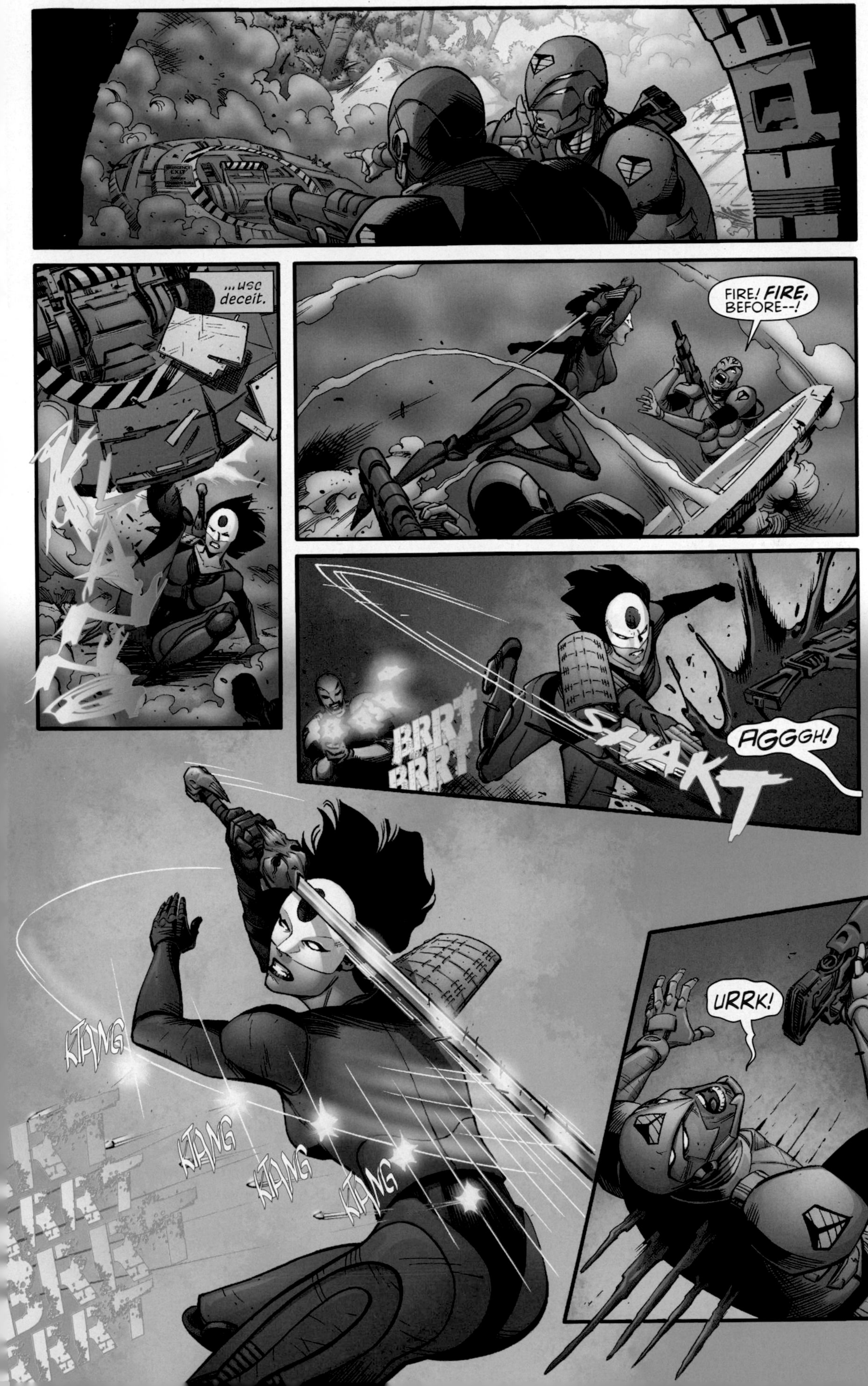

...use deceit.
FIRE! FIRE, BEFORE--!
KLAK
BRRT BRRT
SHAKT
AGGGH!
URRK!
KTANG
KTANG
KTANG
KTANG

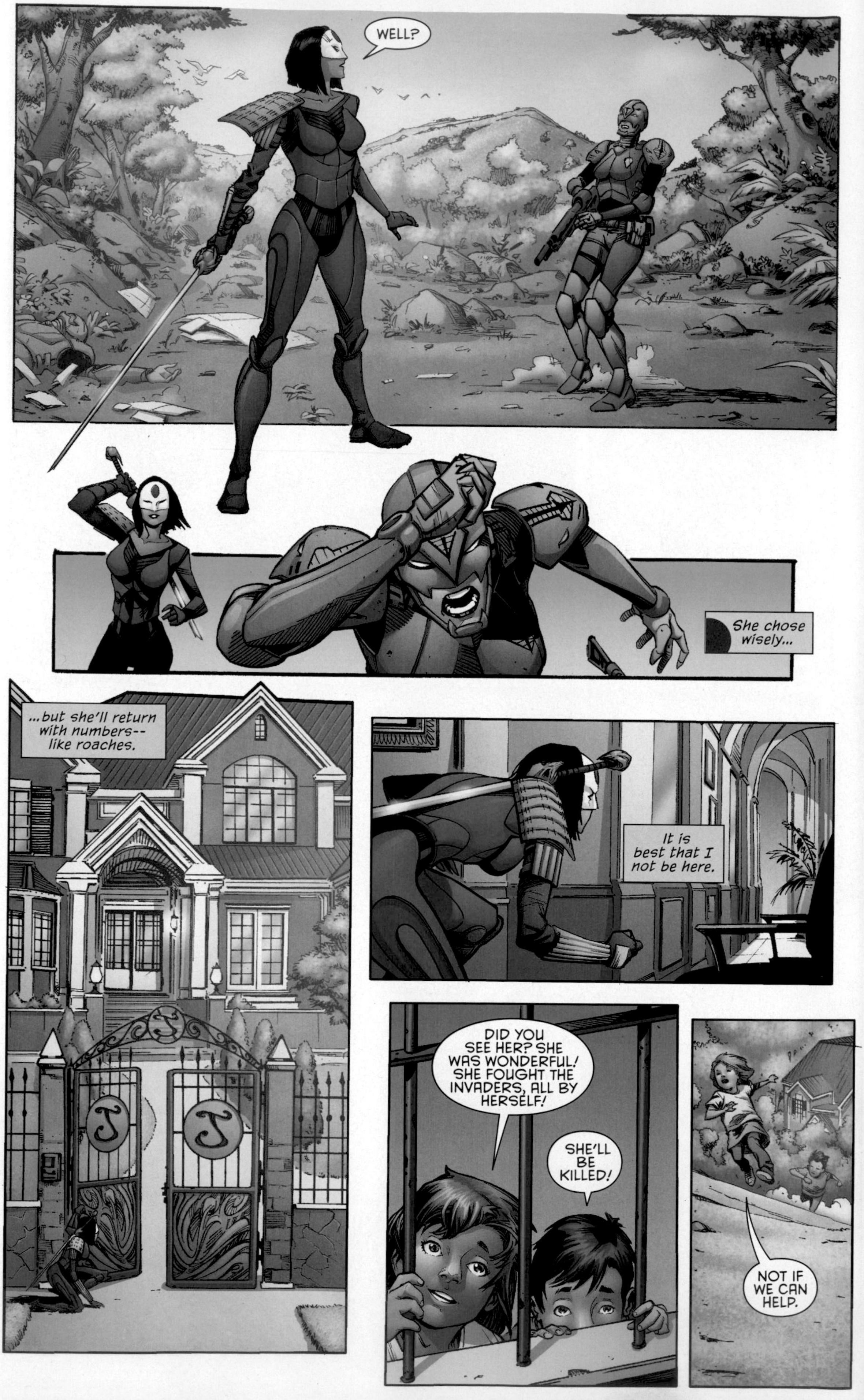
WELL?
She chose wisely...
...but she'll return with numbers--like roaches.
It is best that I not be here.
DID YOU SEE HER? SHE WAS WONDERFUL! SHE FOUGHT THE INVADERS, ALL BY HERSELF!
SHE'LL BE KILLED!
NOT IF WE CAN HELP.

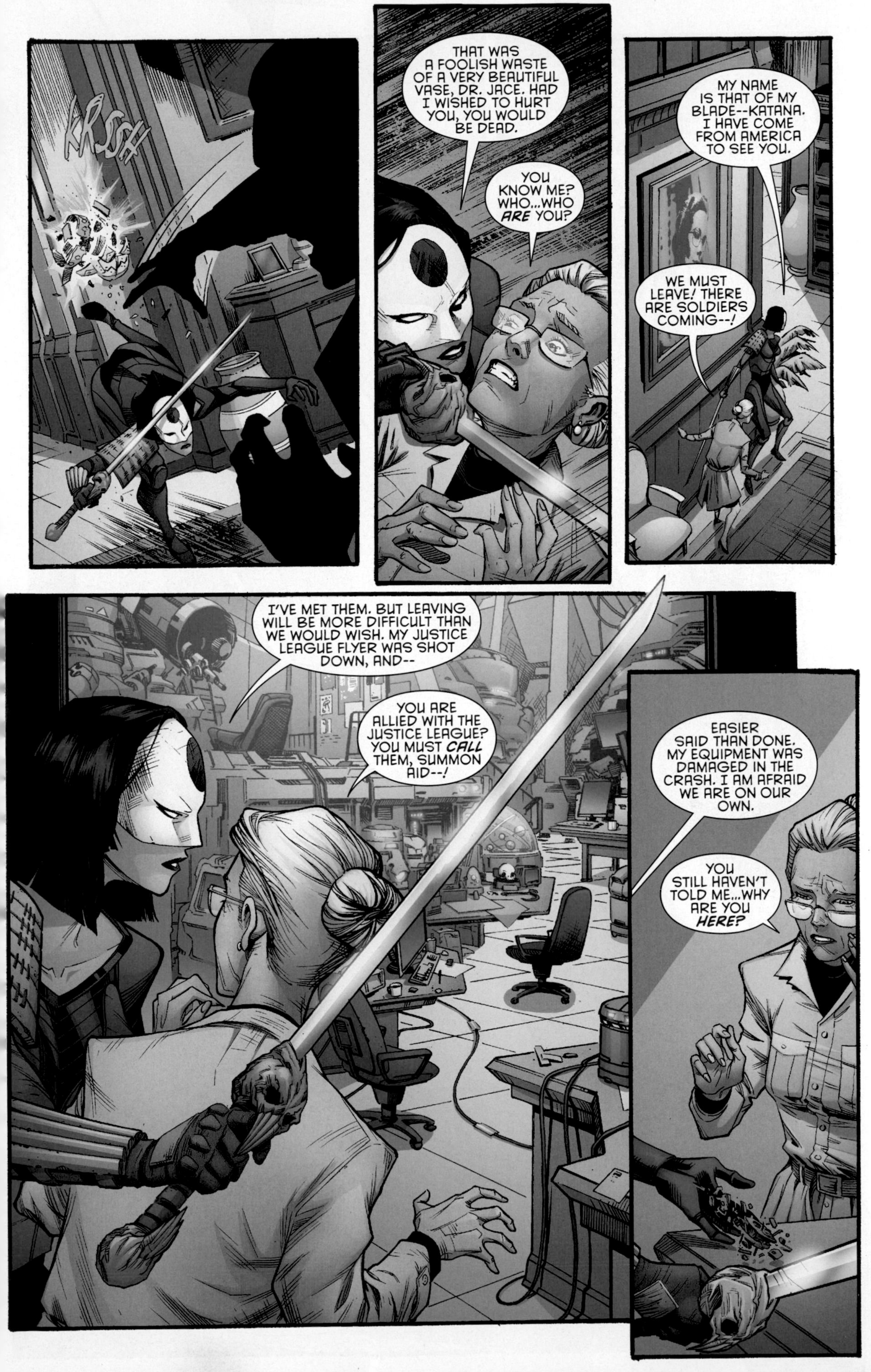
KRSSH
THAT WAS A FOOLISH WASTE OF A VERY BEAUTIFUL VASE, DR. JACE. HAD I WISHED TO HURT YOU, YOU WOULD BE DEAD.
YOU KNOW ME? WHO...WHO ARE YOU?
MY NAME IS THAT OF MY BLADE--KATANA. I HAVE COME FROM AMERICA TO SEE YOU.
WE MUST LEAVE! THERE ARE SOLDIERS COMING--!
I'VE MET THEM. BUT LEAVING WILL BE MORE DIFFICULT THAN WE WOULD WISH. MY JUSTICE LEAGUE FLYER WAS SHOT DOWN, AND--
YOU ARE ALLIED WITH THE JUSTICE LEAGUE? YOU MUST CALL THEM, SUMMON AID--!
EASIER SAID THAN DONE. MY EQUIPMENT WAS DAMAGED IN THE CRASH. I AM AFRAID WE ARE ON OUR OWN.
YOU STILL HAVEN'T TOLD ME...WHY ARE YOU HERE?

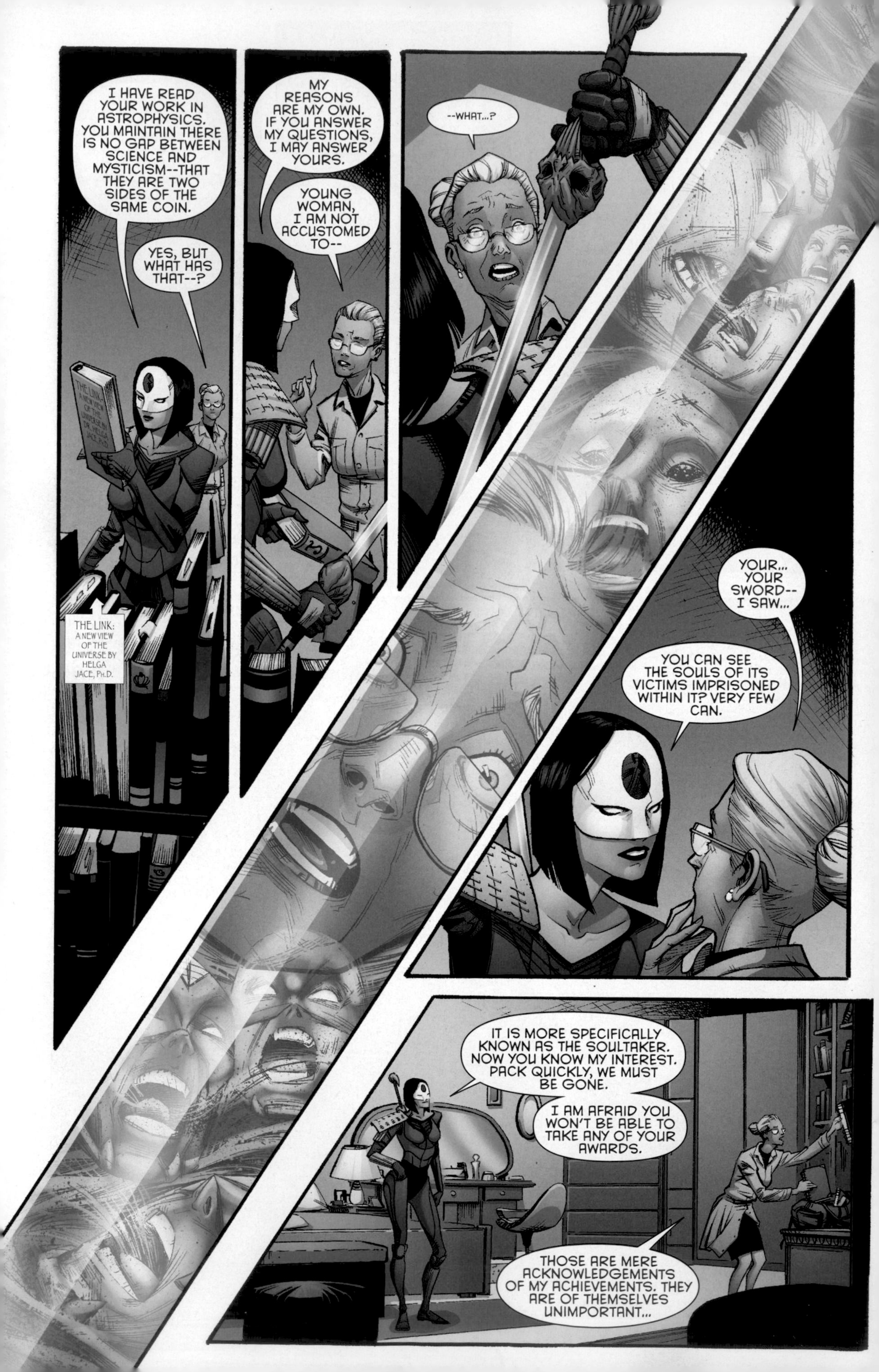

I HAVE READ YOUR WORK IN ASTROPHYSICS. YOU MAINTAIN THERE IS NO GAP BETWEEN SCIENCE AND MYSTICISM--THAT THEY ARE TWO SIDES OF THE SAME COIN.
YES, BUT WHAT HAS THAT--?
THE LINK: A NEW VIEW OF THE UNIVERSE BY HELGA JACE, Ph.D.
MY REASONS ARE MY OWN. IF YOU ANSWER MY QUESTIONS, I MAY ANSWER YOURS.
YOUNG WOMAN, I AM NOT ACCUSTOMED TO--
--WHAT...?
YOUR... YOUR SWORD-- I SAW...
YOU CAN SEE THE SOULS OF ITS VICTIMS IMPRISONED WITHIN IT? VERY FEW CAN.
IT IS MORE SPECIFICALLY KNOWN AS THE SOULTAKER. NOW YOU KNOW MY INTEREST. PACK QUICKLY, WE MUST BE GONE.
I AM AFRAID YOU WON'T BE ABLE TO TAKE ANY OF YOUR AWARDS.
THOSE ARE MERE ACKNOWLEDGEMENTS OF MY ACHIEVEMENTS. THEY ARE OF THEMSELVES UNIMPORTANT...

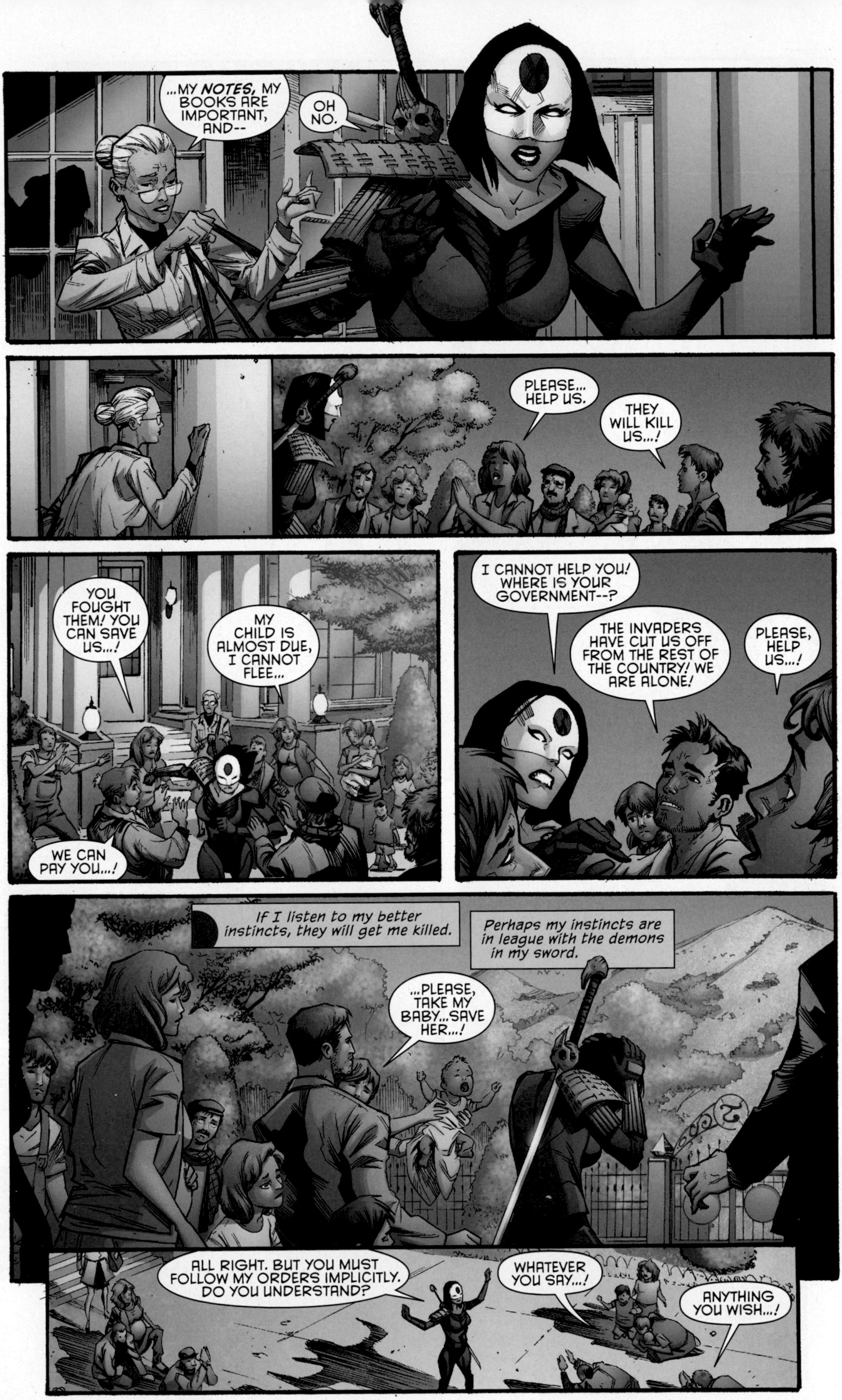
...MY NOTES, MY BOOKS ARE IMPORTANT, AND--
OH NO.
PLEASE... HELP US.
THEY WILL KILL US...!
YOU FOUGHT THEM! YOU CAN SAVE US...!
MY CHILD IS ALMOST DUE, I CANNOT FLEE...
WE CAN PAY YOU...!
I CANNOT HELP YOU! WHERE IS YOUR GOVERNMENT--?
THE INVADERS HAVE CUT US OFF FROM THE REST OF THE COUNTRY! WE ARE ALONE!
PLEASE, HELP US...!
If I listen to my better instincts, they will get me killed.
Perhaps my instincts are in league with the demons in my sword.
...PLEASE, TAKE MY BABY...SAVE HER...!
ALL RIGHT. BUT YOU MUST FOLLOW MY ORDERS IMPLICITLY. DO YOU UNDERSTAND?
WHATEVER YOU SAY...!
ANYTHING YOU WISH...!

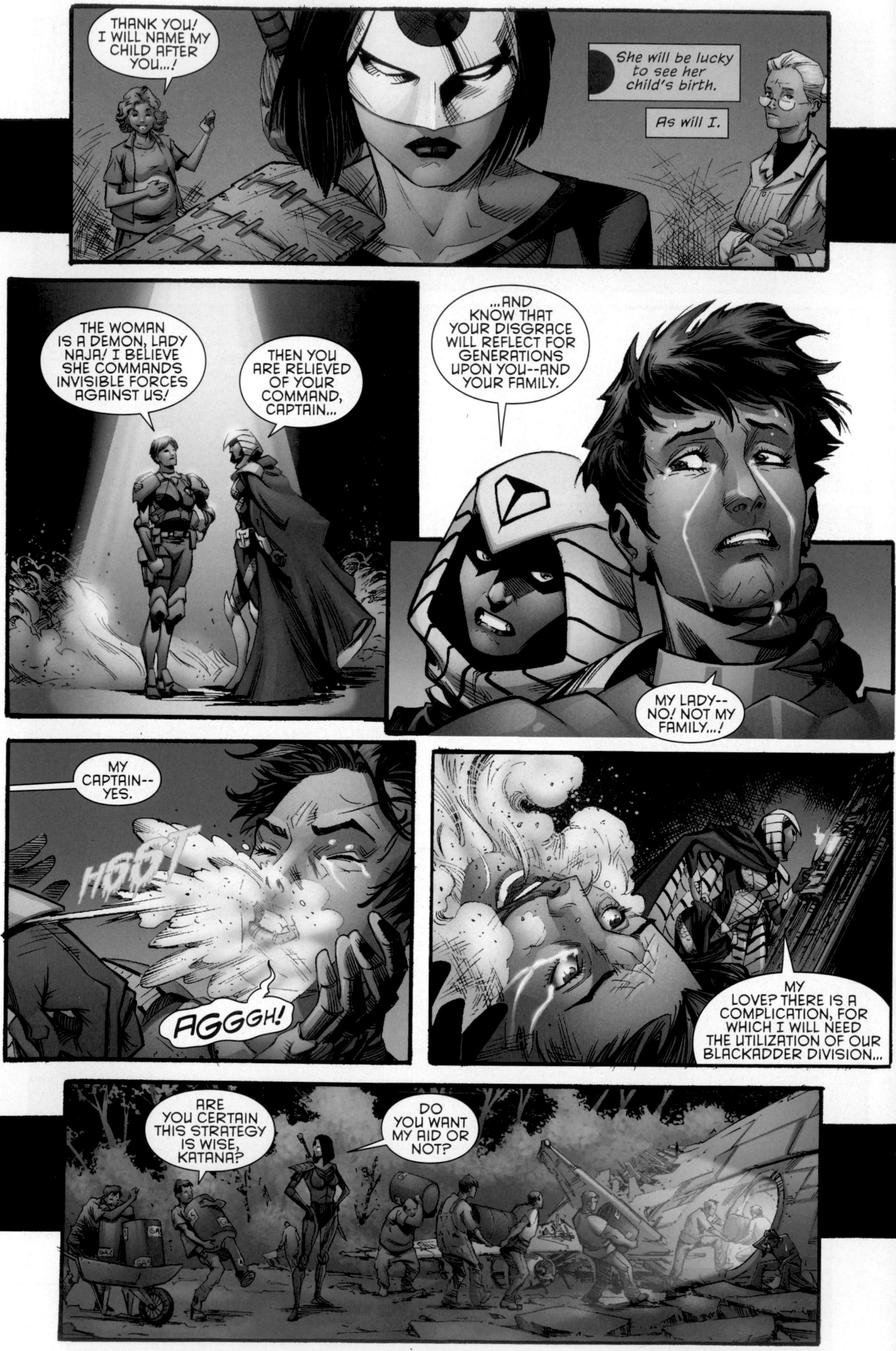

THANK YOU! I WILL NAME MY CHILD AFTER YOU...!
She will be lucky to see her child's birth.
As will I.
THE WOMAN IS A DEMON, LADY NAJA! I BELIEVE SHE COMMANDS INVISIBLE FORCES AGAINST US!
THEN YOU ARE RELIEVED OF YOUR COMMAND, CAPTAIN...
...AND KNOW THAT YOUR DISGRACE WILL REFLECT FOR GENERATIONS UPON YOU--AND YOUR FAMILY.
MY LADY-- NO! NOT MY FAMILY...!
MY CAPTAIN-- YES.
HSST
AGGGH!
MY LOVE? THERE IS A COMPLICATION, FOR WHICH I WILL NEED THE UTILIZATION OF OUR BLACKADDER DIVISION...
ARE YOU CERTAIN THIS STRATEGY IS WISE, KATANA?
DO YOU WANT MY AID OR NOT?

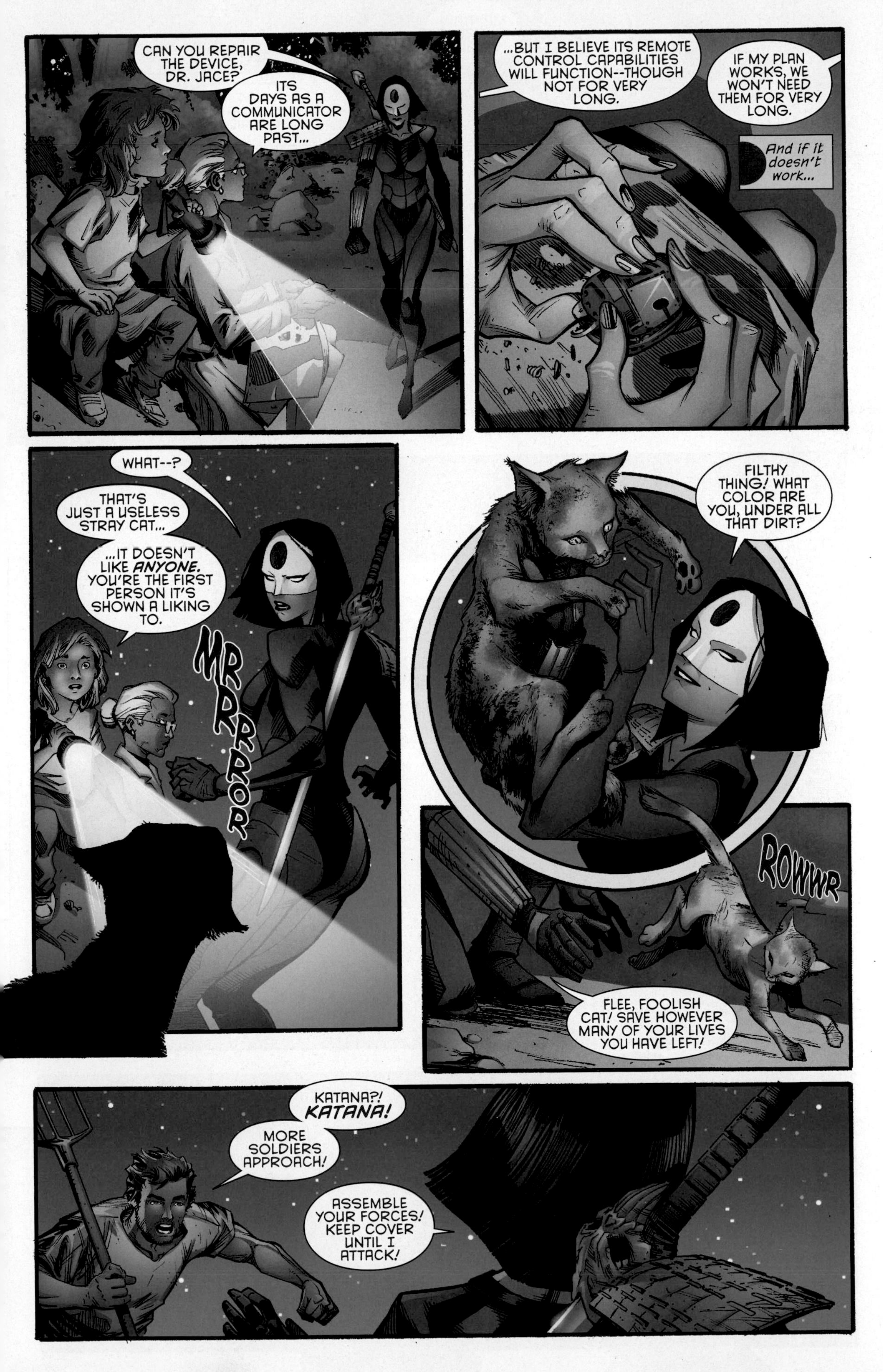
CAN YOU REPAIR THE DEVICE, DR. JACE?
ITS DAYS AS A COMMUNICATOR ARE LONG PAST...
...BUT I BELIEVE ITS REMOTE CONTROL CAPABILITIES WILL FUNCTION--THOUGH NOT FOR VERY LONG.
IF MY PLAN WORKS, WE WON'T NEED THEM FOR VERY LONG.
And if it doesn't work...
WHAT--?
THAT'S JUST A USELESS STRAY CAT...
...IT DOESN'T LIKE ANYONE. YOU'RE THE FIRST PERSON IT'S SHOWN A LIKING TO.
MRRRRROR
FILTHY THING! WHAT COLOR ARE YOU, UNDER ALL THAT DIRT?
ROWWR
FLEE, FOOLISH CAT! SAVE HOWEVER MANY OF YOUR LIVES YOU HAVE LEFT!
KATANA?! KATANA!
MORE SOLDIERS APPROACH!
ASSEMBLE YOUR FORCES! KEEP COVER UNTIL I ATTACK!

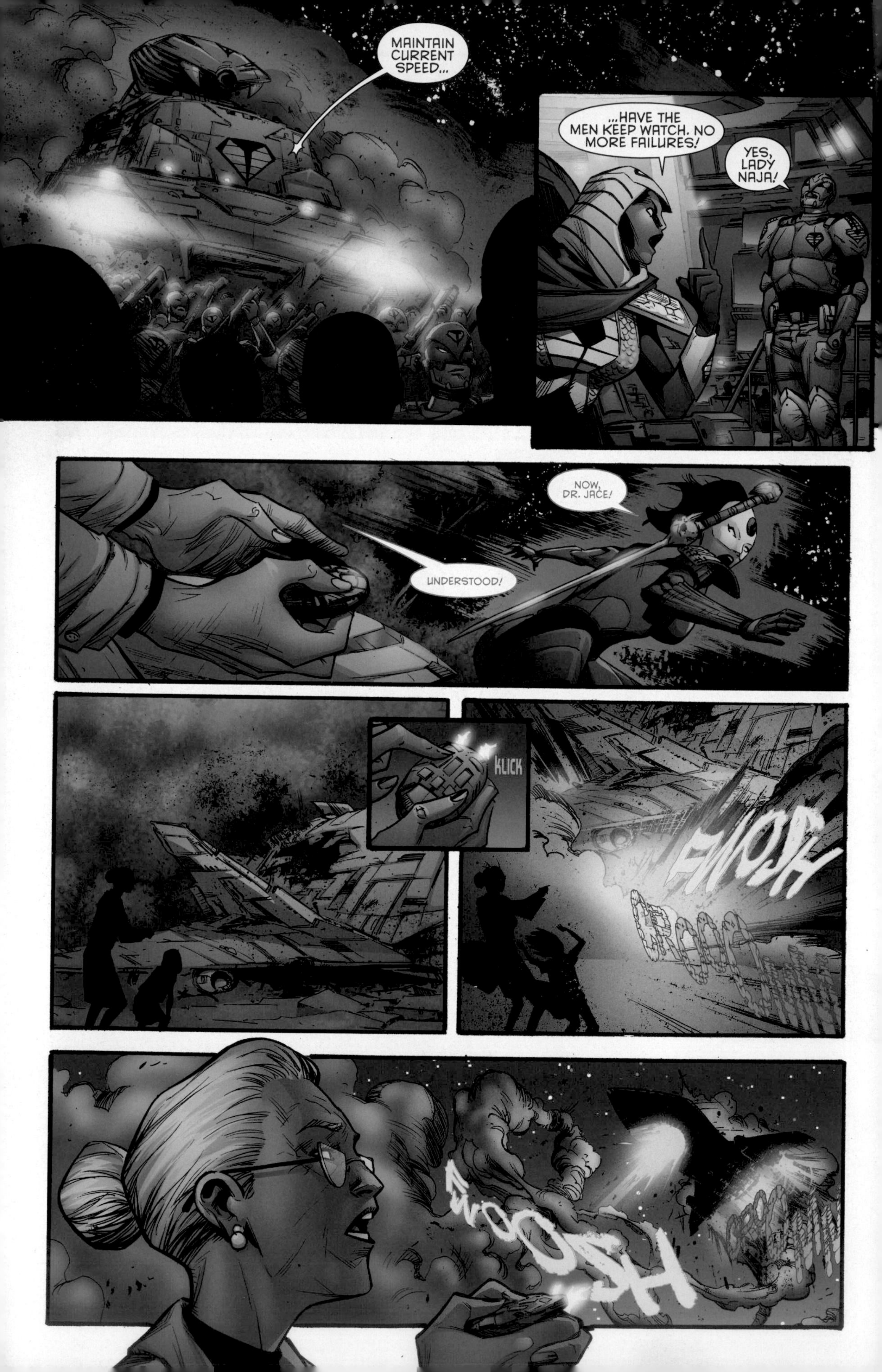
MAINTAIN CURRENT SPEED...
...HAVE THE MEN KEEP WATCH. NO MORE FAILURES!
YES, LADY NAJA!
NOW, DR. JACE!
UNDERSTOOD!
KLICK
FWOSH
BROOOM
FWOOSH

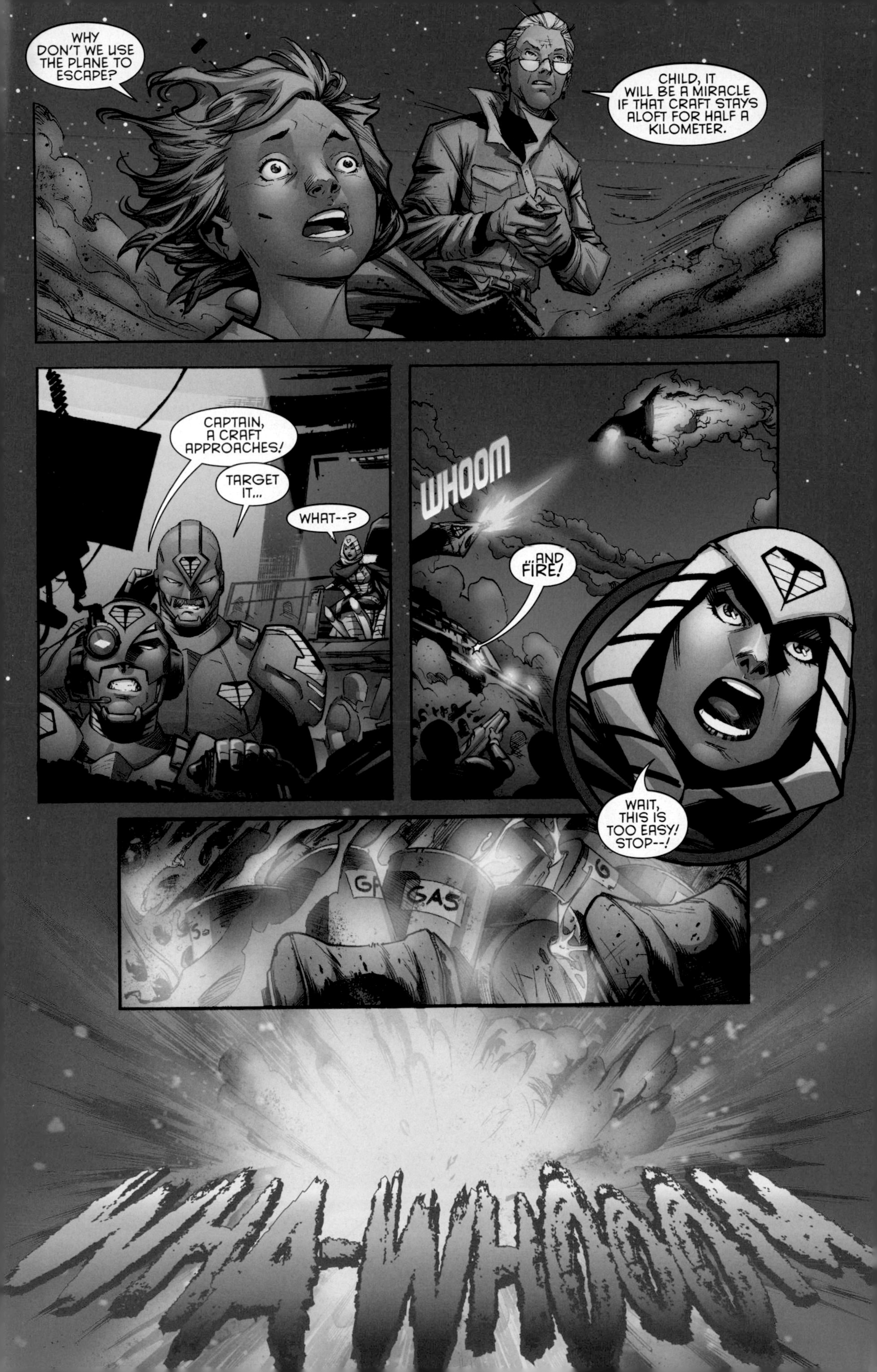
WHY DON'T WE USE THE PLANE TO ESCAPE?
CHILD, IT WILL BE A MIRACLE IF THAT CRAFT STAYS ALOFT FOR HALF A KILOMETER.
CAPTAIN, A CRAFT APPROACHES!
TARGET IT...
WHAT--?
WHOOM
...AND FIRE!
WAIT, THIS IS TOO EASY! STOP--!
GAS

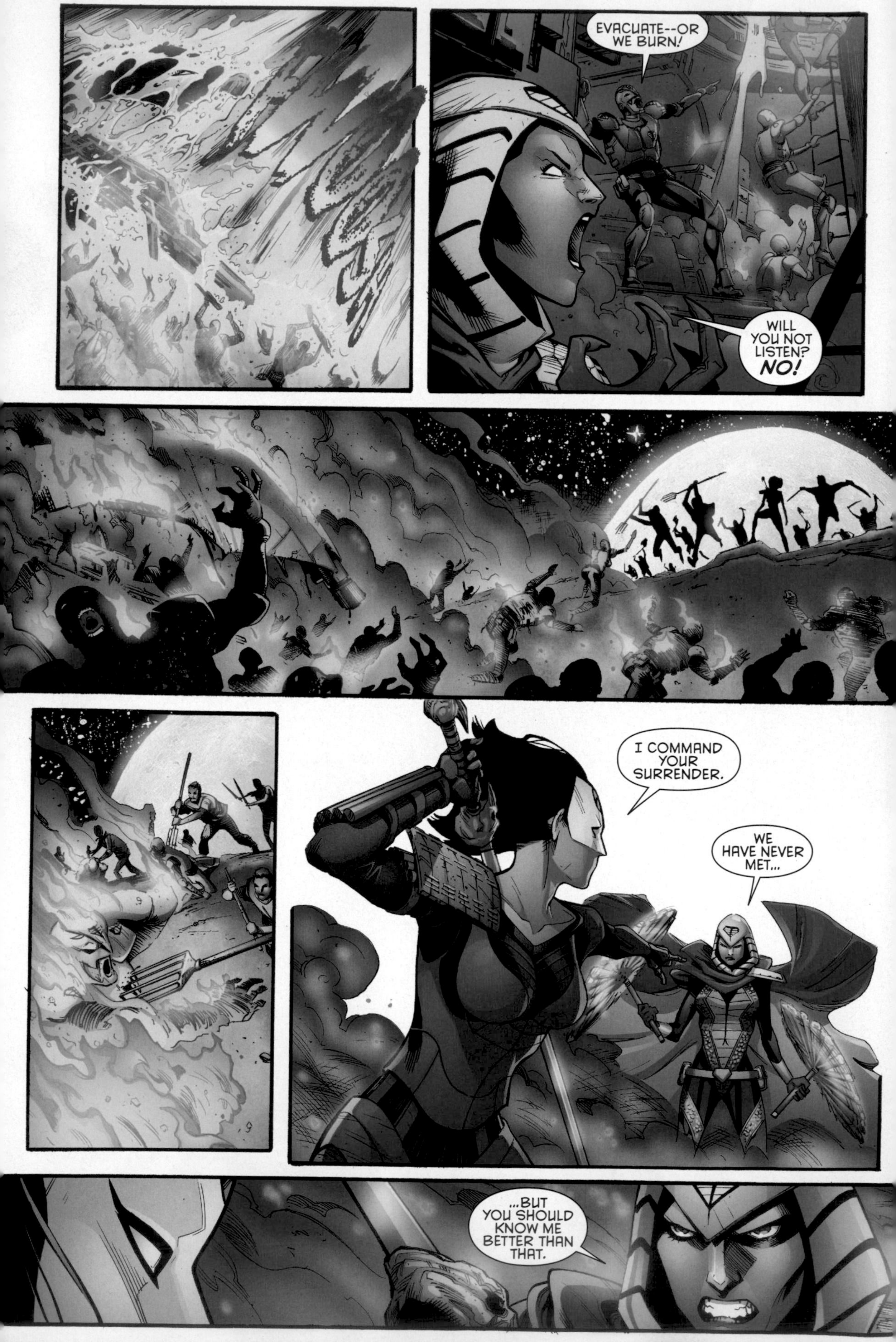
EVACUATE--OR WE BURN!
WILL YOU NOT LISTEN? NO!
I COMMAND YOUR SURRENDER.
WE HAVE NEVER MET...
...BUT YOU SHOULD KNOW ME BETTER THAN THAT.

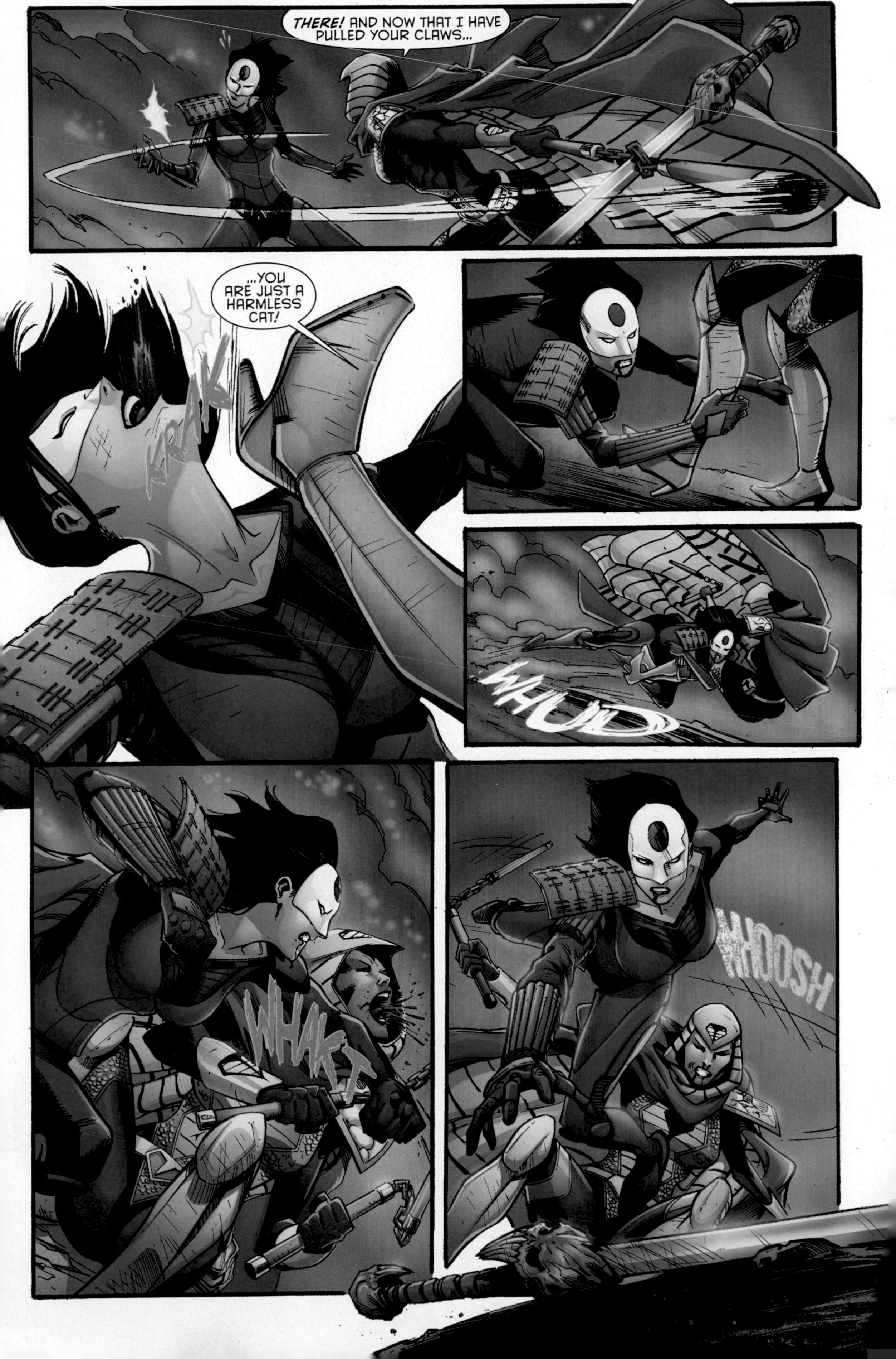

THERE! AND NOW THAT I HAVE PULLED YOUR CLAWS...
...YOU ARE JUST A HARMLESS CAT!
KRAK
WHUD
WHAKT
WHOOSH

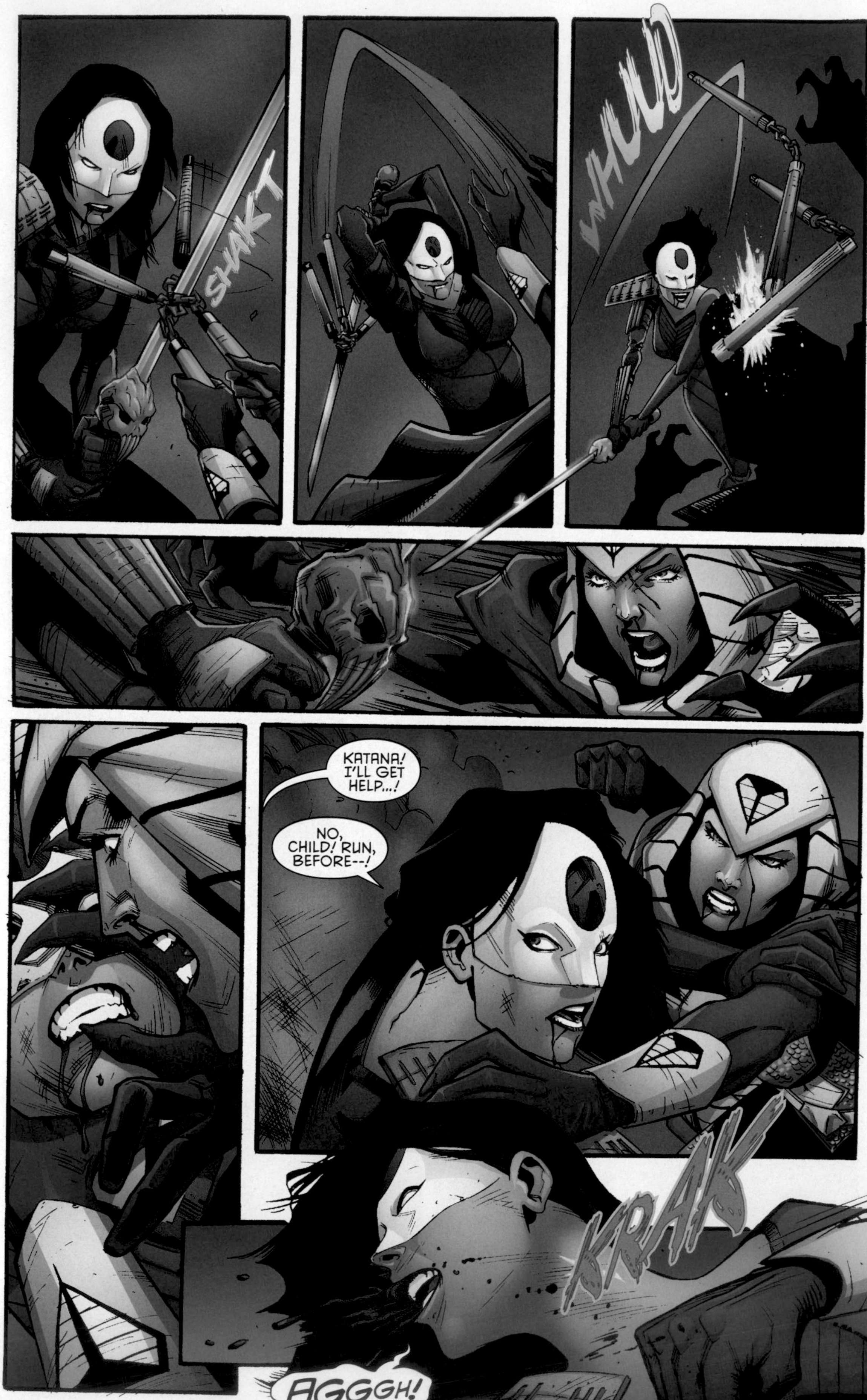
SHAK'T
WHUD
KATANA! I'LL GET HELP...!
NO, CHILD! RUN, BEFORE--!
KRAK
AGGGH!

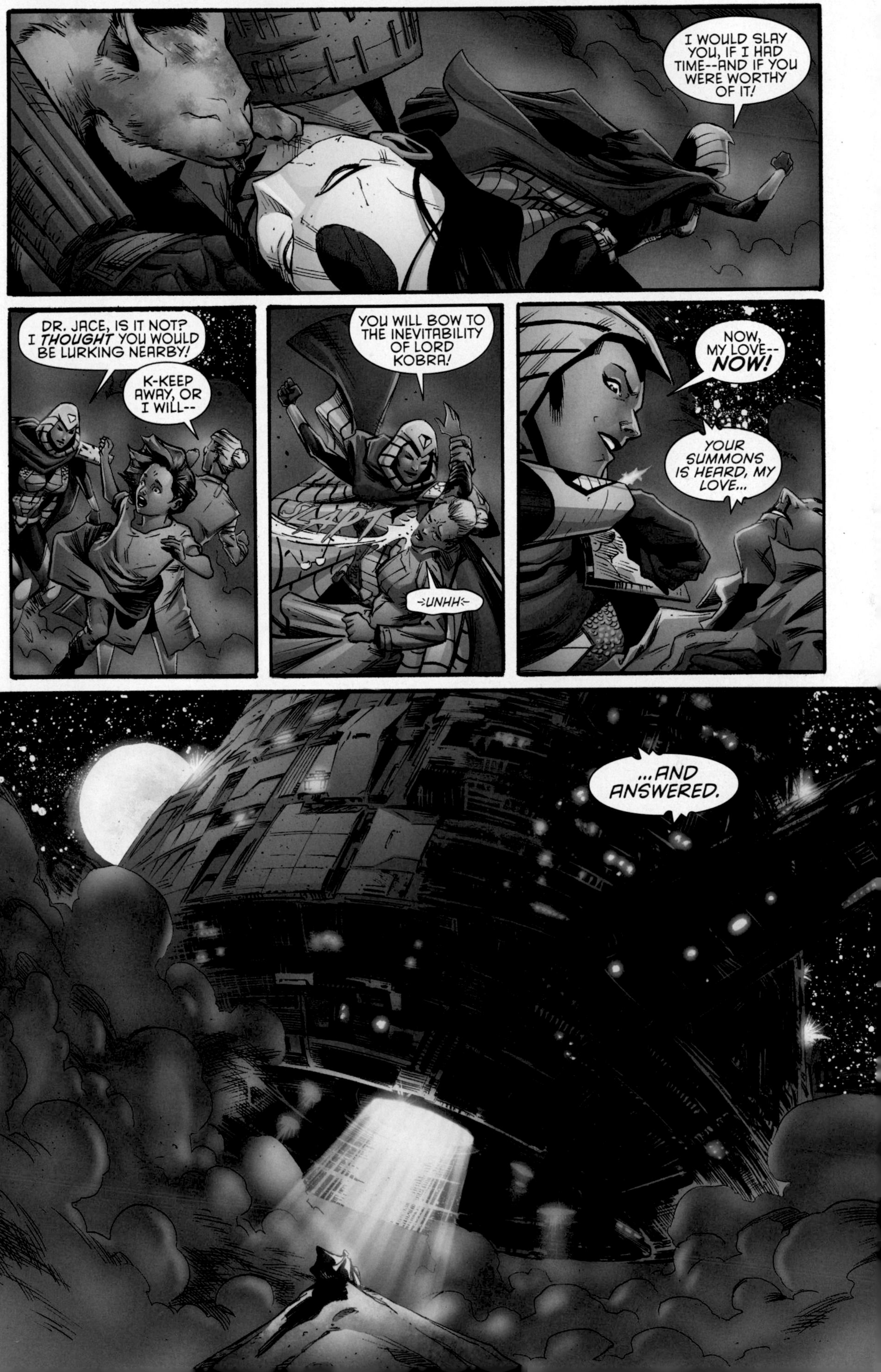
I WOULD SLAY YOU, IF I HAD TIME--AND IF YOU WERE WORTHY OF IT!
DR. JACE, IS IT NOT? I THOUGHT YOU WOULD BE LURKING NEARBY!
K-KEEP AWAY, OR I WILL--
YOU WILL BOW TO THE INEVITABILITY OF LORD KOBRA!
UNHH
NOW, MY LOVE--NOW!
YOUR SUMMONS IS HEARD, MY LOVE...
...AND ANSWERED.

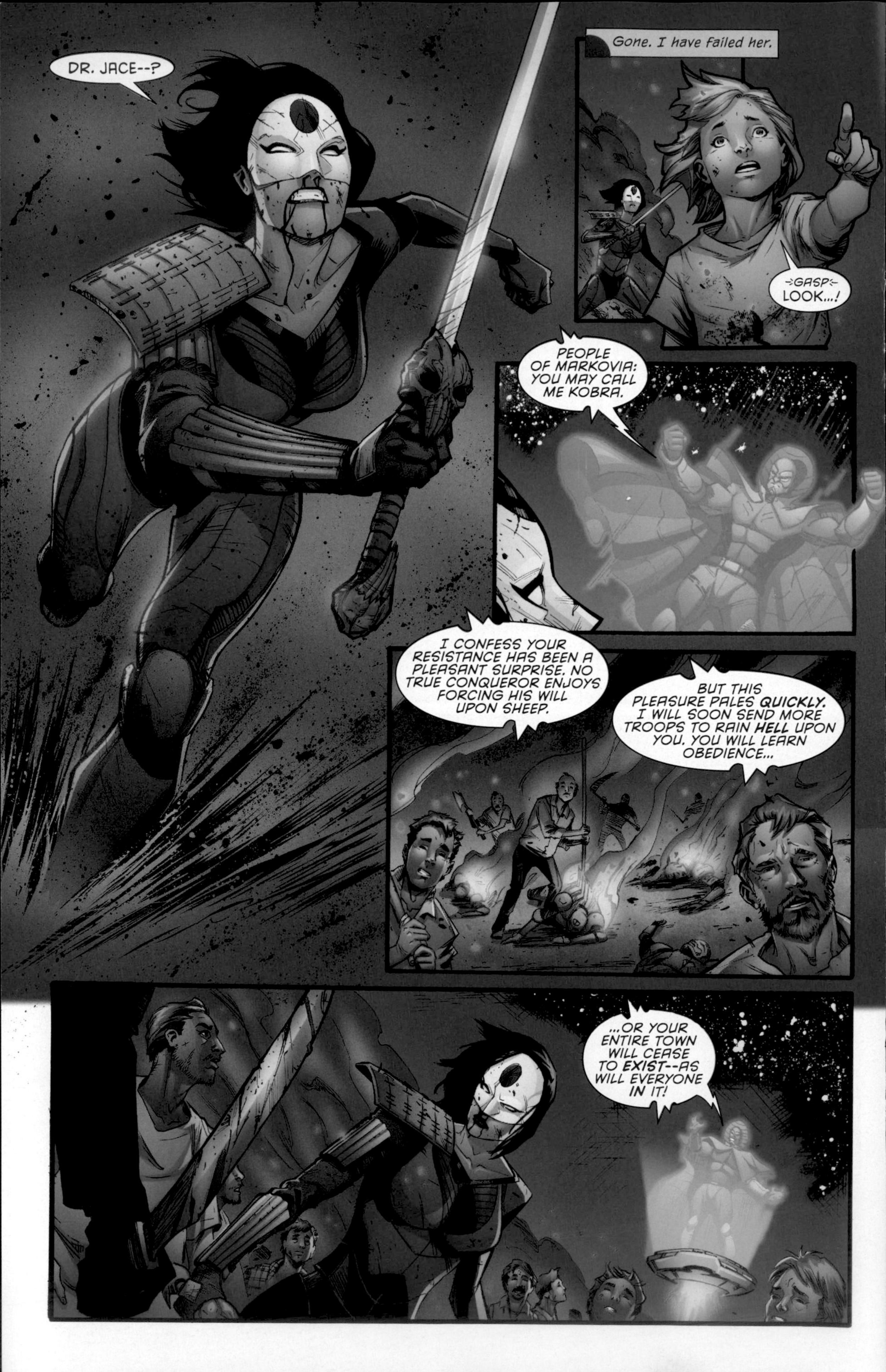
DR. JACE--?
Gone. I have failed her.
-GASP- LOOK...!
PEOPLE OF MARKOVIA: YOU MAY CALL ME KOBRA.
I CONFESS YOUR RESISTANCE HAS BEEN A PLEASANT SURPRISE. NO TRUE CONQUEROR ENJOYS FORCING HIS WILL UPON SHEEP.
BUT THIS PLEASURE PALES QUICKLY. I WILL SOON SEND MORE TROOPS TO RAIN HELL UPON YOU. YOU WILL LEARN OBEDIENCE...
...OR YOUR ENTIRE TOWN WILL CEASE TO EXIST--AS WILL EVERYONE IN IT!

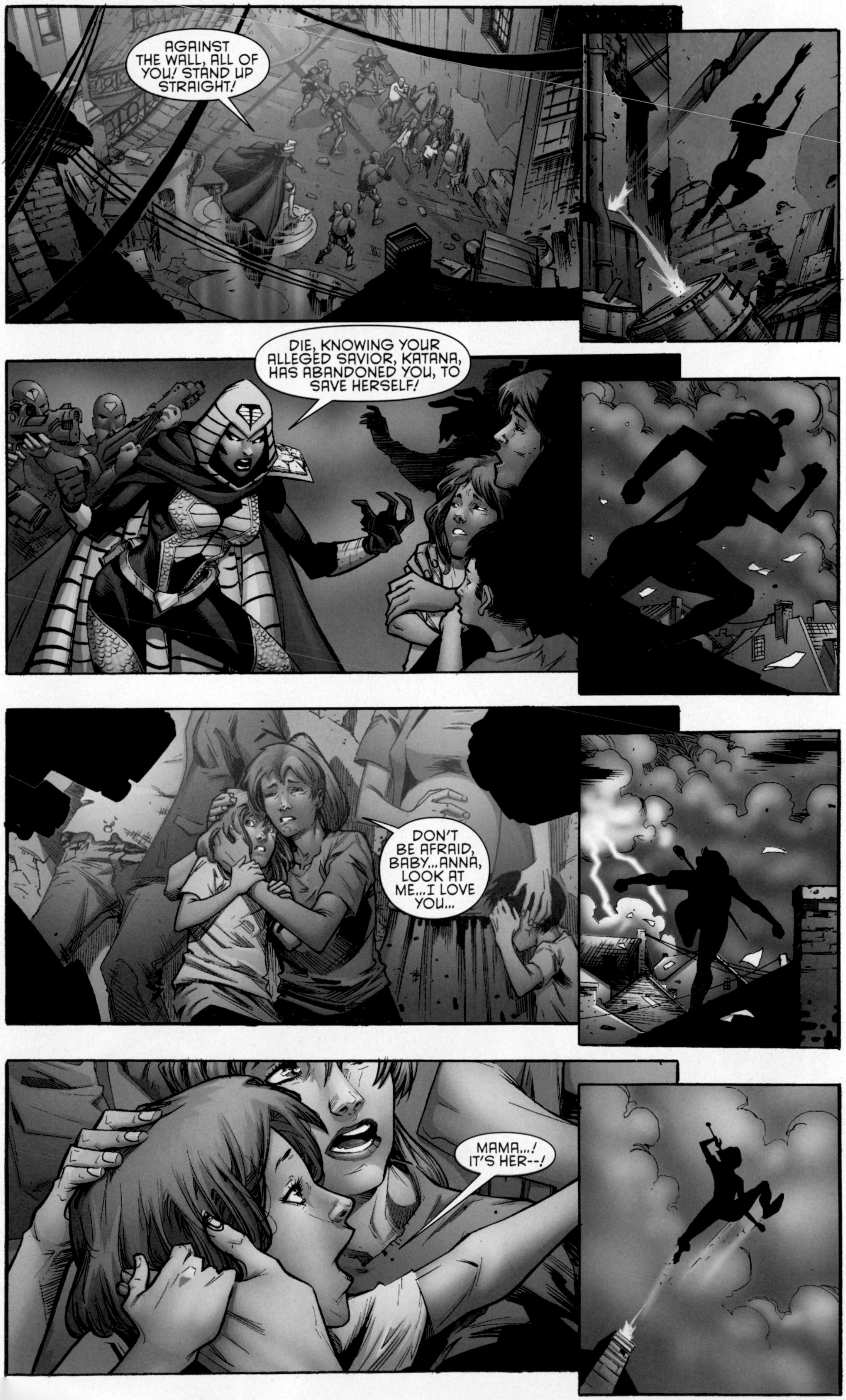
AGAINST THE WALL, ALL OF YOU! STAND UP STRAIGHT!
DIE, KNOWING YOUR ALLEGED SAVIOR, KATANA, HAS ABANDONED YOU, TO SAVE HERSELF!
DON'T BE AFRAID, BABY...ANNA, LOOK AT ME...I LOVE YOU...
MAMA...! IT'S HER--!

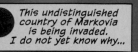

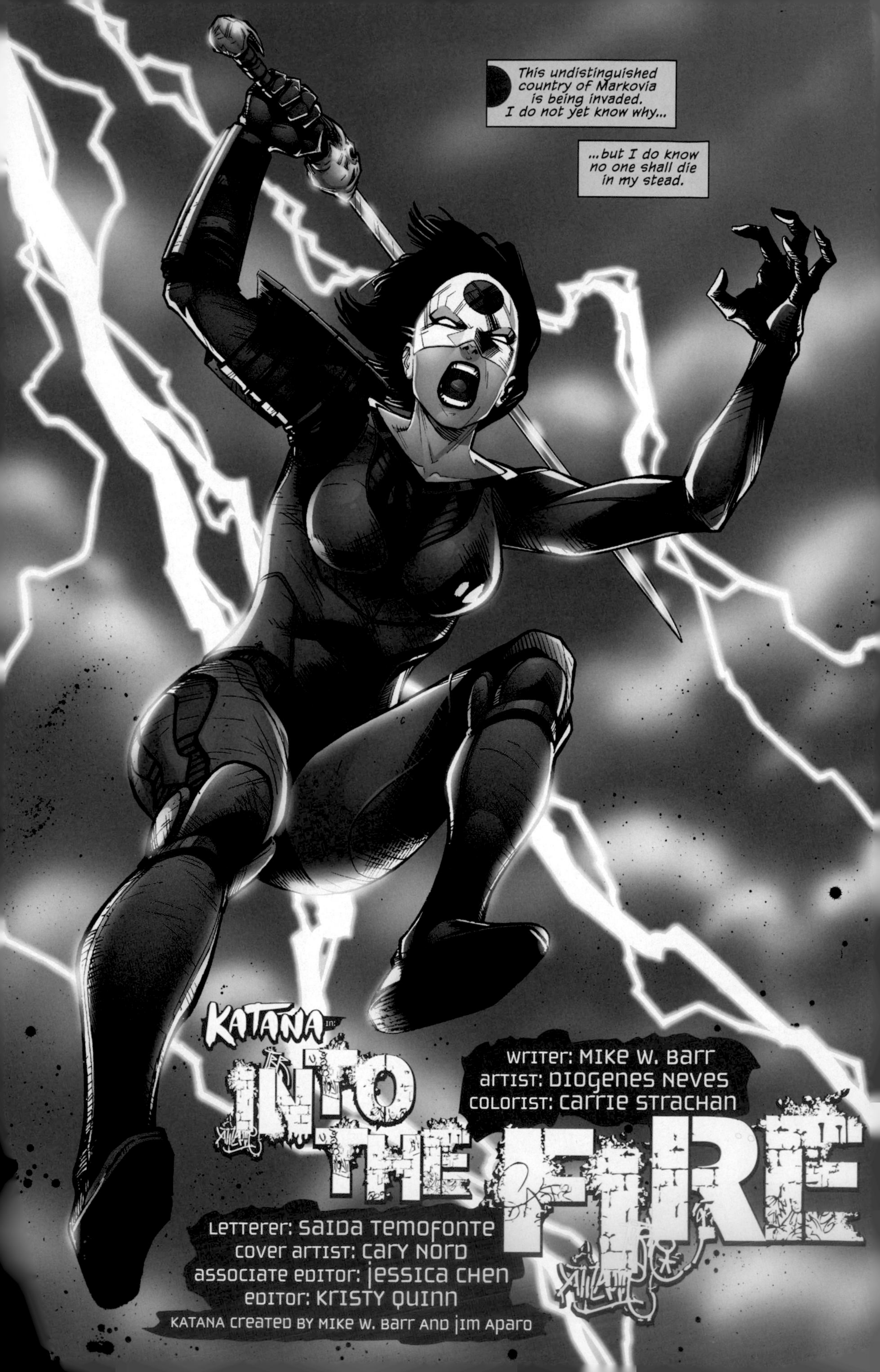

This undistinguished country of Markovia is being invaded. I do not yet know why...

...but I do know no one shall die in my stead.

KATANA in:

INTO THE FIRE

WRITER: MIKE W. BARR
ARTIST: DIOGENES NEVES
COLORIST: CARRIE STRACHAN

LETTERER: SAIDA TEMOFONTE
COVER ARTIST: CARY NORD
ASSOCIATE EDITOR: JESSICA CHEN
EDITOR: KRISTY QUINN

KATANA CREATED BY MIKE W. BARR AND JIM APARO

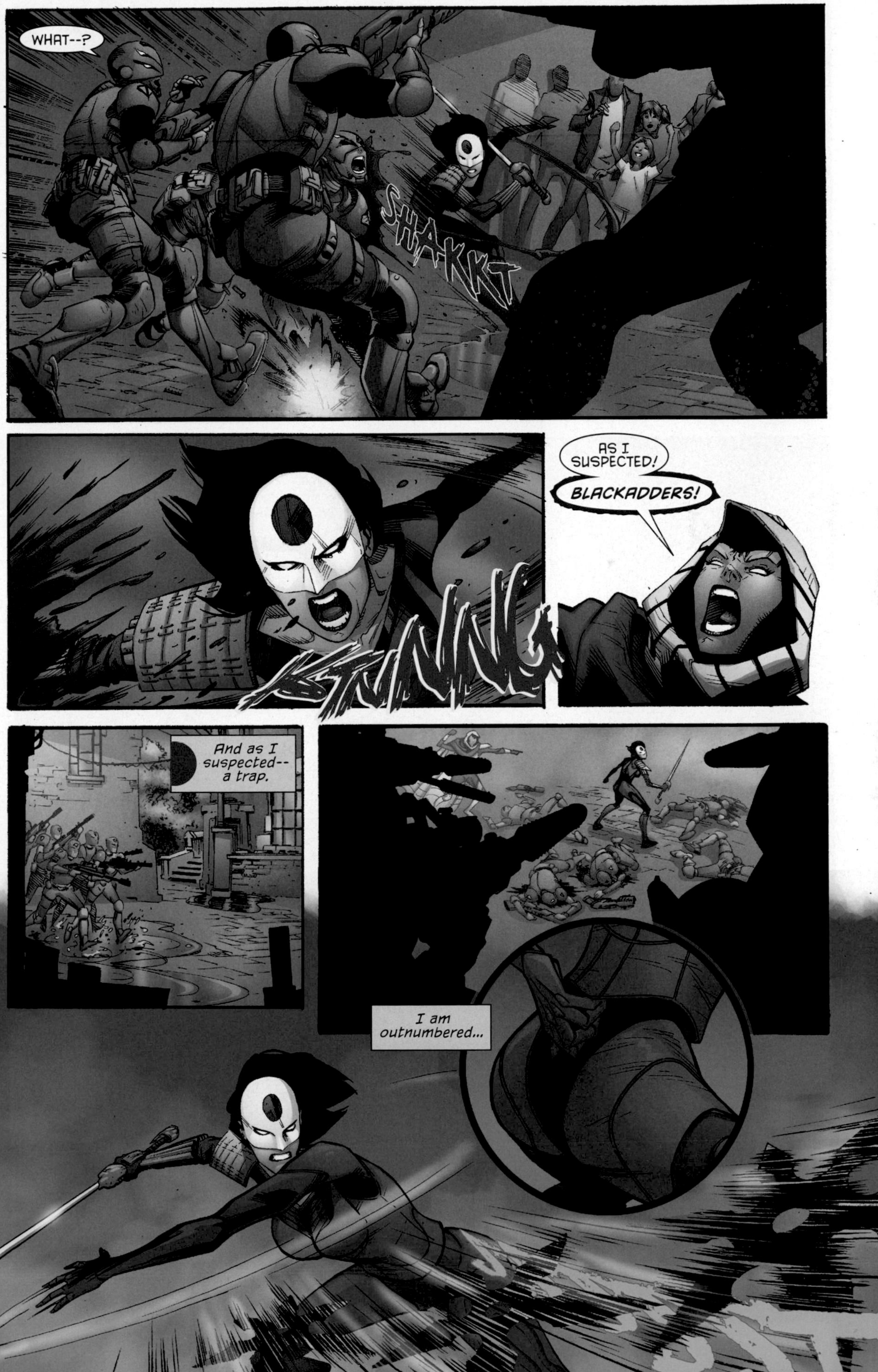

WHAT--?
SHAKKT
AS I SUSPECTED!
BLACKADDERS!
KTUNNG
And as I suspected-- a trap.
I am outnumbered...

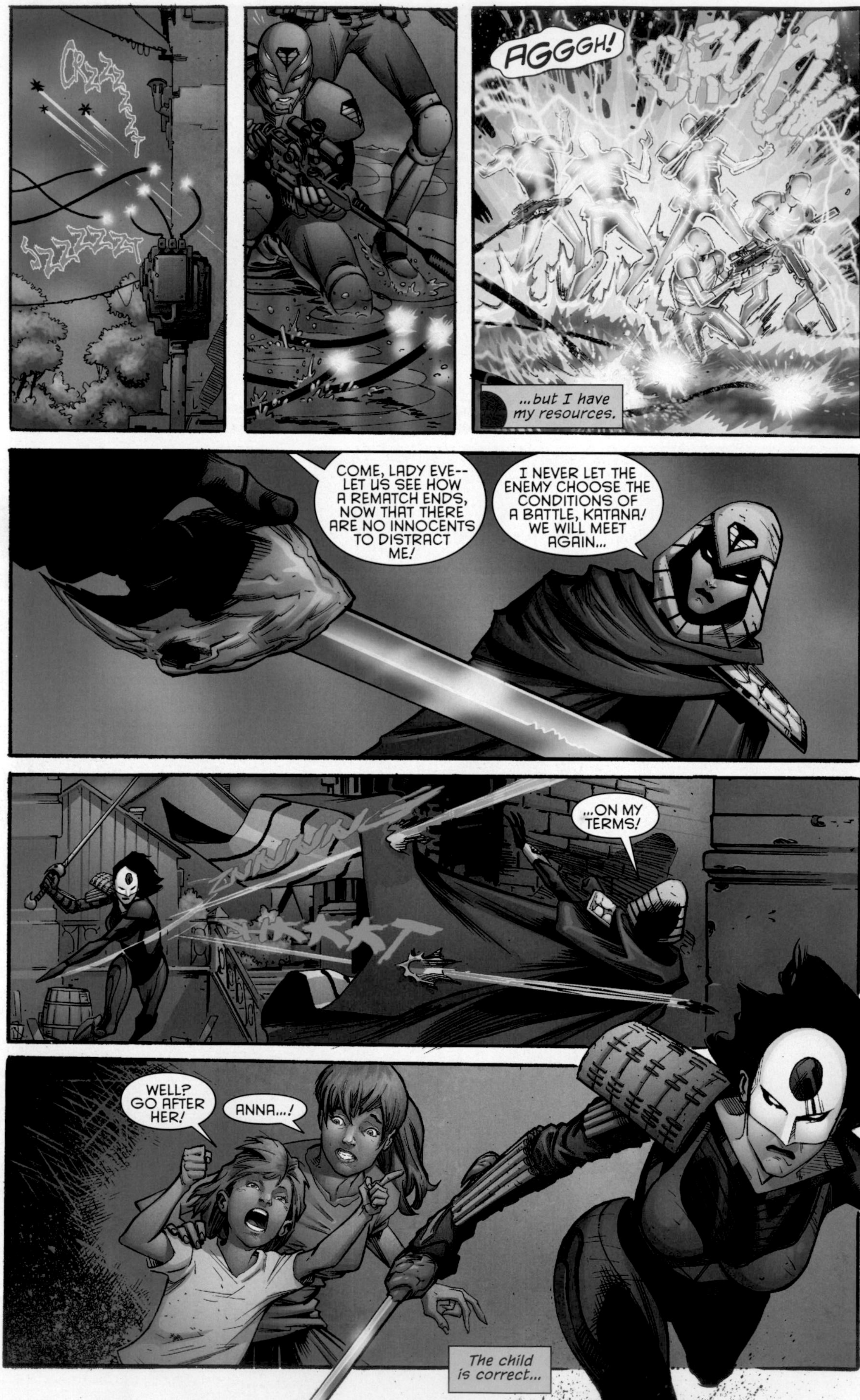
CRZZZZZZT
SZZZZZZZT
AGGGH!
CRAAK
...but I have my resources.
COME, LADY EVE-- LET US SEE HOW A REMATCH ENDS, NOW THAT THERE ARE NO INNOCENTS TO DISTRACT ME!
I NEVER LET THE ENEMY CHOOSE THE CONDITIONS OF A BATTLE, KATANA! WE WILL MEET AGAIN...
...ON MY TERMS!
SHKKKT
WELL? GO AFTER HER!
ANNA...!
The child is correct...

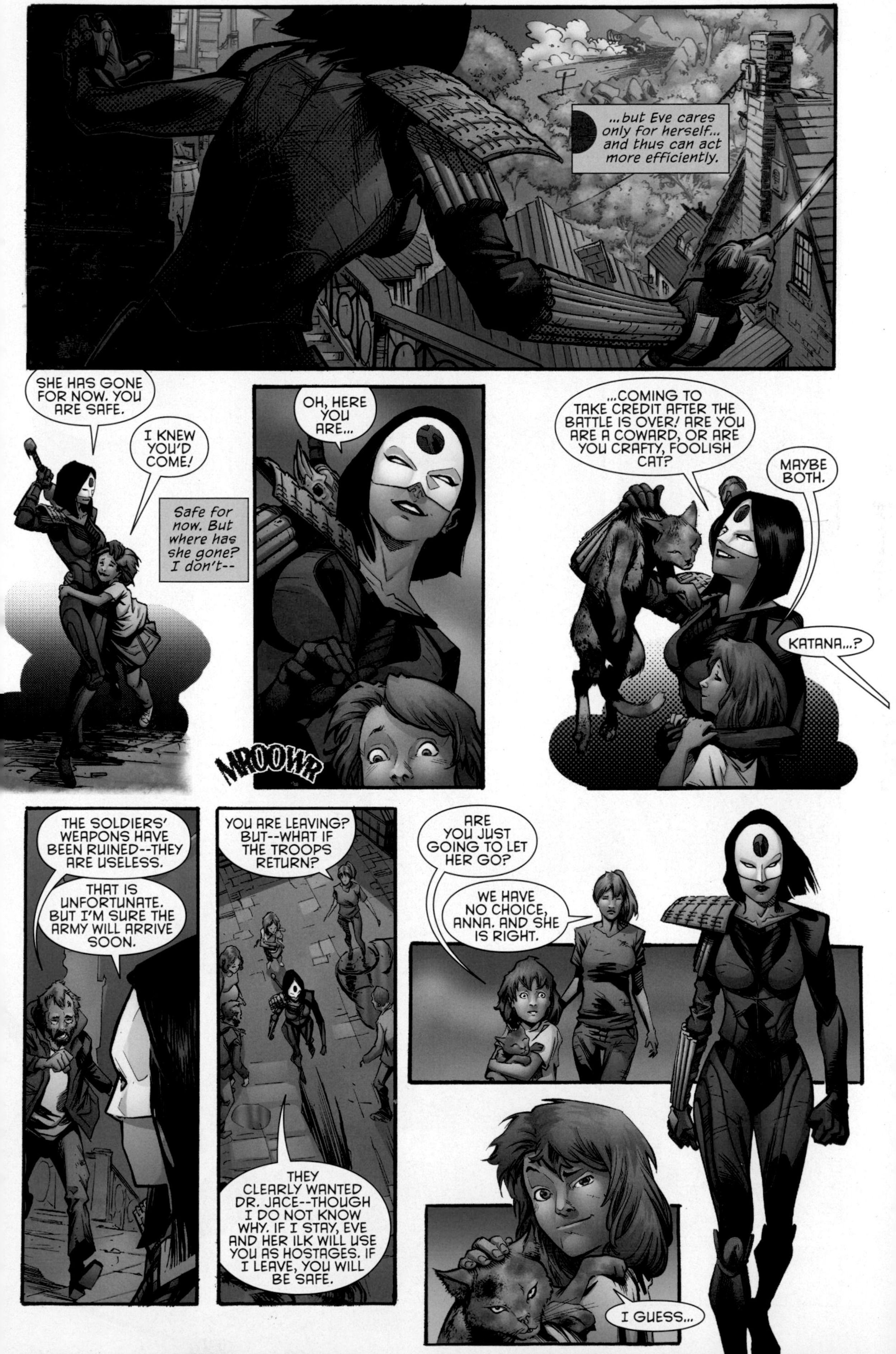
...but Eve cares only for herself... and thus can act more efficiently.
SHE HAS GONE FOR NOW. YOU ARE SAFE.
I KNEW YOU'D COME!
Safe for now. But where has she gone? I don't--
OH, HERE YOU ARE...
MROOWR
...COMING TO TAKE CREDIT AFTER THE BATTLE IS OVER! ARE YOU ARE A COWARD, OR ARE YOU CRAFTY, FOOLISH CAT?
MAYBE BOTH.
KATANA...?
THE SOLDIERS' WEAPONS HAVE BEEN RUINED--THEY ARE USELESS.
THAT IS UNFORTUNATE. BUT I'M SURE THE ARMY WILL ARRIVE SOON.
YOU ARE LEAVING? BUT--WHAT IF THE TROOPS RETURN?
THEY CLEARLY WANTED DR. JACE--THOUGH I DO NOT KNOW WHY. IF I STAY, EVE AND HER ILK WILL USE YOU AS HOSTAGES. IF I LEAVE, YOU WILL BE SAFE.
ARE YOU JUST GOING TO LET HER GO?
WE HAVE NO CHOICE, ANNA. AND SHE IS RIGHT.
I GUESS...

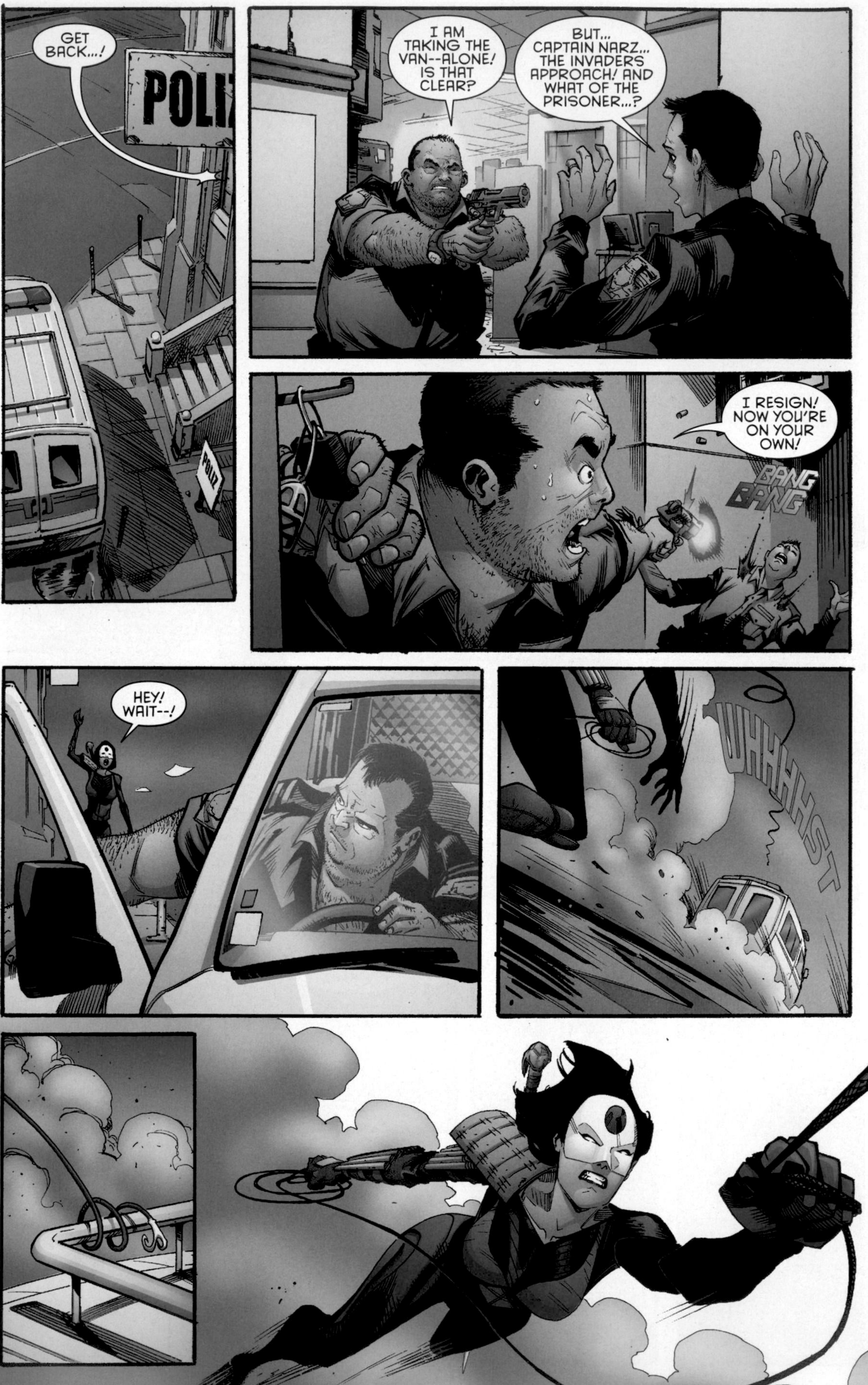
GET BACK...!
POLIZ
I AM TAKING THE VAN--ALONE! IS THAT CLEAR?
BUT... CAPTAIN NARZ... THE INVADERS APPROACH! AND WHAT OF THE PRISONER...?
I RESIGN! NOW YOU'RE ON YOUR OWN!
BANG BANG
HEY! WAIT--!
WHHHHST

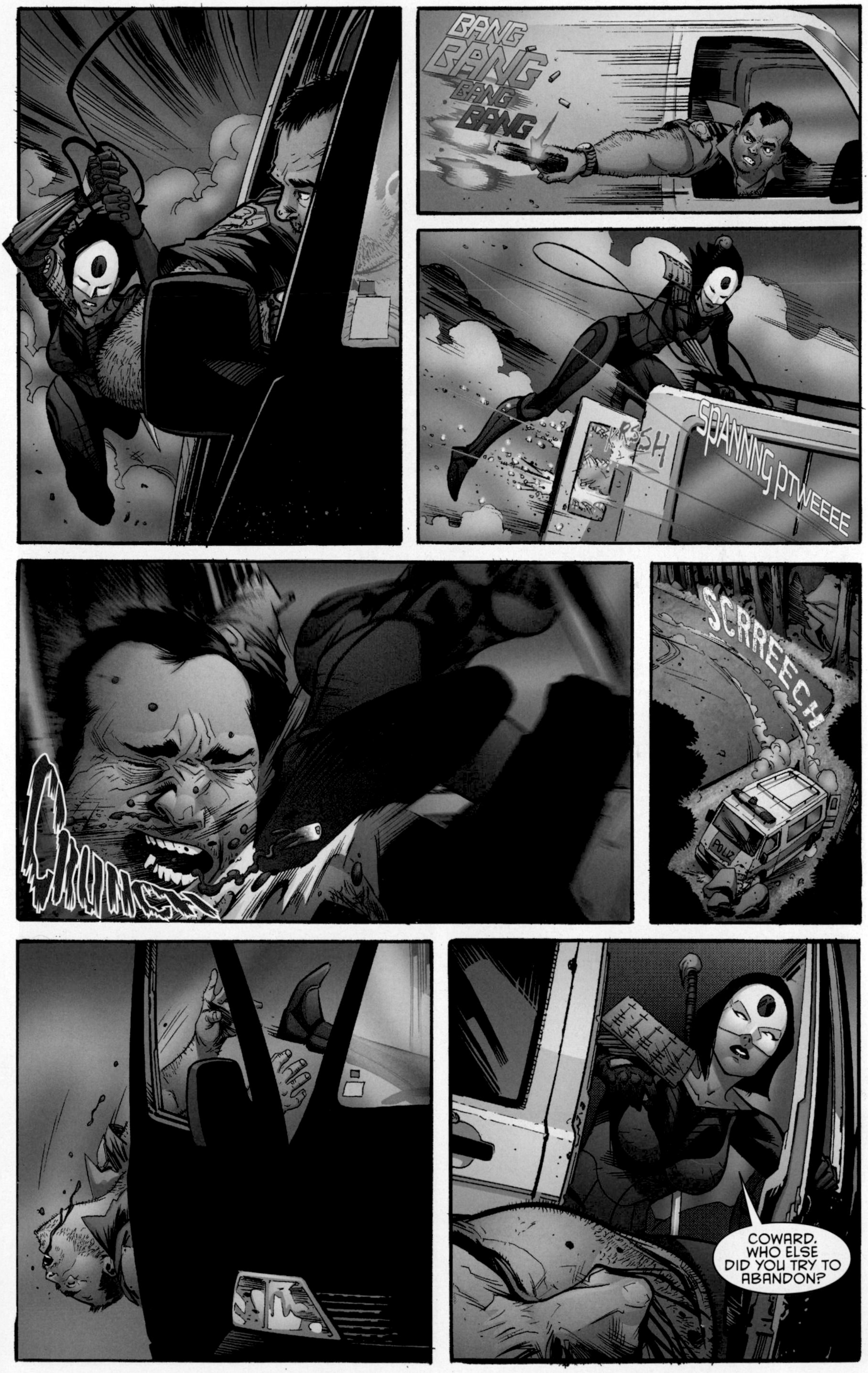
BANG
BANG
BANG
BANG
KRSSH
SPANNNG PTWEEEE
CRUNCH
SCRREECH
POLIZ
COWARD. WHO ELSE DID YOU TRY TO ABANDON?

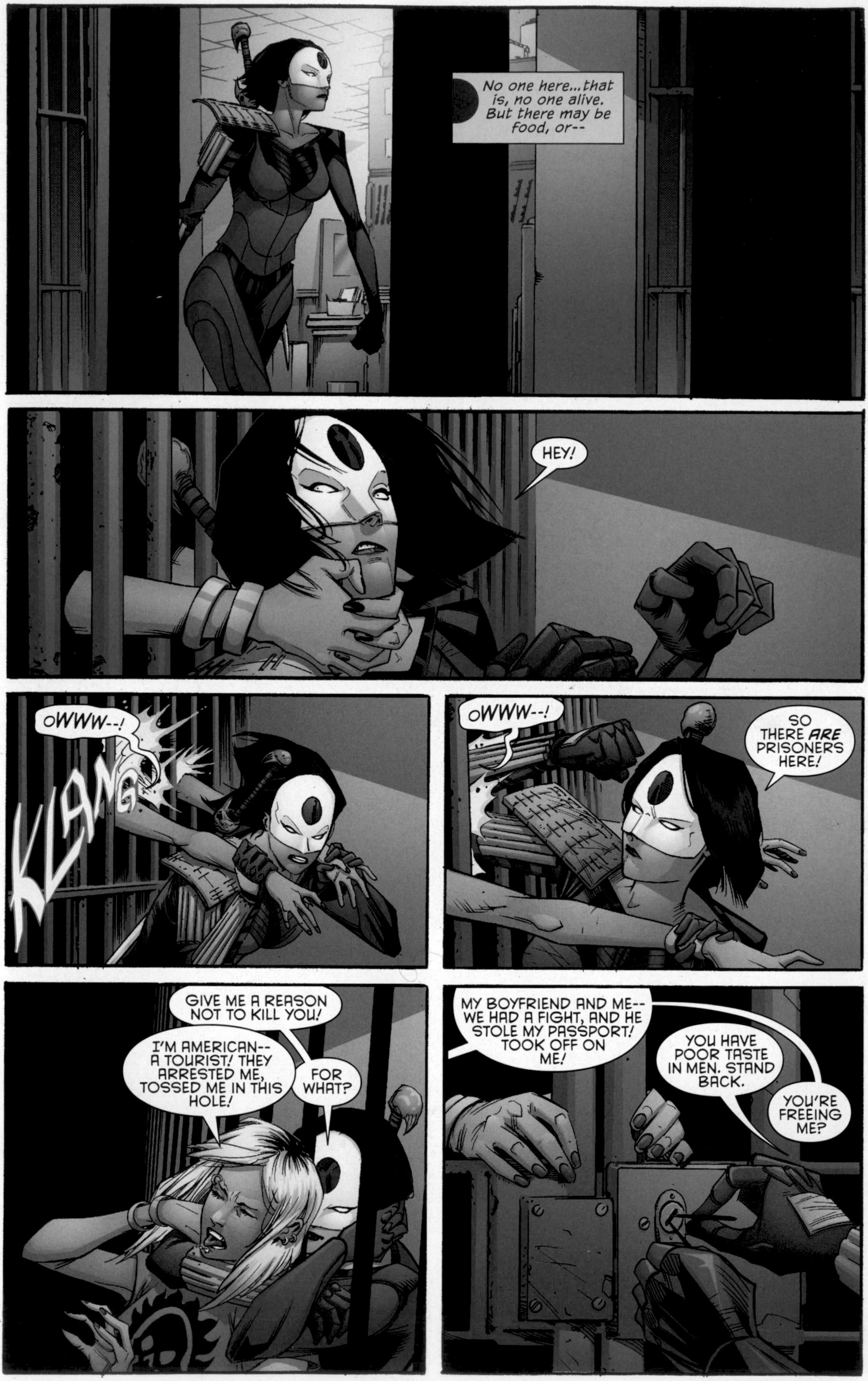

No one here...that is, no one alive. But there may be food, or--
HEY!
oWWW--!
KLANG!
oWWW--!
SO THERE *ARE* PRISONERS HERE!
GIVE ME A REASON NOT TO KILL YOU!
I'M AMERICAN-- A TOURIST! THEY ARRESTED ME, TOSSED ME IN THIS HOLE!
FOR WHAT?
MY BOYFRIEND AND ME-- WE HAD A FIGHT, AND HE STOLE MY PASSPORT! TOOK OFF ON ME!
YOU HAVE POOR TASTE IN MEN. STAND BACK.
YOU'RE FREEING ME?

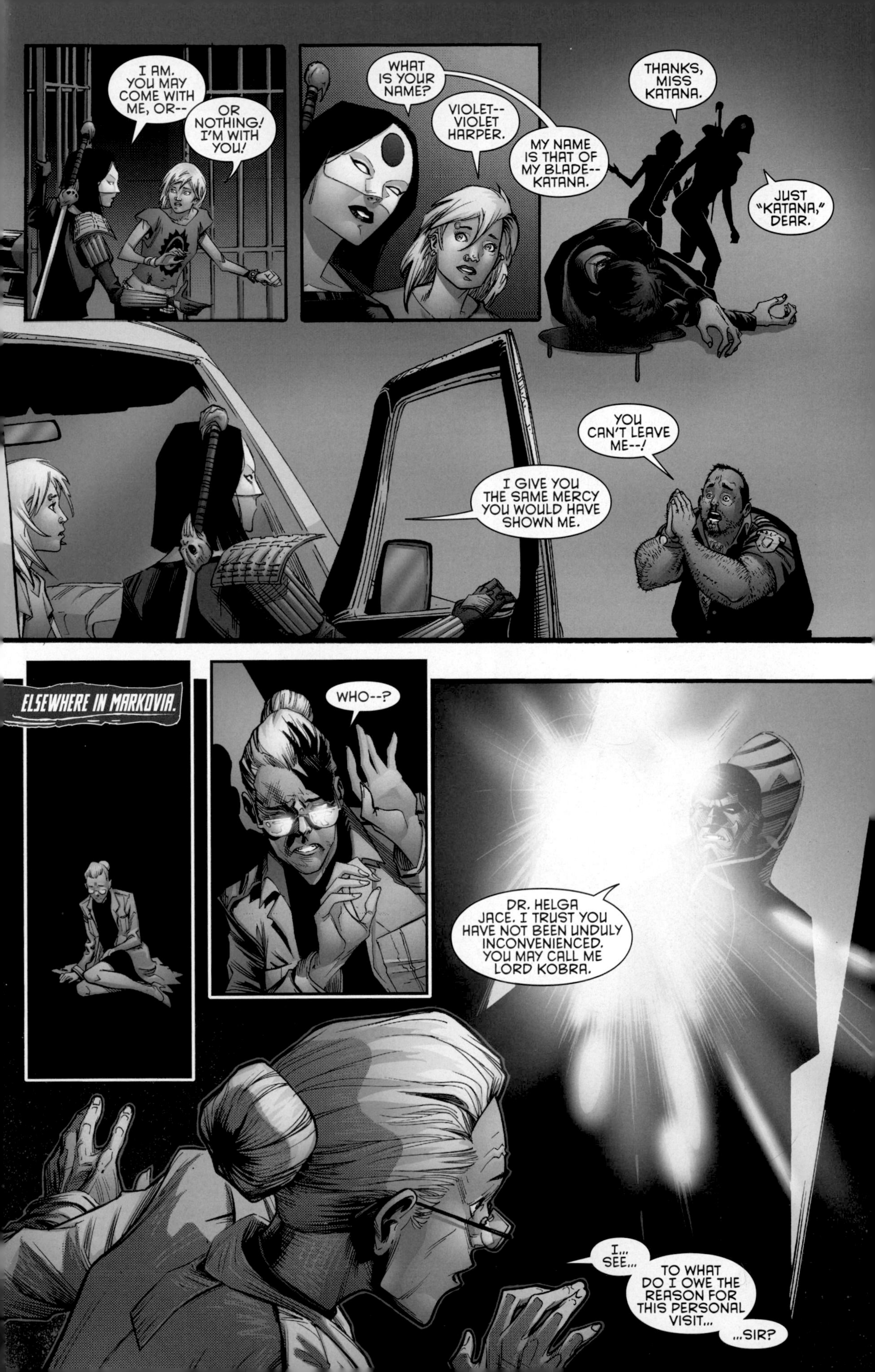
I AM. YOU MAY COME WITH ME, OR--
OR NOTHING! I'M WITH YOU!
WHAT IS YOUR NAME?
VIOLET-- VIOLET HARPER.
MY NAME IS THAT OF MY BLADE-- KATANA.
THANKS, MISS KATANA.
JUST "KATANA," DEAR.
YOU CAN'T LEAVE ME--!
I GIVE YOU THE SAME MERCY YOU WOULD HAVE SHOWN ME.
ELSEWHERE IN MARKOVIA.
WHO--?
DR. HELGA JACE. I TRUST YOU HAVE NOT BEEN UNDULY INCONVENIENCED. YOU MAY CALL ME LORD KOBRA.
I... SEE...
TO WHAT DO I OWE THE REASON FOR THIS PERSONAL VISIT...
...SIR?

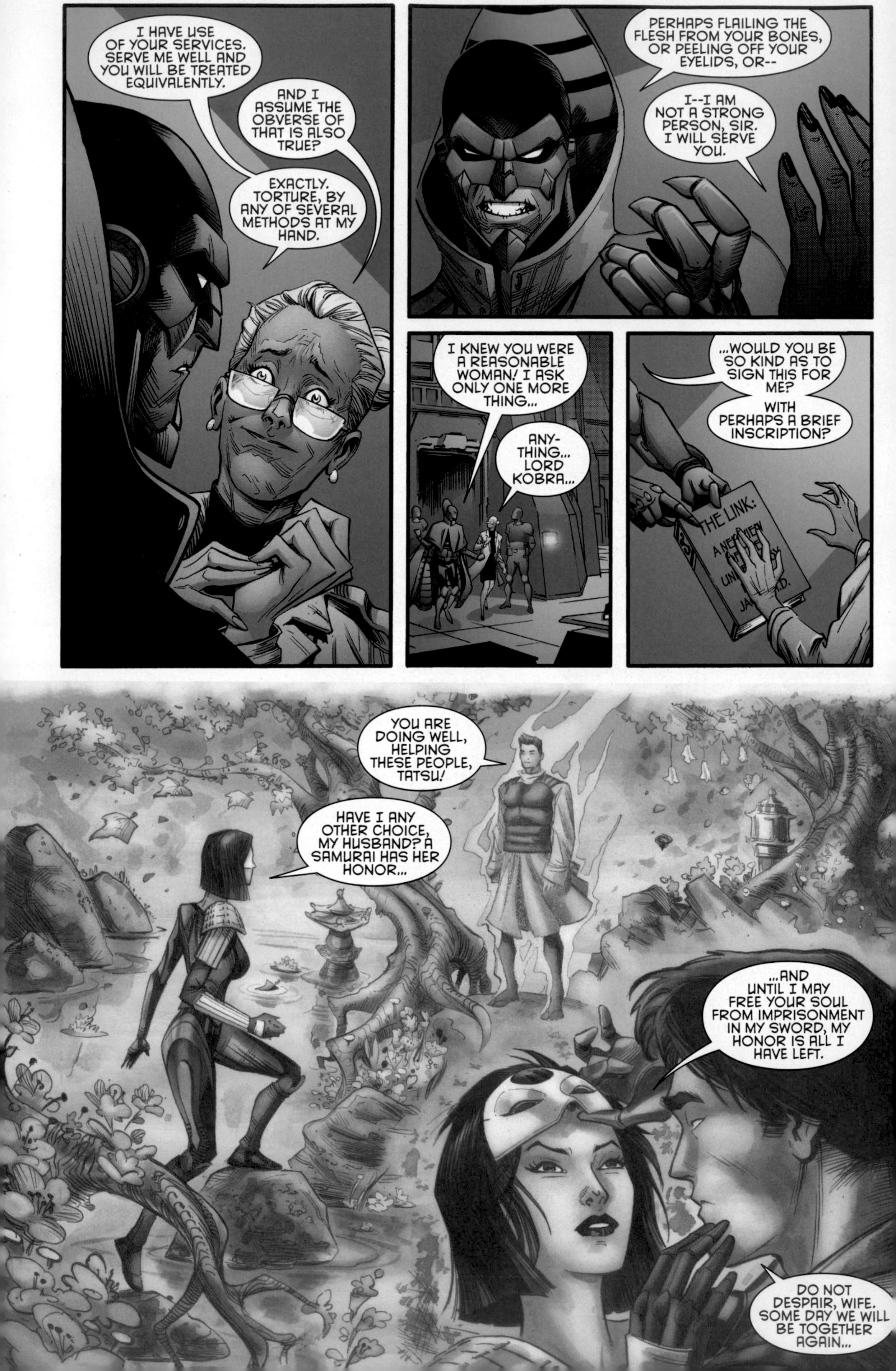
I HAVE USE OF YOUR SERVICES. SERVE ME WELL AND YOU WILL BE TREATED EQUIVALENTLY.
AND I ASSUME THE OBVERSE OF THAT IS ALSO TRUE?
EXACTLY. TORTURE, BY ANY OF SEVERAL METHODS AT MY HAND.
PERHAPS FLAILING THE FLESH FROM YOUR BONES, OR PEELING OFF YOUR EYELIDS, OR--
I--I AM NOT A STRONG PERSON, SIR. I WILL SERVE YOU.
I KNEW YOU WERE A REASONABLE WOMAN! I ASK ONLY ONE MORE THING...
ANY-THING... LORD KOBRA...
...WOULD YOU BE SO KIND AS TO SIGN THIS FOR ME?
WITH PERHAPS A BRIEF INSCRIPTION?
THE LINK:
YOU ARE DOING WELL, HELPING THESE PEOPLE, TATSU!
HAVE I ANY OTHER CHOICE, MY HUSBAND? A SAMURAI HAS HER HONOR...
...AND UNTIL I MAY FREE YOUR SOUL FROM IMPRISONMENT IN MY SWORD, MY HONOR IS ALL I HAVE LEFT.
DO NOT DESPAIR, WIFE. SOME DAY WE WILL BE TOGETHER AGAIN...

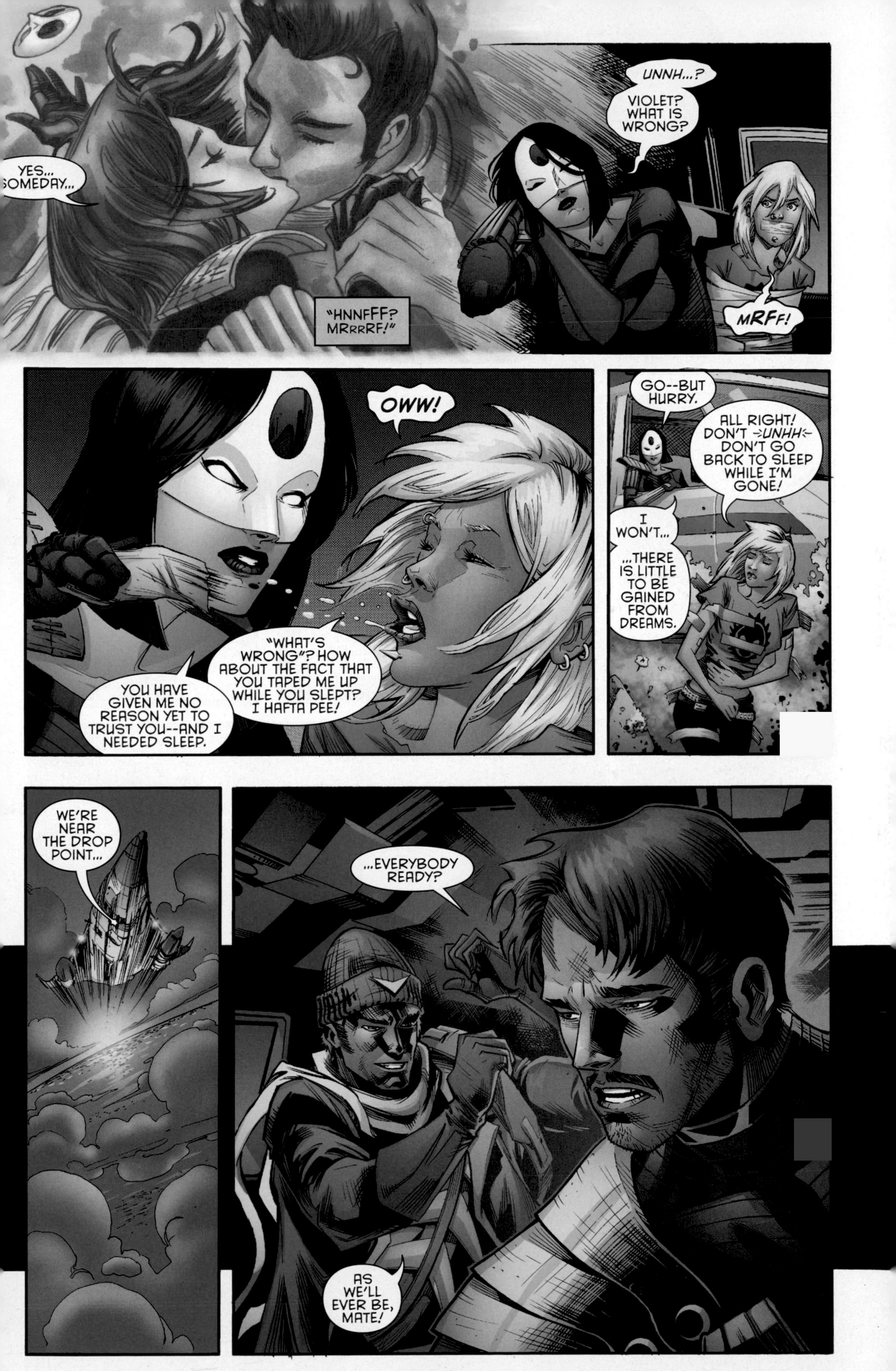
YES... SOMEDAY...
"HNNFFF? MRrrRF!"
UNNH...?
VIOLET? WHAT IS WRONG?
MRFf!
OWW!
"WHAT'S WRONG"? HOW ABOUT THE FACT THAT YOU TAPED ME UP WHILE YOU SLEPT? I HAFTA PEE!
YOU HAVE GIVEN ME NO REASON YET TO TRUST YOU--AND I NEEDED SLEEP.
GO--BUT HURRY.
ALL RIGHT! DON'T UNHH DON'T GO BACK TO SLEEP WHILE I'M GONE!
I WON'T...
...THERE IS LITTLE TO BE GAINED FROM DREAMS.
WE'RE NEAR THE DROP POINT...
...EVERYBODY READY?
AS WE'LL EVER BE, MATE!

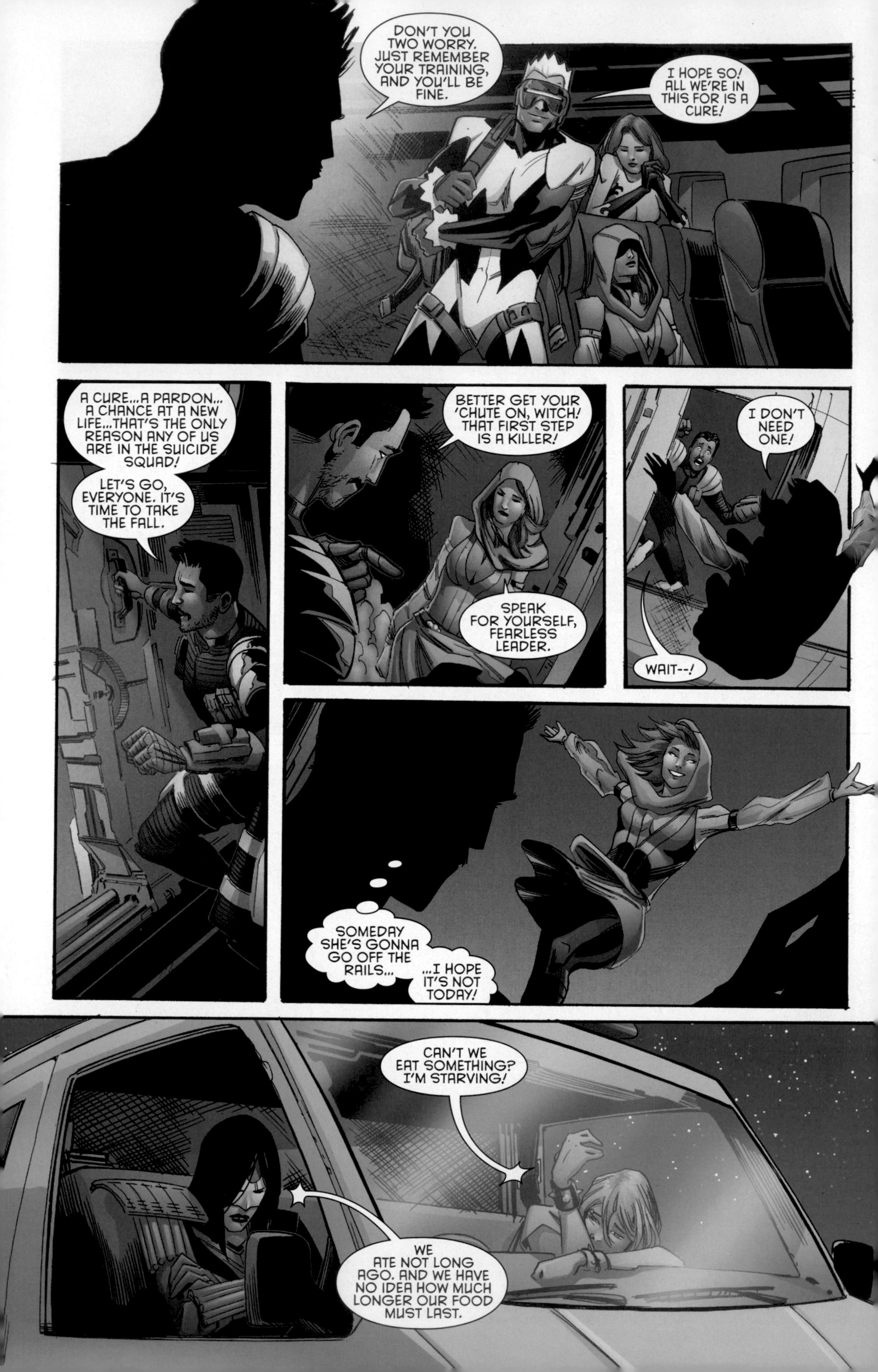

DON'T YOU TWO WORRY. JUST REMEMBER YOUR TRAINING, AND YOU'LL BE FINE.
I HOPE SO! ALL WE'RE IN THIS FOR IS A CURE!
A CURE...A PARDON... A CHANCE AT A NEW LIFE...THAT'S THE ONLY REASON ANY OF US ARE IN THE SUICIDE SQUAD!
LET'S GO, EVERYONE. IT'S TIME TO TAKE THE FALL.
BETTER GET YOUR 'CHUTE ON, WITCH! THAT FIRST STEP IS A KILLER!
SPEAK FOR YOURSELF, FEARLESS LEADER.
I DON'T NEED ONE!
WAIT--!
SOMEDAY SHE'S GONNA GO OFF THE RAILS...
...I HOPE IT'S NOT TODAY!
CAN'T WE EAT SOMETHING? I'M STARVING!
WE ATE NOT LONG AGO. AND WE HAVE NO IDEA HOW MUCH LONGER OUR FOOD MUST LAST.

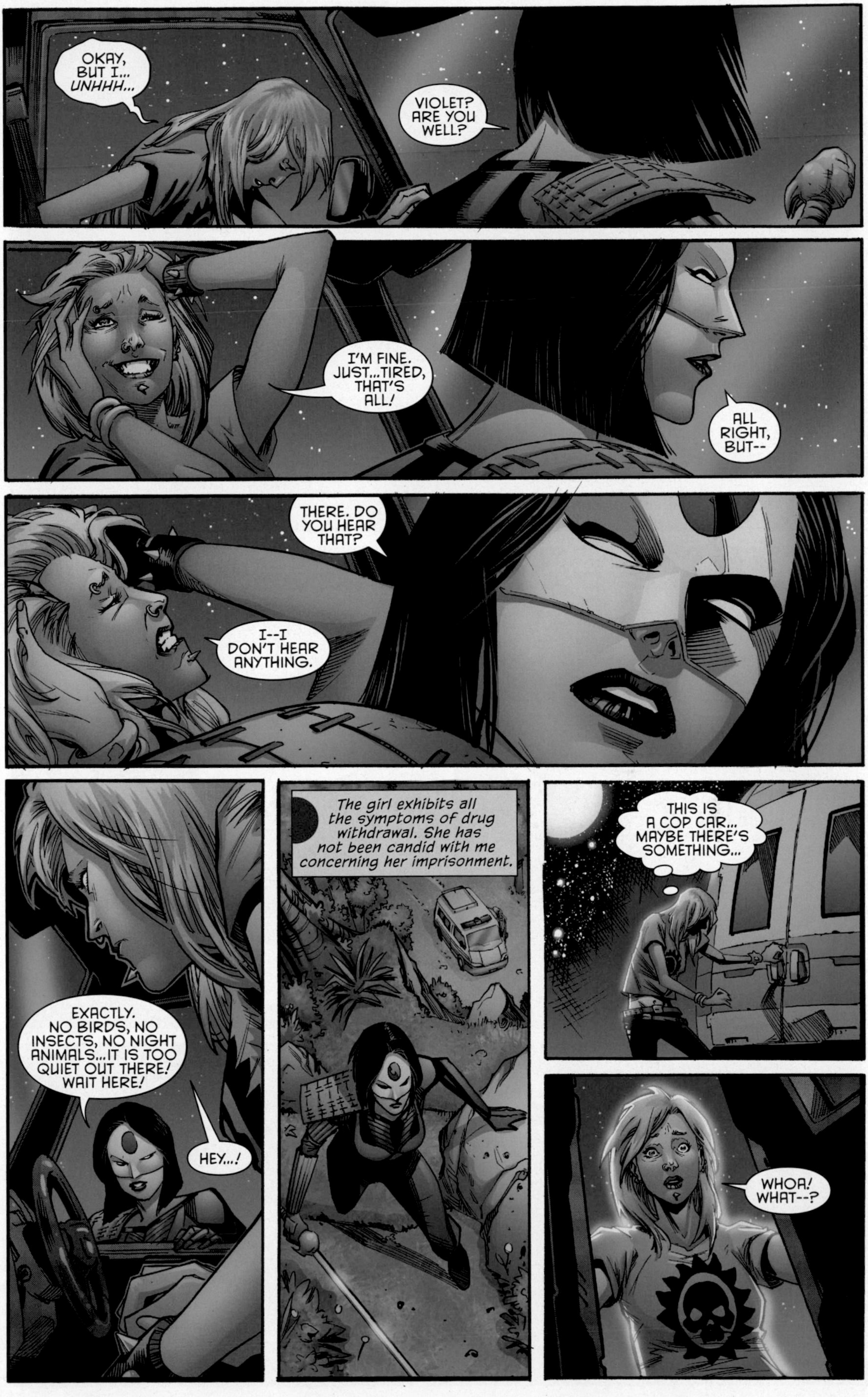
OKAY, BUT I... UNHHH...
VIOLET? ARE YOU WELL?
I'M FINE. JUST...TIRED, THAT'S ALL!
ALL RIGHT, BUT--
THERE. DO YOU HEAR THAT?
I--I DON'T HEAR ANYTHING.
EXACTLY. NO BIRDS, NO INSECTS, NO NIGHT ANIMALS...IT IS TOO QUIET OUT THERE! WAIT HERE!
HEY...!
The girl exhibits all the symptoms of drug withdrawal. She has not been candid with me concerning her imprisonment.
THIS IS A COP CAR... MAYBE THERE'S SOMETHING...
WHOA! WHAT--?

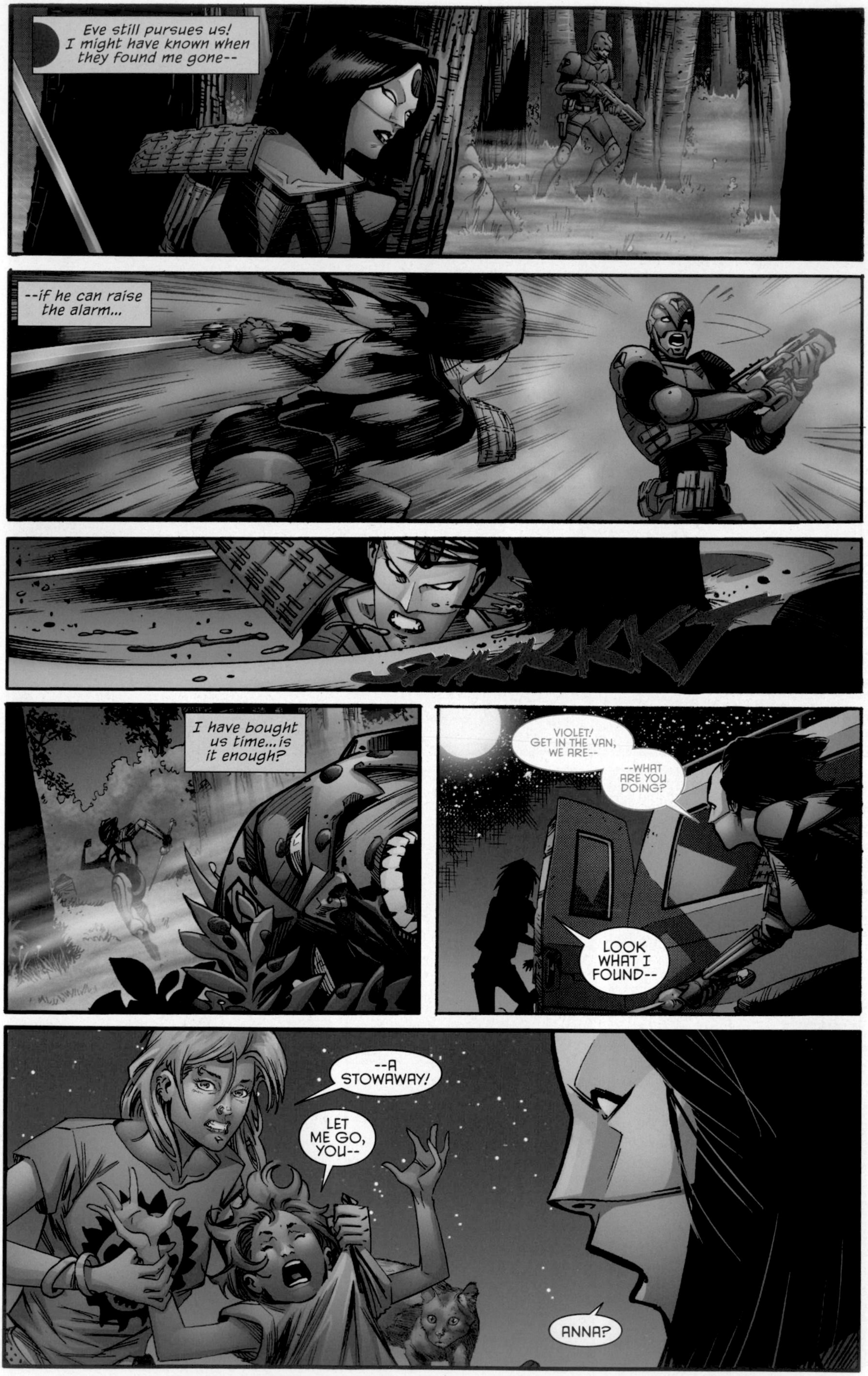
Eve still pursues us! I might have known when they found me gone--
--if he can raise the alarm...
I have bought us time...is it enough?
VIOLET! GET IN THE VAN, WE ARE--
--WHAT ARE YOU DOING?
LOOK WHAT I FOUND--
--A STOWAWAY!
LET ME GO, YOU--
ANNA?

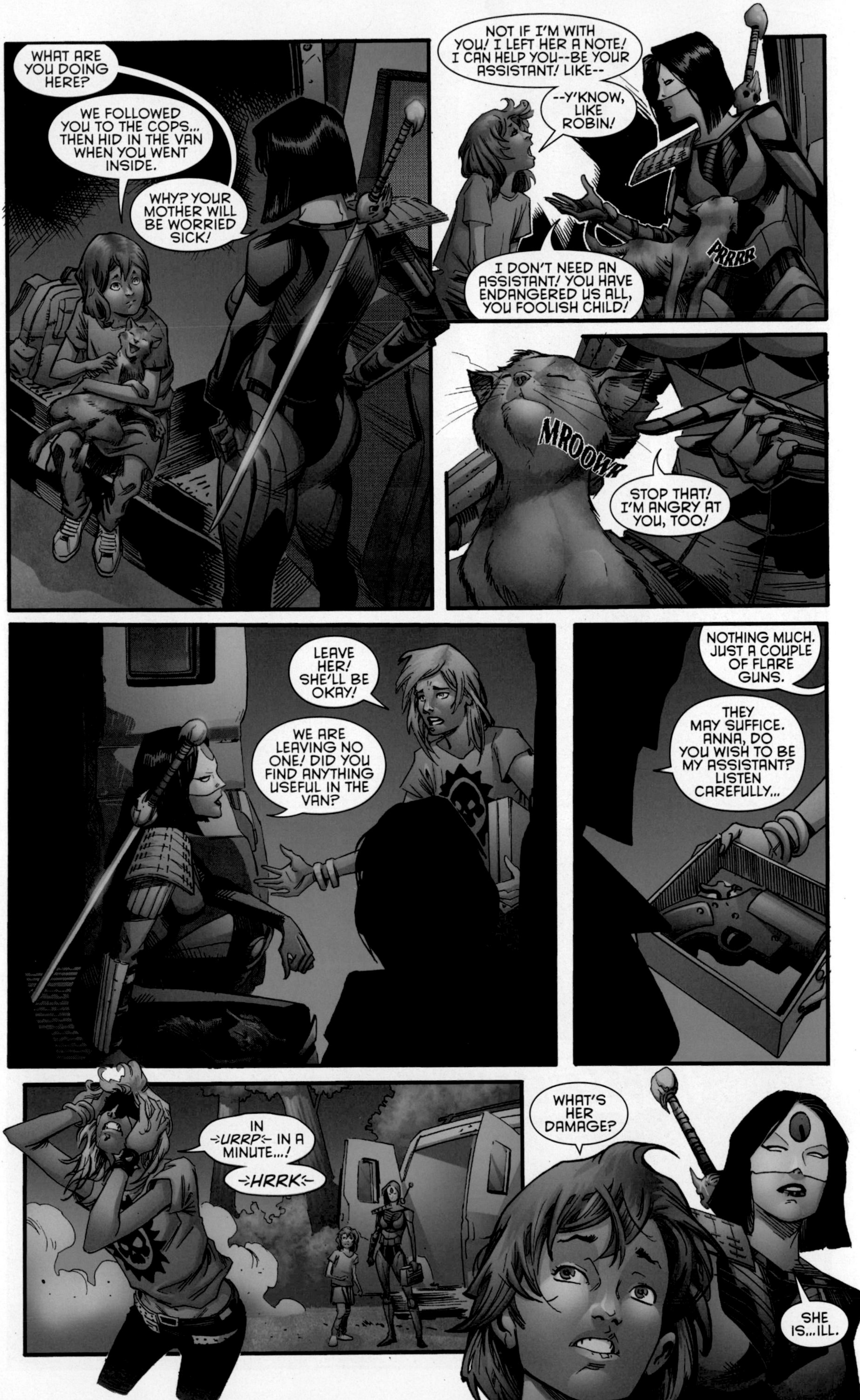
WHAT ARE YOU DOING HERE?
WE FOLLOWED YOU TO THE COPS... THEN HID IN THE VAN WHEN YOU WENT INSIDE.
WHY? YOUR MOTHER WILL BE WORRIED SICK!
NOT IF I'M WITH YOU! I LEFT HER A NOTE! I CAN HELP YOU--BE YOUR ASSISTANT! LIKE--
--Y'KNOW, LIKE ROBIN!
I DON'T NEED AN ASSISTANT! YOU HAVE ENDANGERED US ALL, YOU FOOLISH CHILD!
PRRRR
MROOWR
STOP THAT! I'M ANGRY AT YOU, TOO!
LEAVE HER! SHE'LL BE OKAY!
WE ARE LEAVING NO ONE! DID YOU FIND ANYTHING USEFUL IN THE VAN?
NOTHING MUCH. JUST A COUPLE OF FLARE GUNS.
THEY MAY SUFFICE. ANNA, DO YOU WISH TO BE MY ASSISTANT? LISTEN CAREFULLY...
IN -URRP- IN A MINUTE...!
-HRRK-
WHAT'S HER DAMAGE?
SHE IS...ILL.

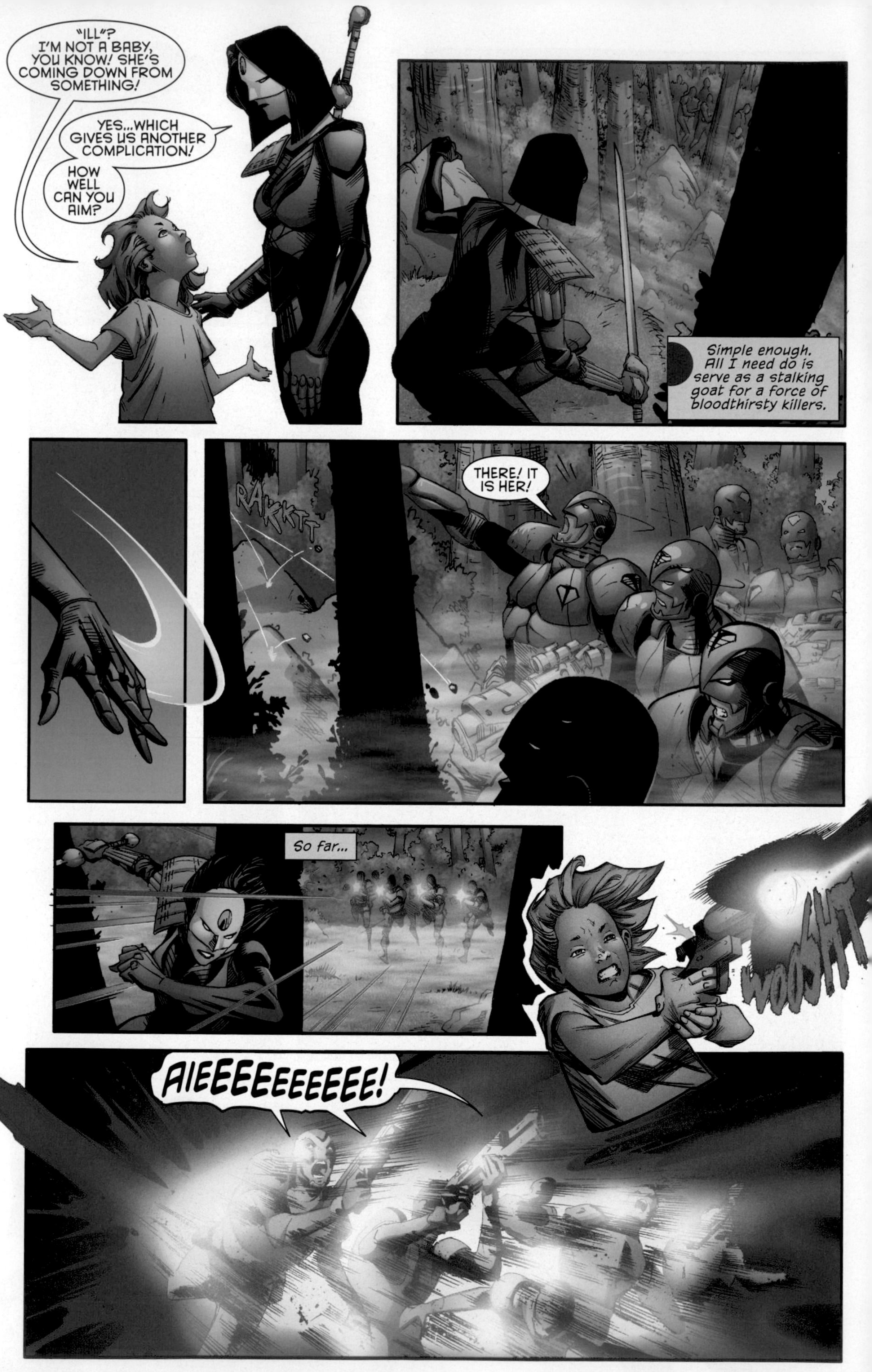
"ILL"? I'M NOT A BABY, YOU KNOW! SHE'S COMING DOWN FROM SOMETHING!
YES...WHICH GIVES US ANOTHER COMPLICATION!
HOW WELL CAN YOU AIM?
Simple enough. All I need do is serve as a stalking goat for a force of bloodthirsty killers.
RAKKTT
THERE! IT IS HER!
So far...
WOOSHT
AIEEEEEEEEEEE!

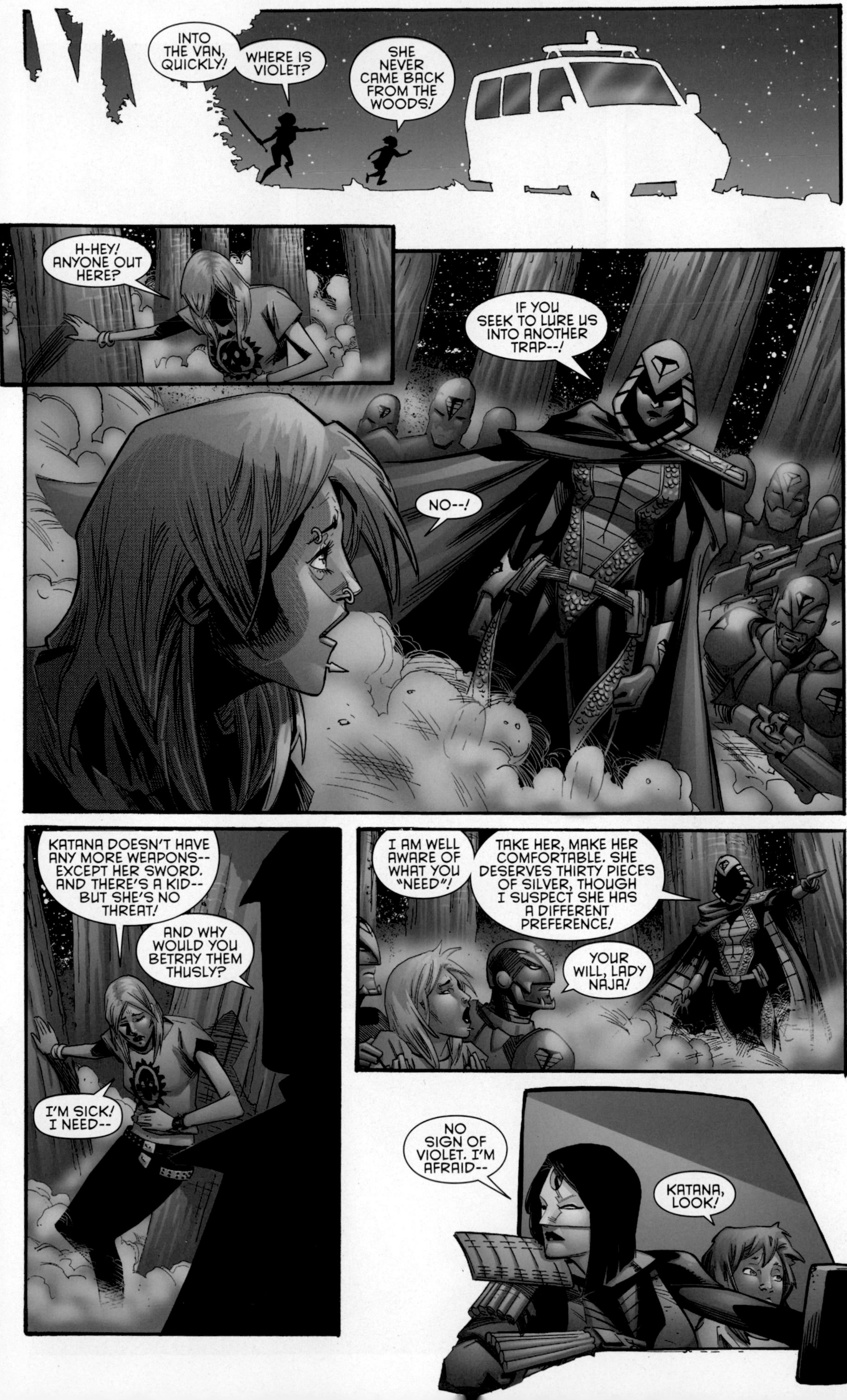
INTO THE VAN, QUICKLY!
WHERE IS VIOLET?
SHE NEVER CAME BACK FROM THE WOODS!
H-HEY! ANYONE OUT HERE?
IF YOU SEEK TO LURE US INTO ANOTHER TRAP--!
NO--!
KATANA DOESN'T HAVE ANY MORE WEAPONS-- EXCEPT HER SWORD. AND THERE'S A KID-- BUT SHE'S NO THREAT!
AND WHY WOULD YOU BETRAY THEM THUSLY?
I'M SICK! I NEED--
I AM WELL AWARE OF WHAT YOU "NEED"!
TAKE HER, MAKE HER COMFORTABLE. SHE DESERVES THIRTY PIECES OF SILVER, THOUGH I SUSPECT SHE HAS A DIFFERENT PREFERENCE!
YOUR WILL, LADY NAJA!
NO SIGN OF VIOLET. I'M AFRAID--
KATANA, LOOK!

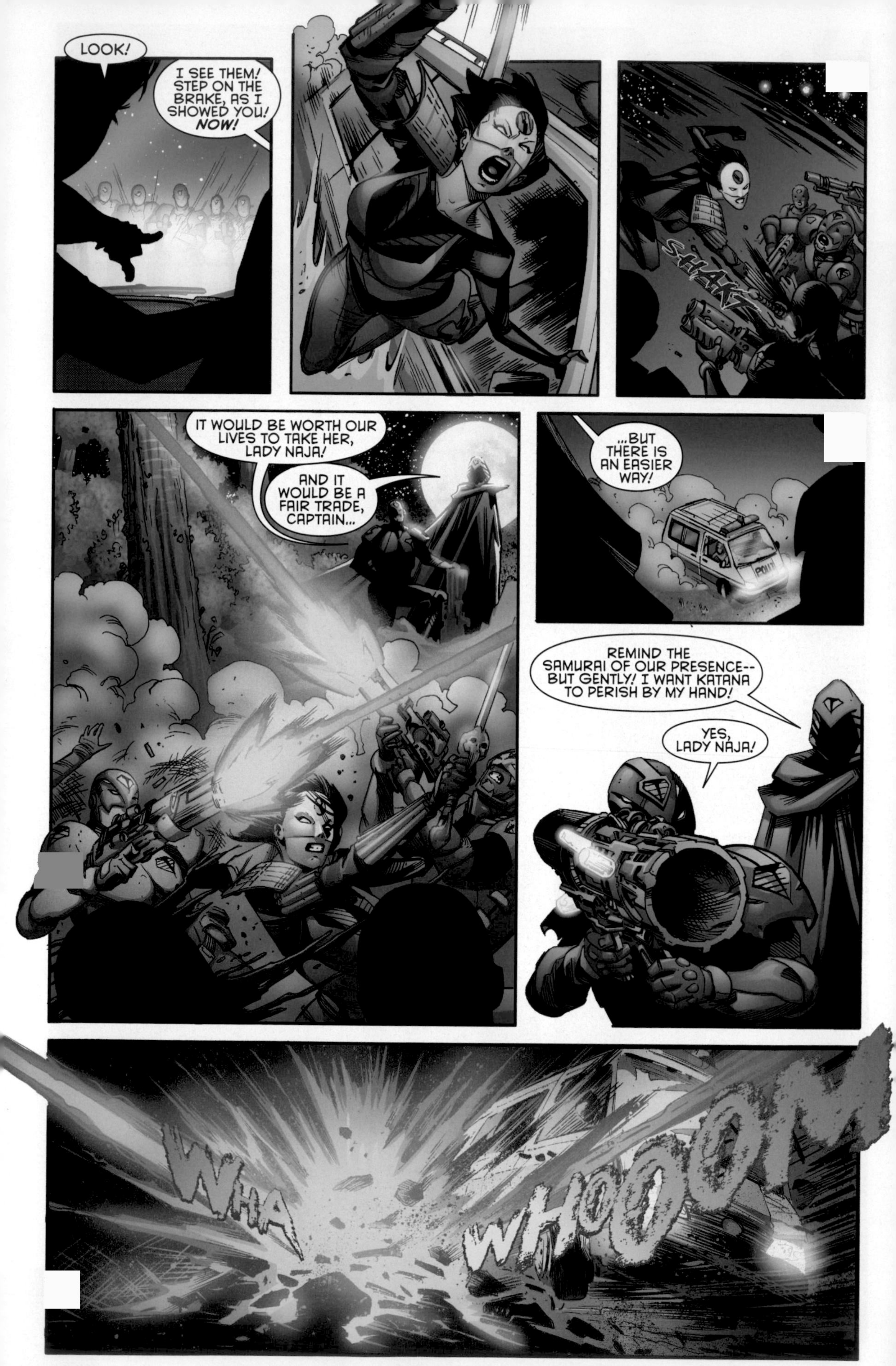
LOOK!
I SEE THEM! STEP ON THE BRAKE, AS I SHOWED YOU! *NOW!*
SHAKT
IT WOULD BE WORTH OUR LIVES TO TAKE HER, LADY NAJA!
AND IT WOULD BE A FAIR TRADE, CAPTAIN...
...BUT THERE IS AN EASIER WAY!
REMIND THE SAMURAI OF OUR PRESENCE-- BUT GENTLY! I WANT KATANA TO PERISH BY MY HAND!
YES, LADY NAJA!
WHA
WHOOOOM

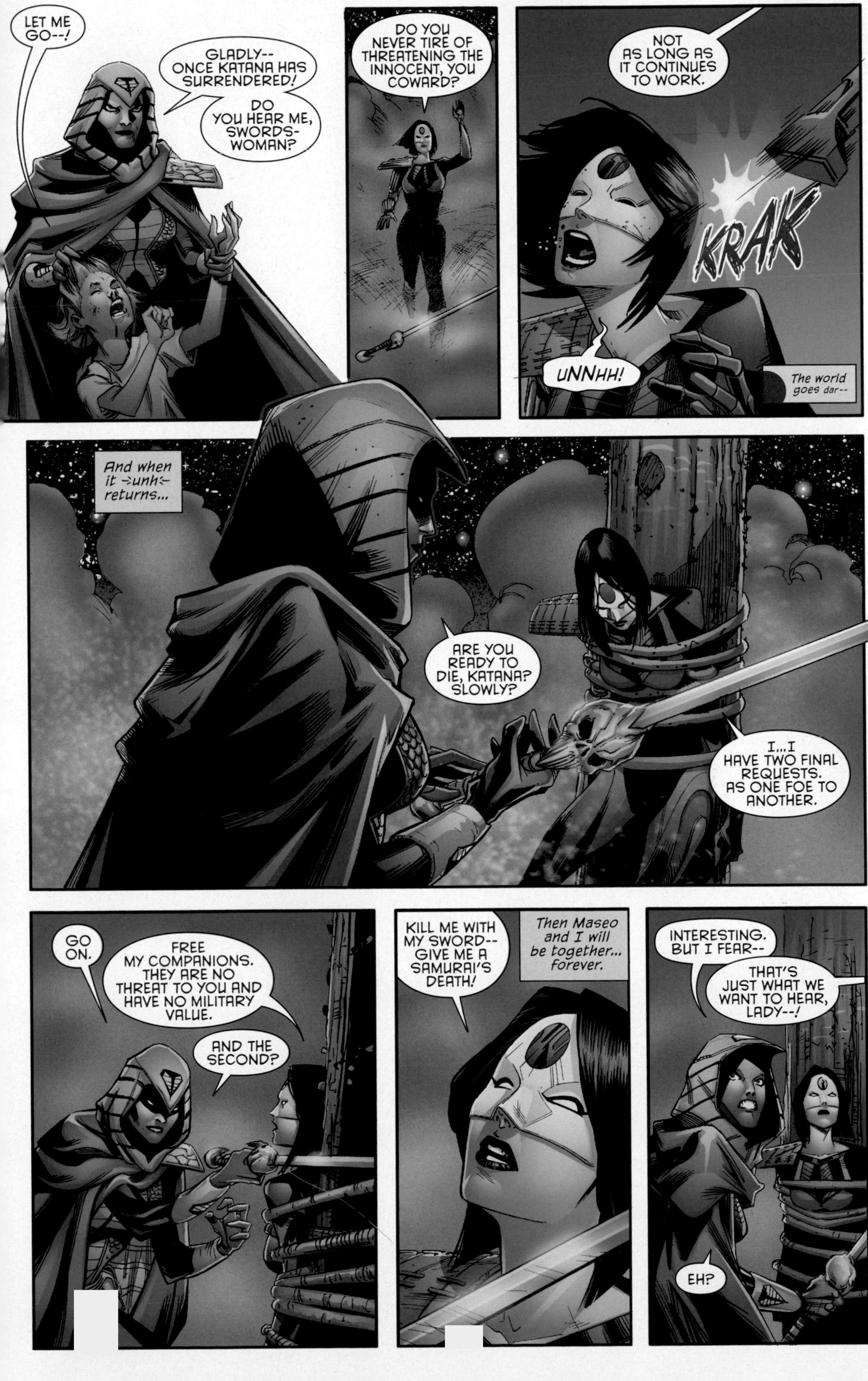
LET ME GO--!
GLADLY-- ONCE KATANA HAS SURRENDERED!
DO YOU HEAR ME, SWORDS-WOMAN?
DO YOU NEVER TIRE OF THREATENING THE INNOCENT, YOU COWARD?
NOT AS LONG AS IT CONTINUES TO WORK.
KRAK
UNNHH!
The world goes dar--
And when it ⇒unh⇐ returns...
ARE YOU READY TO DIE, KATANA? SLOWLY?
I...I HAVE TWO FINAL REQUESTS. AS ONE FOE TO ANOTHER.
GO ON.
FREE MY COMPANIONS. THEY ARE NO THREAT TO YOU AND HAVE NO MILITARY VALUE.
AND THE SECOND?
KILL ME WITH MY SWORD-- GIVE ME A SAMURAI'S DEATH!
Then Maseo and I will be together... forever.
INTERESTING. BUT I FEAR--
THAT'S JUST WHAT WE WANT TO HEAR, LADY--!
EH?

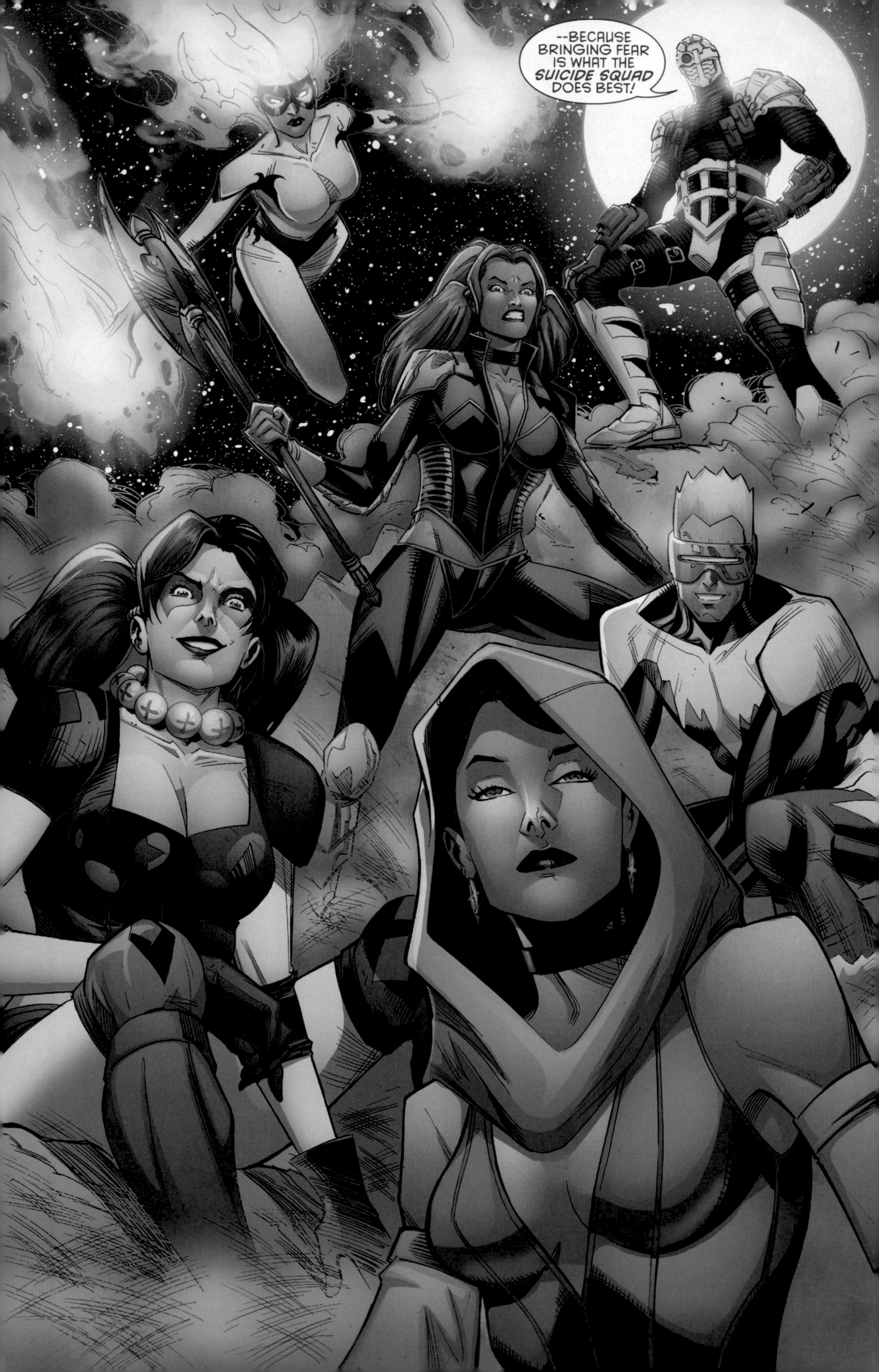
--BECAUSE BRINGING FEAR IS WHAT THE SUICIDE SQUAD DOES BEST!

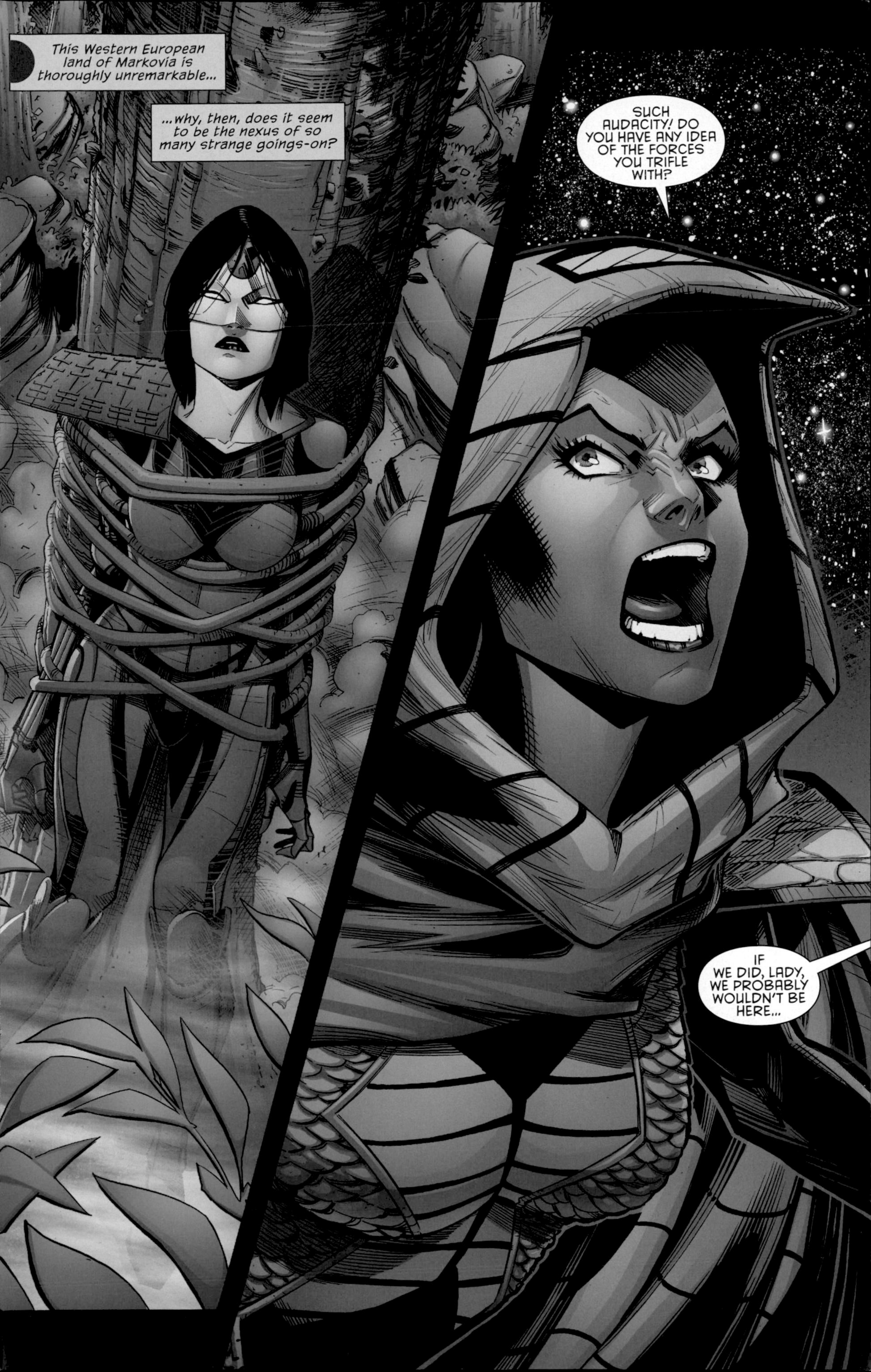
This Western European land of Markovia is thoroughly unremarkable...
...why, then, does it seem to be the nexus of so many strange goings-on?
SUCH AUDACITY! DO YOU HAVE ANY IDEA OF THE FORCES YOU TRIFLE WITH?
IF WE DID, LADY, WE PROBABLY WOULDN'T BE HERE...

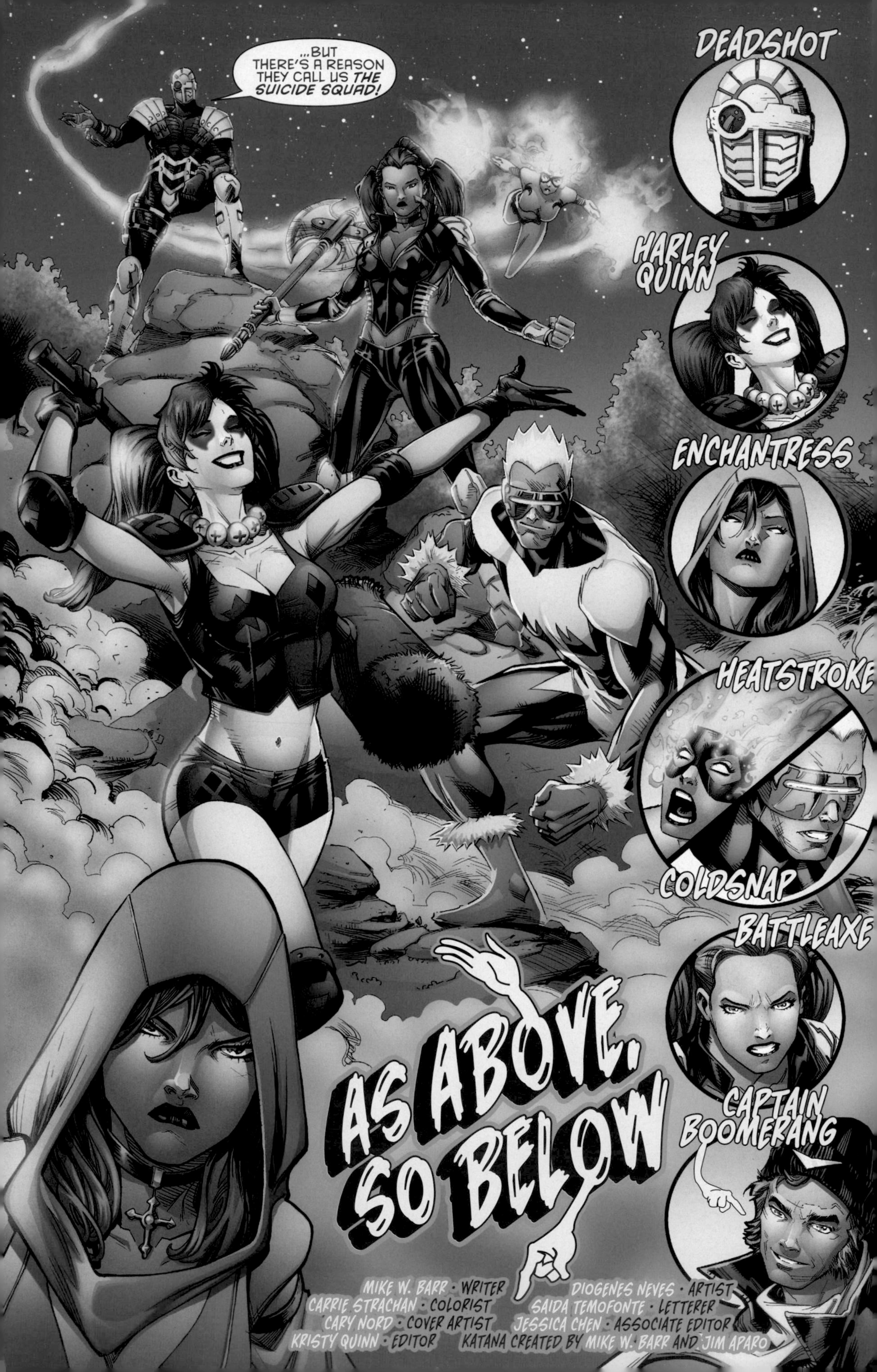

...BUT THERE'S A REASON THEY CALL US THE SUICIDE SQUAD!
DEADSHOT
HARLEY QUINN
ENCHANTRESS
HEATSTROKE
COLDSNAP
BATTLEAXE
CAPTAIN BOOMERANG
AS ABOVE, SO BELOW
MIKE W. BARR · WRITER
DIOGENES NEVES · ARTIST
CARRIE STRACHAN · COLORIST
SAIDA TEMOFONTE · LETTERER
CARY NORD · COVER ARTIST
JESSICA CHEN · ASSOCIATE EDITOR
KRISTY QUINN · EDITOR
KATANA CREATED BY MIKE W. BARR AND JIM APARO

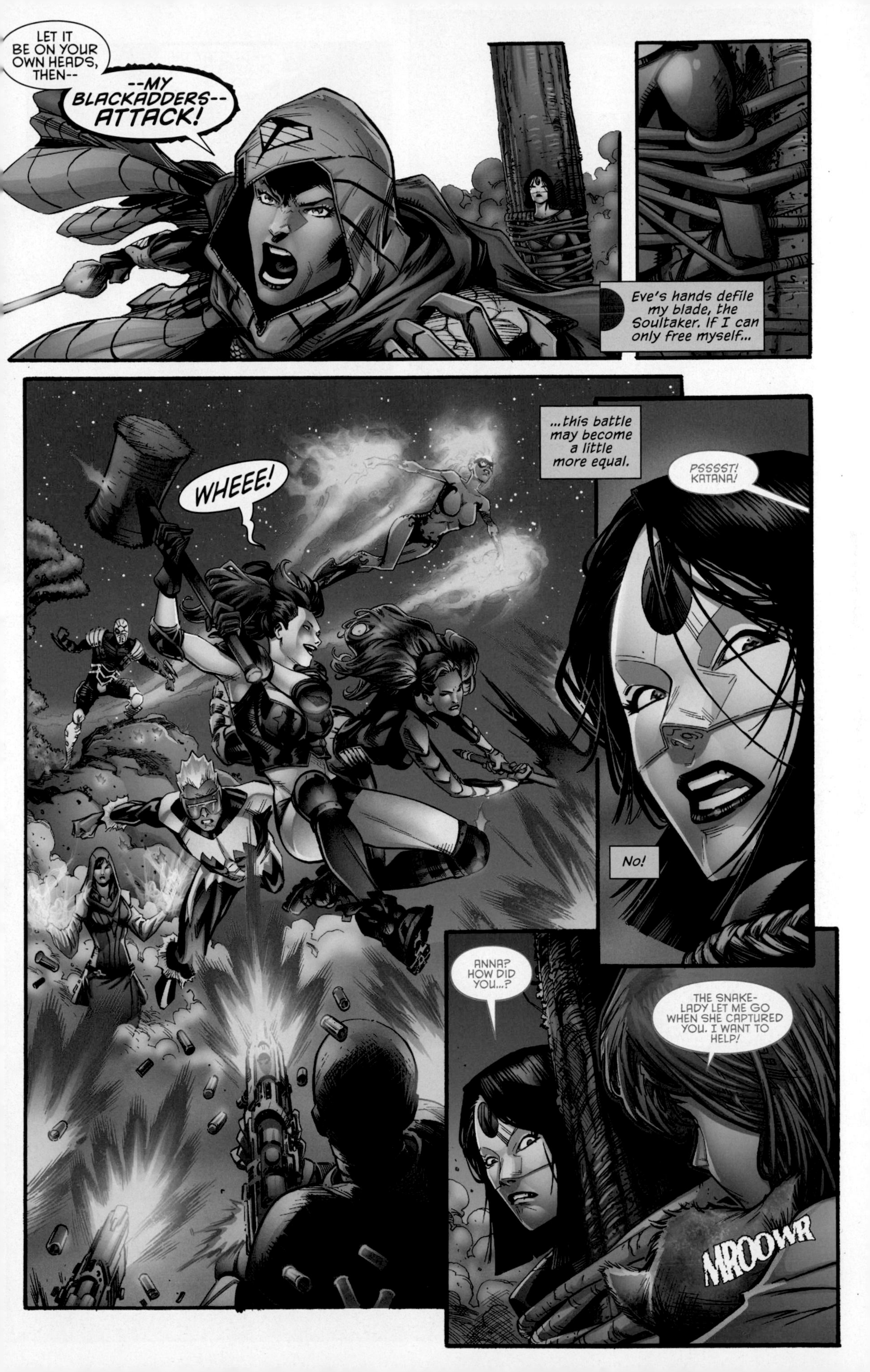
LET IT BE ON YOUR OWN HEADS, THEN--
--MY BLACKADDERS-- ATTACK!
Eve's hands defile my blade, the Soultaker. If I can only free myself...
...this battle may become a little more equal.
WHEEE!
PSSSST! KATANA!
No!
ANNA? HOW DID YOU...?
THE SNAKE-LADY LET ME GO WHEN SHE CAPTURED YOU. I WANT TO HELP!
MROOWR

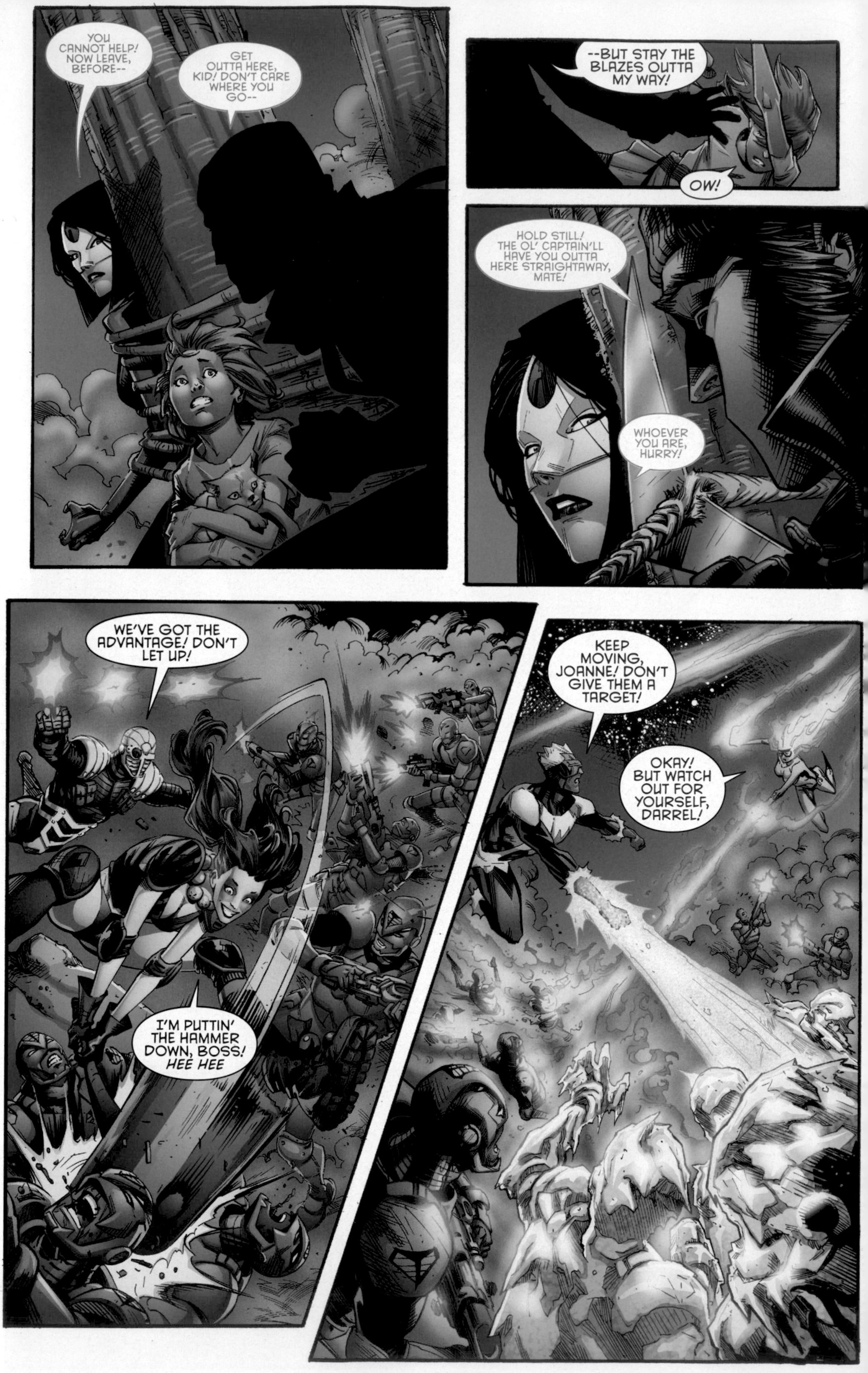
YOU CANNOT HELP! NOW LEAVE, BEFORE--
GET OUTTA HERE, KID! DON'T CARE WHERE YOU GO--
--BUT STAY THE BLAZES OUTTA MY WAY!
OW!
HOLD STILL! THE OL' CAPTAIN'LL HAVE YOU OUTTA HERE STRAIGHTAWAY, MATE!
WHOEVER YOU ARE, HURRY!
WE'VE GOT THE ADVANTAGE! DON'T LET UP!
I'M PUTTIN' THE HAMMER DOWN, BOSS! HEE HEE
KEEP MOVING, JOANNE! DON'T GIVE THEM A TARGET!
OKAY! BUT WATCH OUT FOR YOURSELF, DARREL!

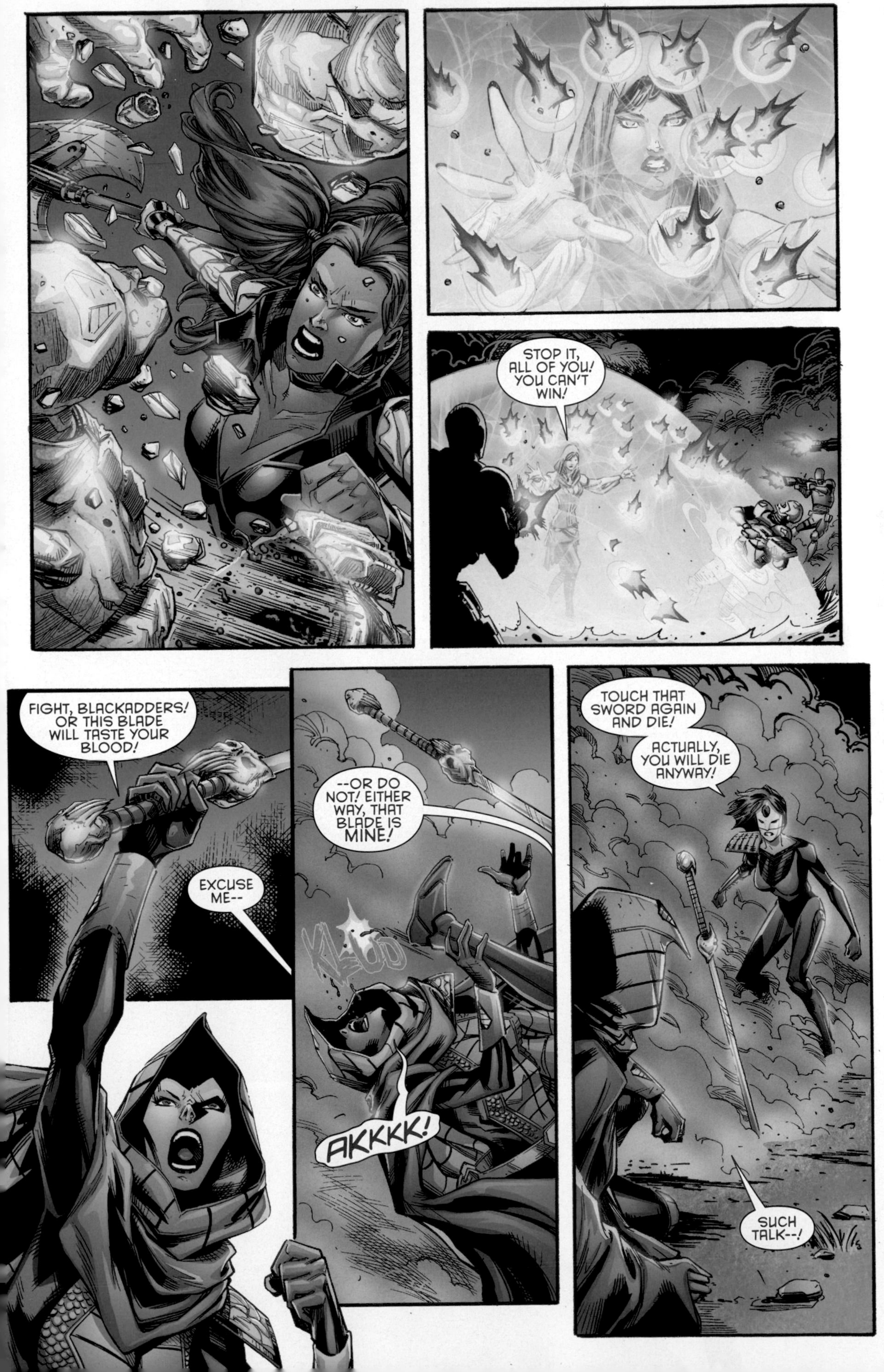
STOP IT, ALL OF YOU! YOU CAN'T WIN!
FIGHT, BLACKADDERS! OR THIS BLADE WILL TASTE YOUR BLOOD!
EXCUSE ME--
--OR DO NOT! EITHER WAY, THAT BLADE IS MINE!
KLUD
AKKKK!
TOUCH THAT SWORD AGAIN AND DIE!
ACTUALLY, YOU WILL DIE ANYWAY!
SUCH TALK--!

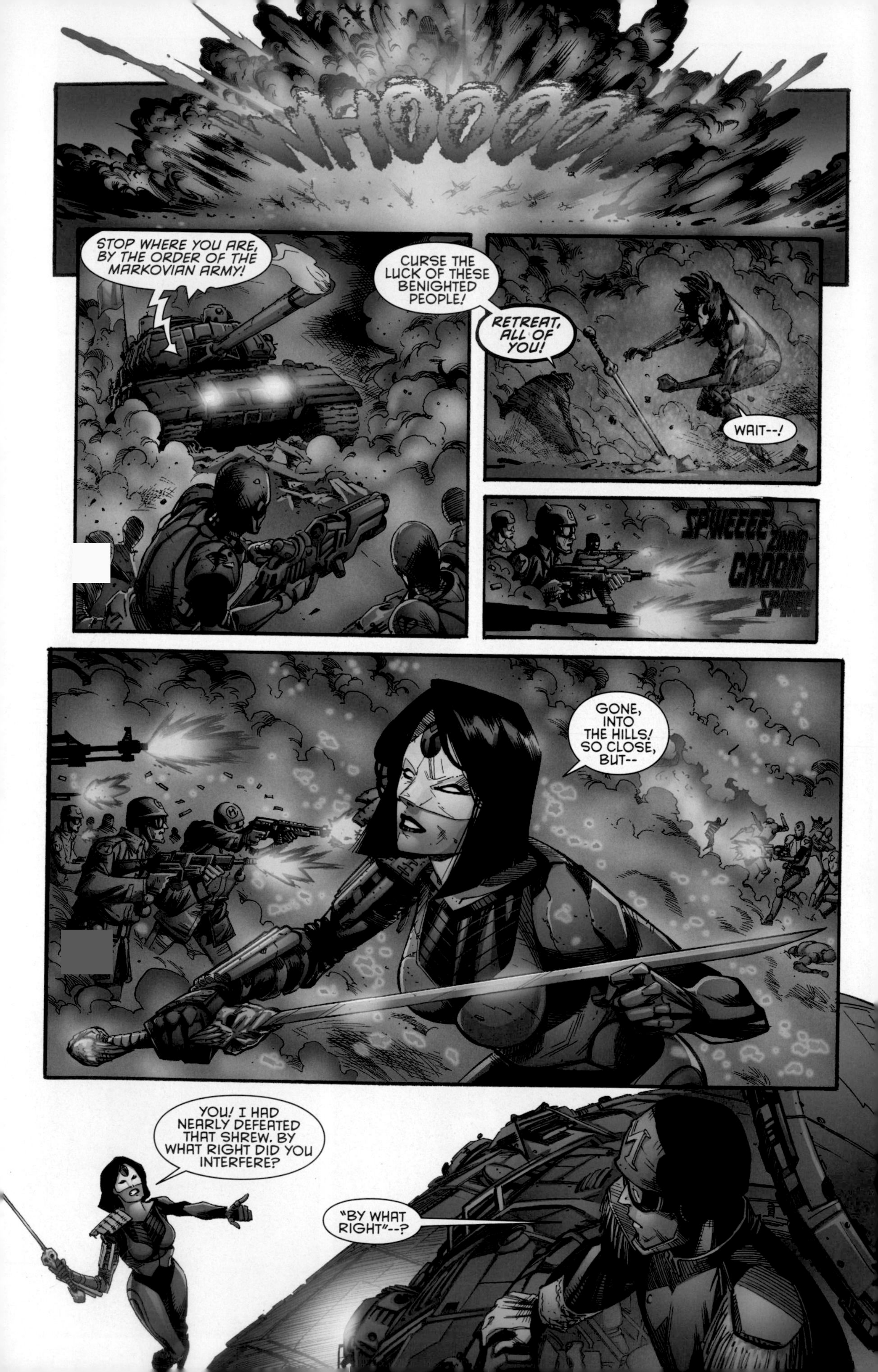
WHOOOOM
STOP WHERE YOU ARE, BY THE ORDER OF THE MARKOVIAN ARMY!
CURSE THE LUCK OF THESE BENIGHTED PEOPLE!
RETREAT, ALL OF YOU!
WAIT--!
SPWEEE
ZANG
CROOM
GONE, INTO THE HILLS! SO CLOSE, BUT--
YOU! I HAD NEARLY DEFEATED THAT SHREW. BY WHAT RIGHT DID YOU INTERFERE?
"BY WHAT RIGHT"--?

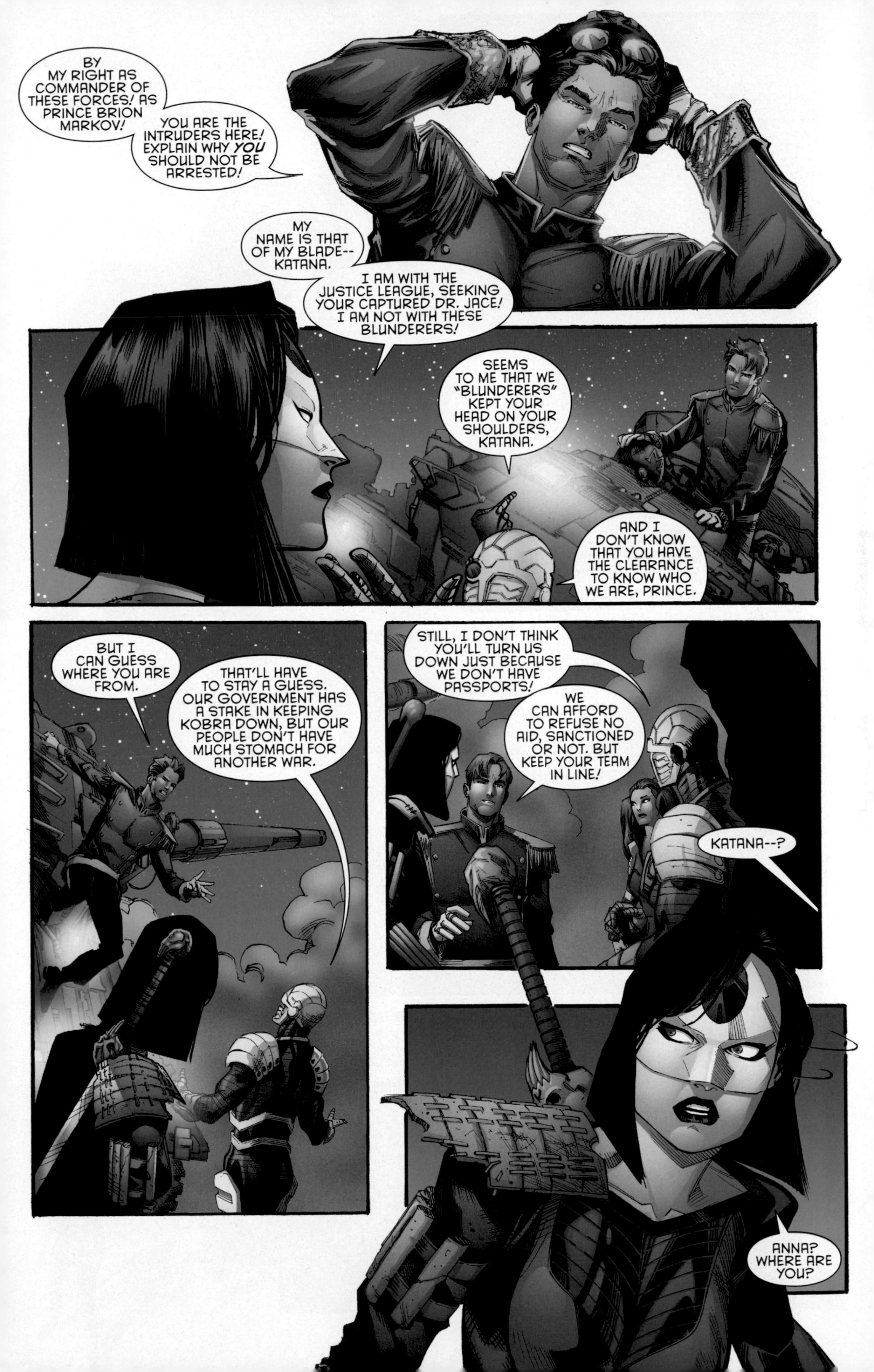
BY MY RIGHT AS COMMANDER OF THESE FORCES! AS PRINCE BRION MARKOV!
YOU ARE THE INTRUDERS HERE! EXPLAIN WHY YOU SHOULD NOT BE ARRESTED!
MY NAME IS THAT OF MY BLADE-- KATANA.
I AM WITH THE JUSTICE LEAGUE, SEEKING YOUR CAPTURED DR. JACE! I AM NOT WITH THESE BLUNDERERS!
SEEMS TO ME THAT WE "BLUNDERERS" KEPT YOUR HEAD ON YOUR SHOULDERS, KATANA.
AND I DON'T KNOW THAT YOU HAVE THE CLEARANCE TO KNOW WHO WE ARE, PRINCE.
BUT I CAN GUESS WHERE YOU ARE FROM.
THAT'LL HAVE TO STAY A GUESS. OUR GOVERNMENT HAS A STAKE IN KEEPING KOBRA DOWN, BUT OUR PEOPLE DON'T HAVE MUCH STOMACH FOR ANOTHER WAR.
STILL, I DON'T THINK YOU'LL TURN US DOWN JUST BECAUSE WE DON'T HAVE PASSPORTS!
WE CAN AFFORD TO REFUSE NO AID, SANCTIONED OR NOT. BUT KEEP YOUR TEAM IN LINE!
KATANA--?
ANNA? WHERE ARE YOU?

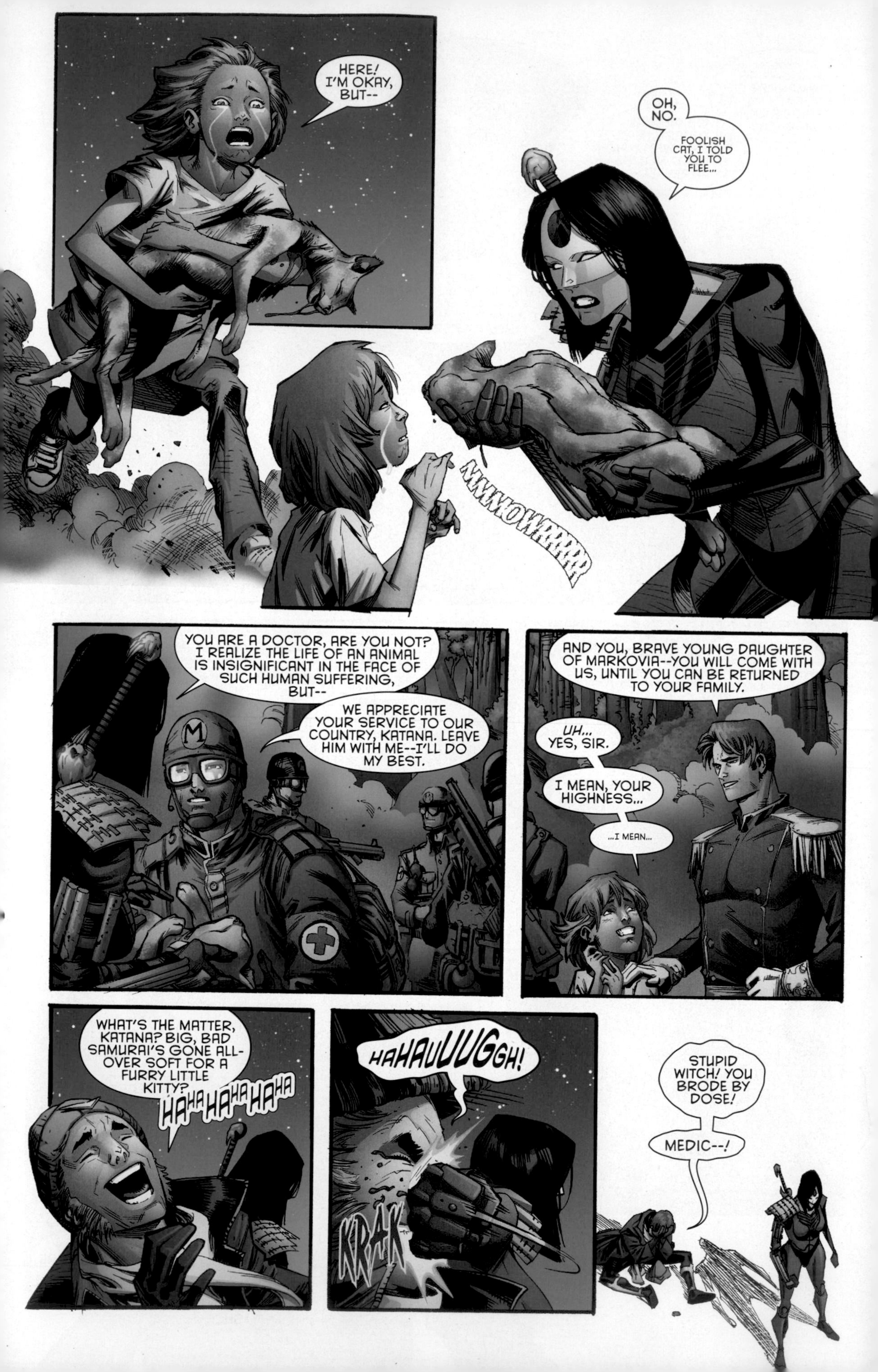
HERE! I'M OKAY, BUT--
OH, NO.
FOOLISH CAT, I TOLD YOU TO FLEE...
MMMOWRRRR
YOU ARE A DOCTOR, ARE YOU NOT? I REALIZE THE LIFE OF AN ANIMAL IS INSIGNIFICANT IN THE FACE OF SUCH HUMAN SUFFERING, BUT--
WE APPRECIATE YOUR SERVICE TO OUR COUNTRY, KATANA. LEAVE HIM WITH ME--I'LL DO MY BEST.
AND YOU, BRAVE YOUNG DAUGHTER OF MARKOVIA--YOU WILL COME WITH US, UNTIL YOU CAN BE RETURNED TO YOUR FAMILY.
UH... YES, SIR.
I MEAN, YOUR HIGHNESS...
...I MEAN...
WHAT'S THE MATTER, KATANA? BIG, BAD SAMURAI'S GONE ALL-OVER SOFT FOR A FURRY LITTLE KITTY?
HAHA HAHA HAHA
HAHAUUUGGH!
KRAK
STUPID WITCH! YOU BRODE BY DOSE!
MEDIC--!

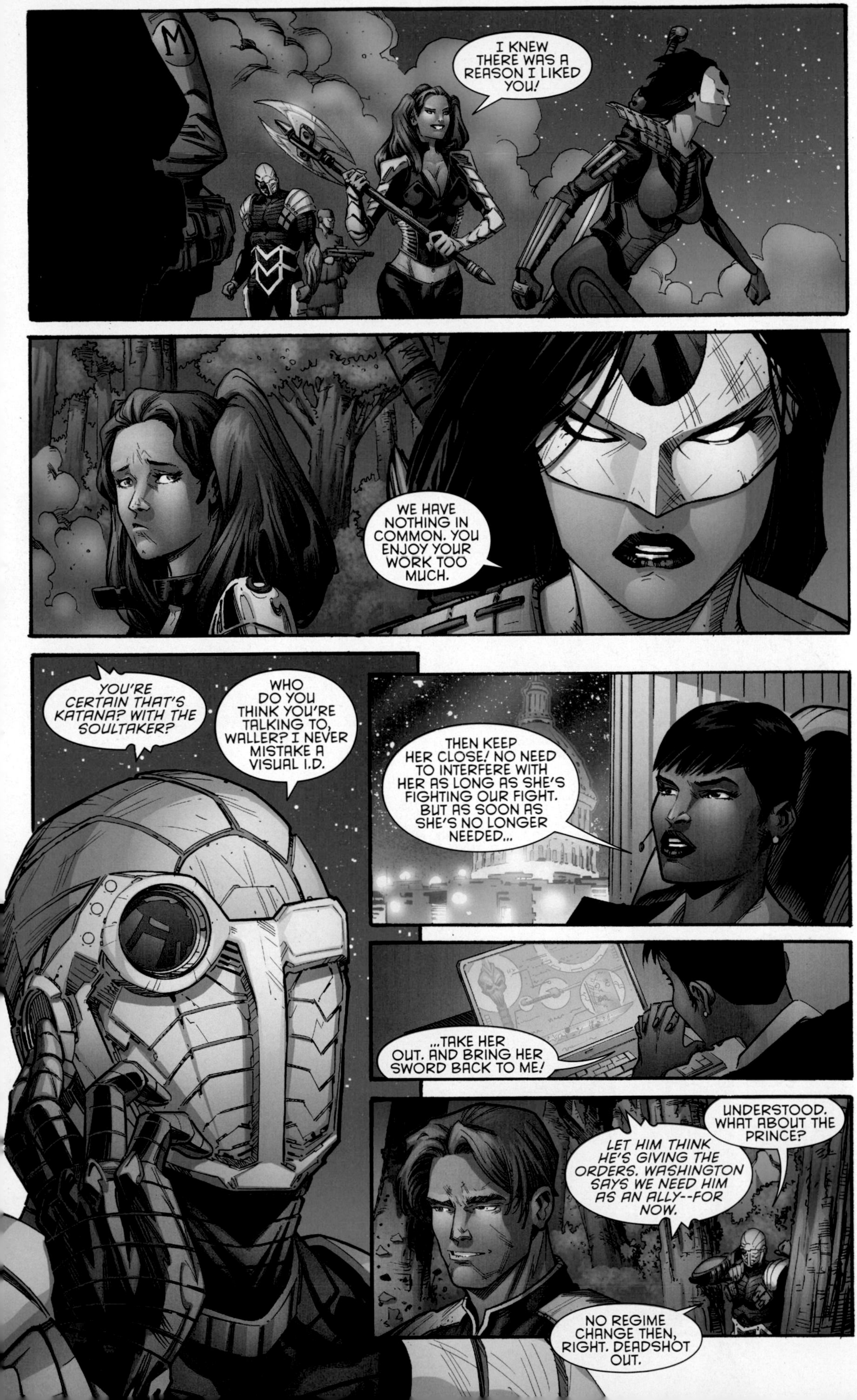
I KNEW THERE WAS A REASON I LIKED YOU!
WE HAVE NOTHING IN COMMON. YOU ENJOY YOUR WORK TOO MUCH.
YOU'RE CERTAIN THAT'S KATANA? WITH THE SOULTAKER?
WHO DO YOU THINK YOU'RE TALKING TO, WALLER? I NEVER MISTAKE A VISUAL I.D.
THEN KEEP HER CLOSE! NO NEED TO INTERFERE WITH HER AS LONG AS SHE'S FIGHTING OUR FIGHT. BUT AS SOON AS SHE'S NO LONGER NEEDED...
...TAKE HER OUT. AND BRING HER SWORD BACK TO ME!
UNDERSTOOD. WHAT ABOUT THE PRINCE?
LET HIM THINK HE'S GIVING THE ORDERS. WASHINGTON SAYS WE NEED HIM AS AN ALLY--FOR NOW.
NO REGIME CHANGE THEN, RIGHT. DEADSHOT OUT.

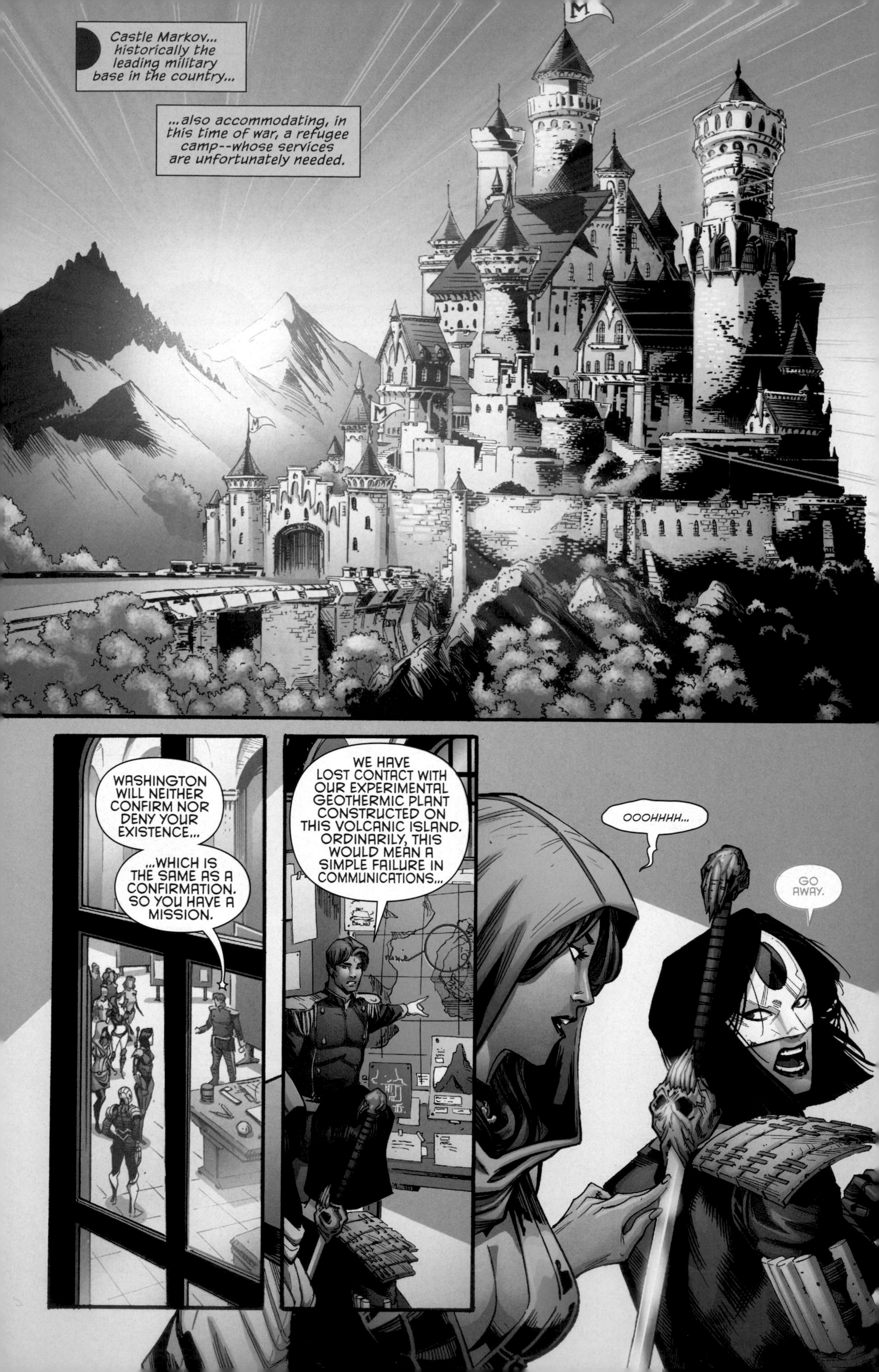
Castle Markov... historically the leading military base in the country...
...also accommodating, in this time of war, a refugee camp--whose services are unfortunately needed.
WASHINGTON WILL NEITHER CONFIRM NOR DENY YOUR EXISTENCE...
...WHICH IS THE SAME AS A CONFIRMATION. SO YOU HAVE A MISSION.
WE HAVE LOST CONTACT WITH OUR EXPERIMENTAL GEOTHERMIC PLANT CONSTRUCTED ON THIS VOLCANIC ISLAND. ORDINARILY, THIS WOULD MEAN A SIMPLE FAILURE IN COMMUNICATIONS...
OOOHHHH...
GO AWAY.

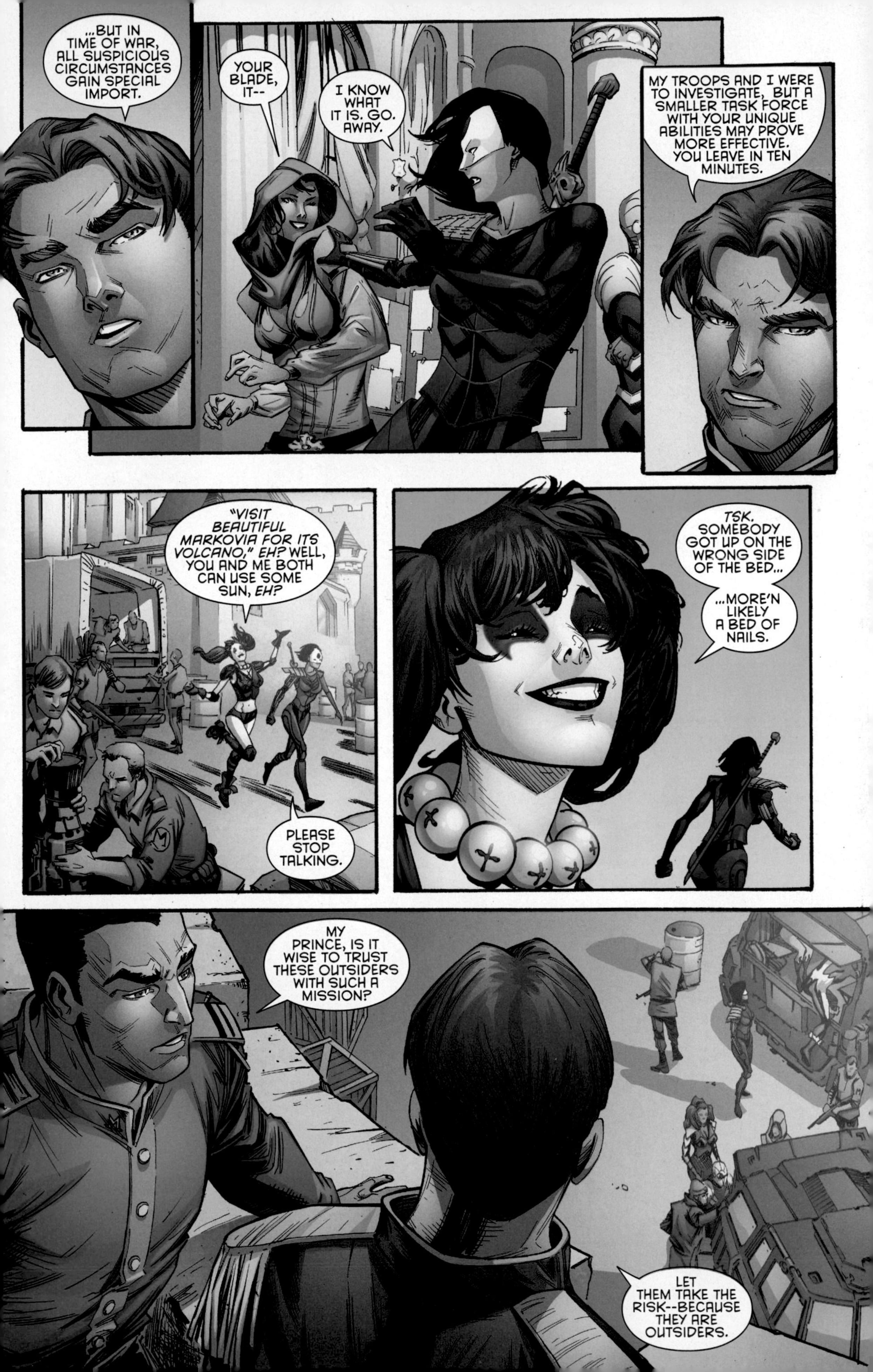
...BUT IN TIME OF WAR, ALL SUSPICIOUS CIRCUMSTANCES GAIN SPECIAL IMPORT.
YOUR BLADE, IT--
I KNOW WHAT IT IS. GO. AWAY.
MY TROOPS AND I WERE TO INVESTIGATE, BUT A SMALLER TASK FORCE WITH YOUR UNIQUE ABILITIES MAY PROVE MORE EFFECTIVE. YOU LEAVE IN TEN MINUTES.
"VISIT BEAUTIFUL MARKOVIA FOR ITS VOLCANO," EH? WELL, YOU AND ME BOTH CAN USE SOME SUN, EH?
PLEASE STOP TALKING.
TSK. SOMEBODY GOT UP ON THE WRONG SIDE OF THE BED...
...MORE'N LIKELY A BED OF NAILS.
MY PRINCE, IS IT WISE TO TRUST THESE OUTSIDERS WITH SUCH A MISSION?
LET THEM TAKE THE RISK--BECAUSE THEY ARE OUTSIDERS.

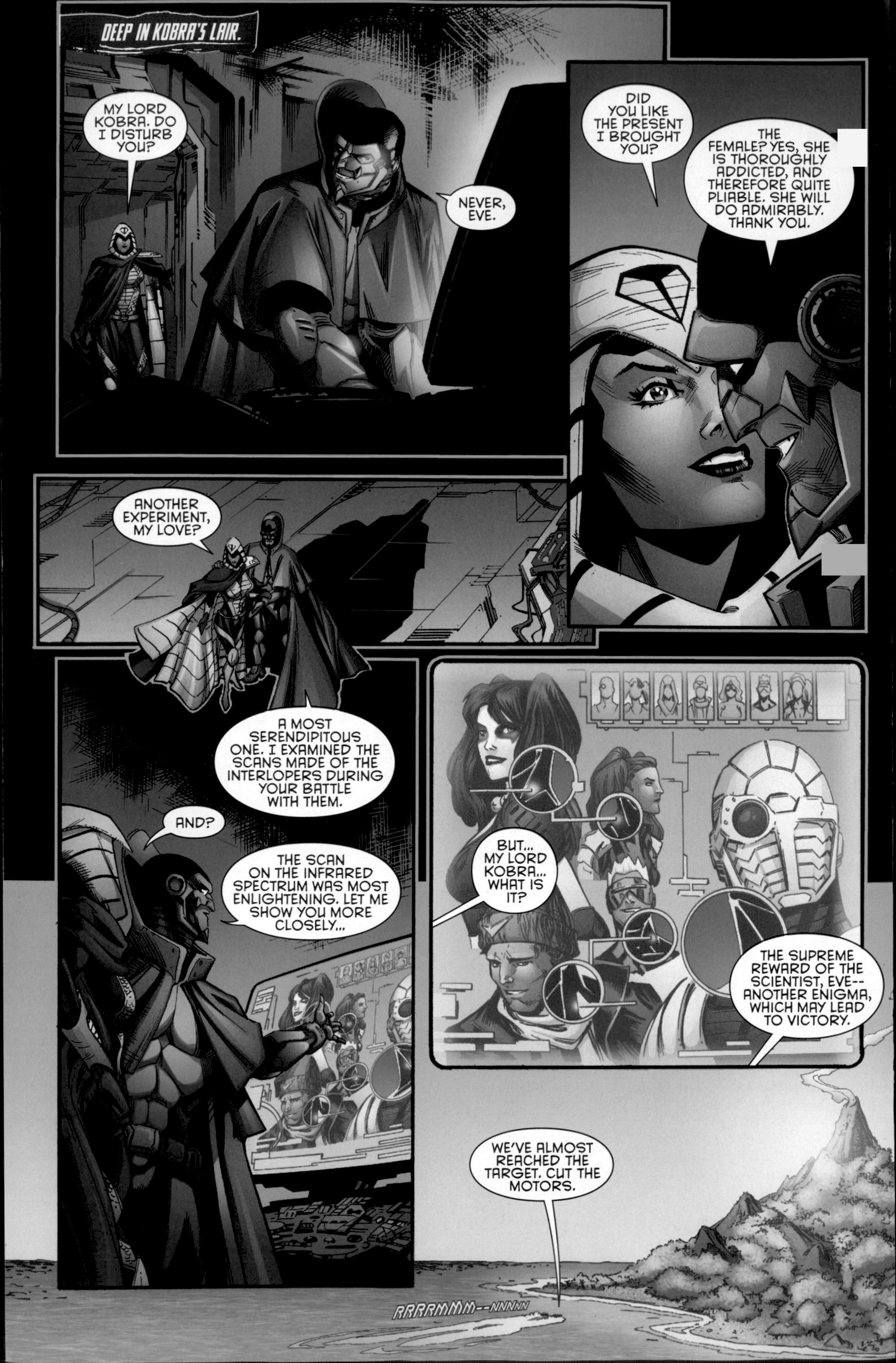

DEEP IN KOBRA'S LAIR.
MY LORD KOBRA. DO I DISTURB YOU?
NEVER, EVE.
DID YOU LIKE THE PRESENT I BROUGHT YOU?
THE FEMALE? YES, SHE IS THOROUGHLY ADDICTED, AND THEREFORE QUITE PLIABLE. SHE WILL DO ADMIRABLY. THANK YOU.
ANOTHER EXPERIMENT, MY LOVE?
A MOST SERENDIPITOUS ONE. I EXAMINED THE SCANS MADE OF THE INTERLOPERS DURING YOUR BATTLE WITH THEM.
AND?
THE SCAN ON THE INFRARED SPECTRUM WAS MOST ENLIGHTENING. LET ME SHOW YOU MORE CLOSELY...
BUT... MY LORD KOBRA... WHAT IS IT?
THE SUPREME REWARD OF THE SCIENTIST, EVE-- ANOTHER ENIGMA, WHICH MAY LEAD TO VICTORY.
WE'VE ALMOST REACHED THE TARGET. CUT THE MOTORS.
RRRRMMM--NNNNN

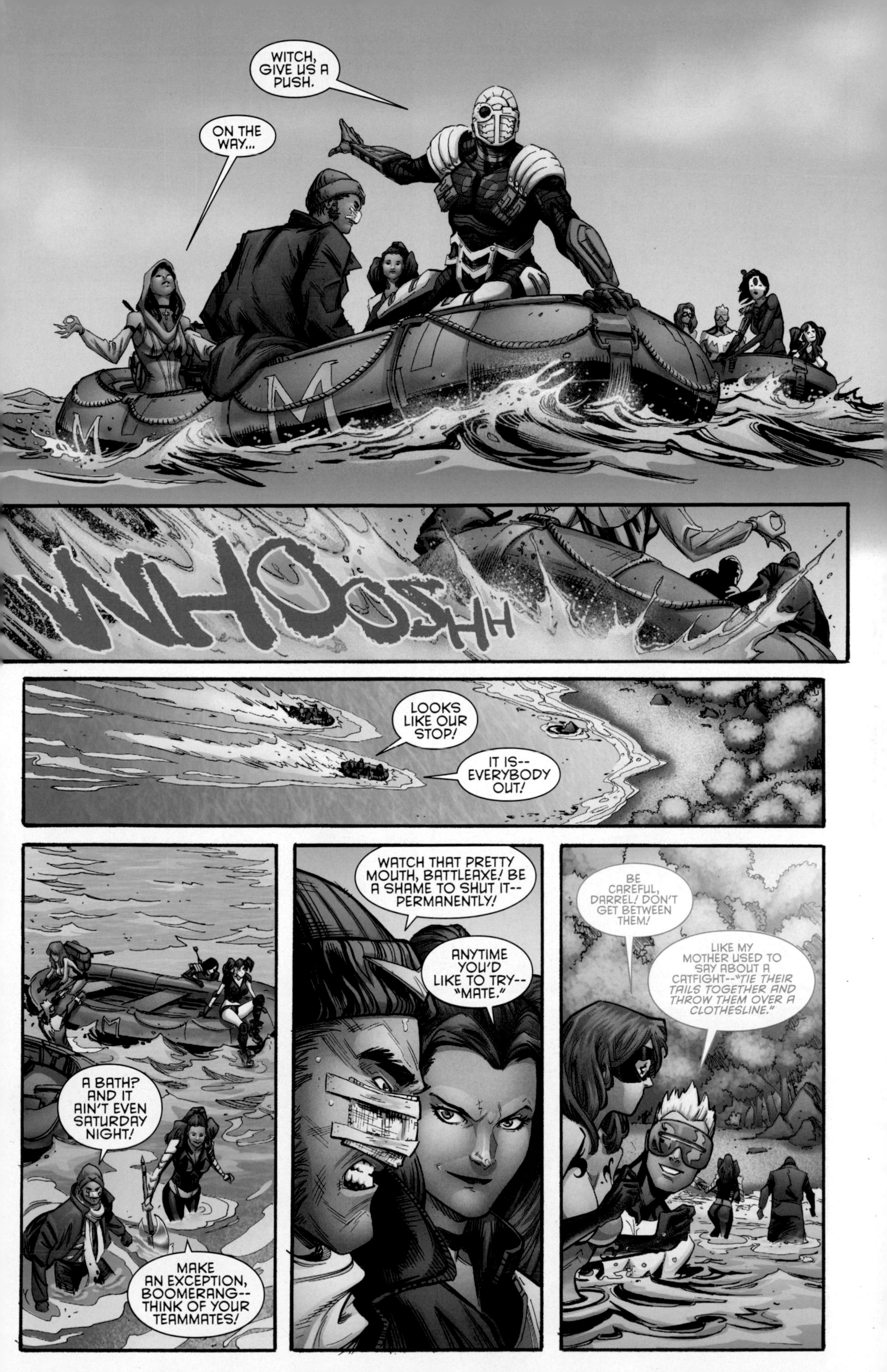
WITCH, GIVE US A PUSH.
ON THE WAY...
WHOOSHH
LOOKS LIKE OUR STOP!
IT IS-- EVERYBODY OUT!
A BATH? AND IT AIN'T EVEN SATURDAY NIGHT!
MAKE AN EXCEPTION, BOOMERANG-- THINK OF YOUR TEAMMATES!
WATCH THAT PRETTY MOUTH, BATTLEAXE! BE A SHAME TO SHUT IT-- PERMANENTLY!
ANYTIME YOU'D LIKE TO TRY-- "MATE."
BE CAREFUL, DARREL! DON'T GET BETWEEN THEM!
LIKE MY MOTHER USED TO SAY ABOUT A CATFIGHT--"TIE THEIR TAILS TOGETHER AND THROW THEM OVER A CLOTHESLINE."

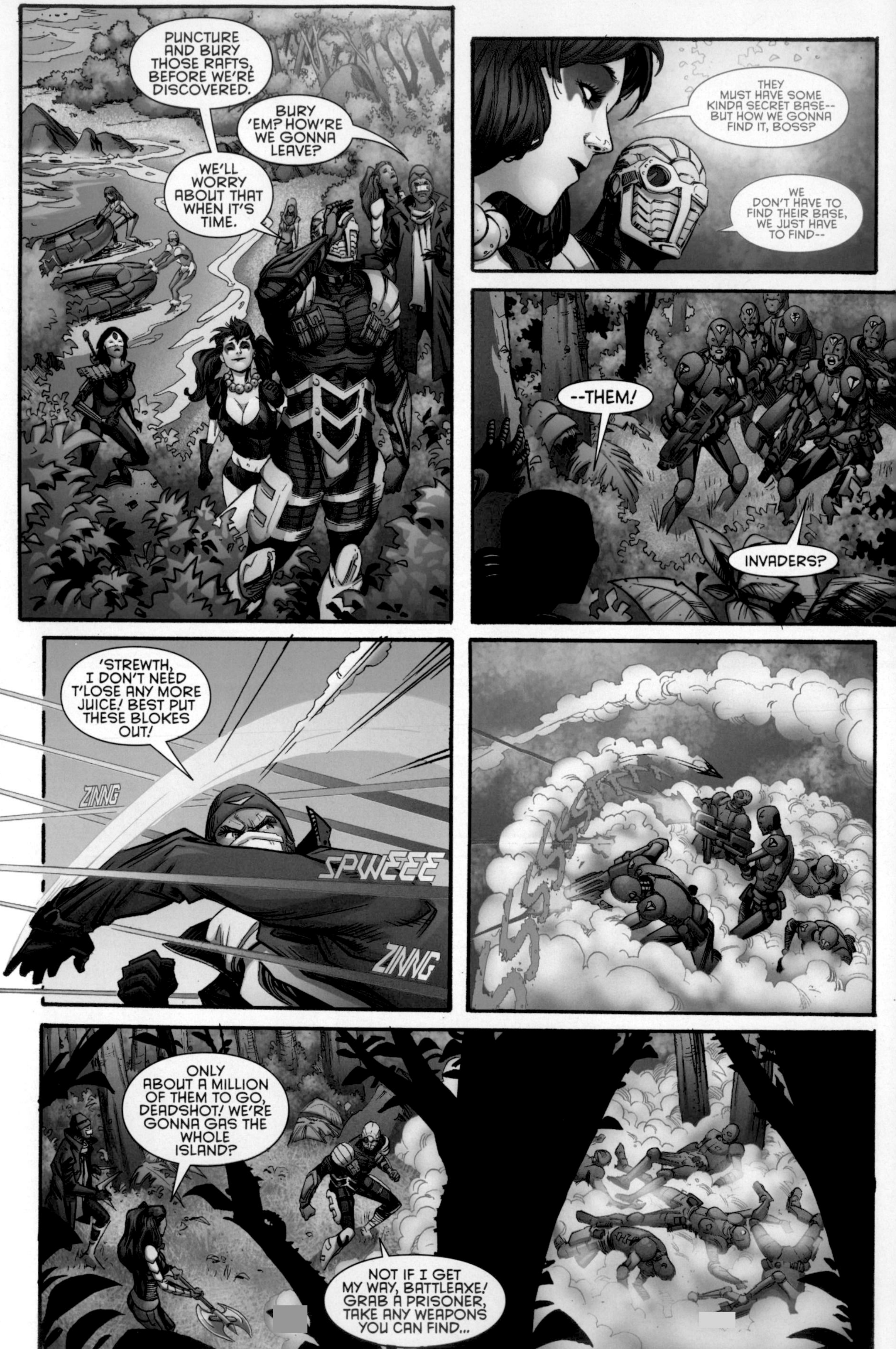
PUNCTURE AND BURY THOSE RAFTS, BEFORE WE'RE DISCOVERED.
BURY 'EM? HOW'RE WE GONNA LEAVE?
WE'LL WORRY ABOUT THAT WHEN IT'S TIME.
THEY MUST HAVE SOME KINDA SECRET BASE-- BUT HOW WE GONNA FIND IT, BOSS?
WE DON'T HAVE TO FIND THEIR BASE, WE JUST HAVE TO FIND--
--THEM!
INVADERS?
'STREWTH, I DON'T NEED T'LOSE ANY MORE JUICE! BEST PUT THESE BLOKES OUT!
ZINNG
SPWEEE
ZINNG
ONLY ABOUT A MILLION OF THEM TO GO, DEADSHOT! WE'RE GONNA GAS THE WHOLE ISLAND?
NOT IF I GET MY WAY, BATTLEAXE! GRAB A PRISONER, TAKE ANY WEAPONS YOU CAN FIND...

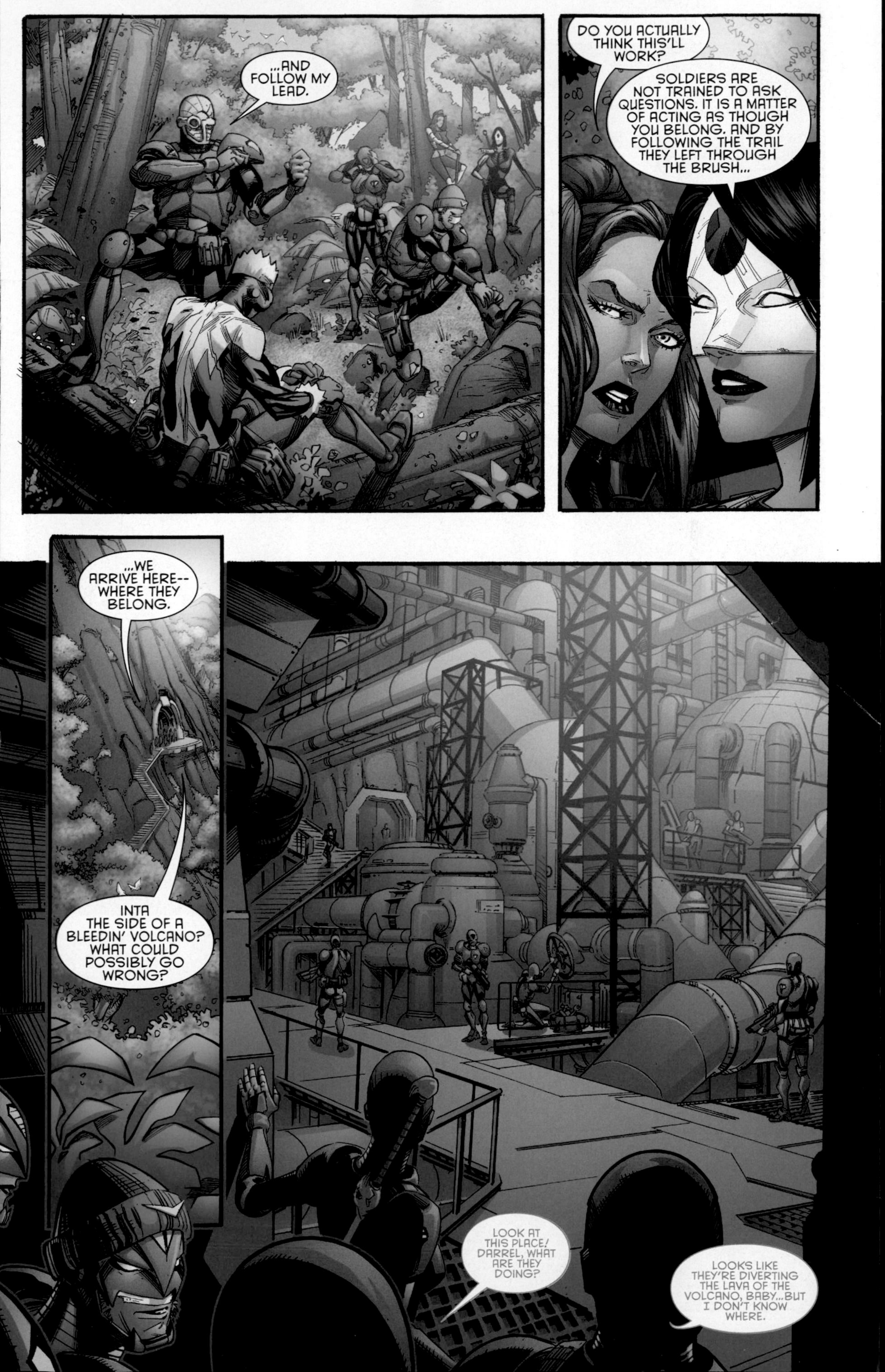
...AND FOLLOW MY LEAD.
DO YOU ACTUALLY THINK THIS'LL WORK?
SOLDIERS ARE NOT TRAINED TO ASK QUESTIONS. IT IS A MATTER OF ACTING AS THOUGH YOU BELONG. AND BY FOLLOWING THE TRAIL THEY LEFT THROUGH THE BRUSH...
...WE ARRIVE HERE-- WHERE THEY BELONG.
INTA THE SIDE OF A BLEEDIN' VOLCANO? WHAT COULD POSSIBLY GO WRONG?
LOOK AT THIS PLACE! DARREL, WHAT ARE THEY DOING?
LOOKS LIKE THEY'RE DIVERTING THE LAVA OF THE VOLCANO, BABY...BUT I DON'T KNOW WHERE.

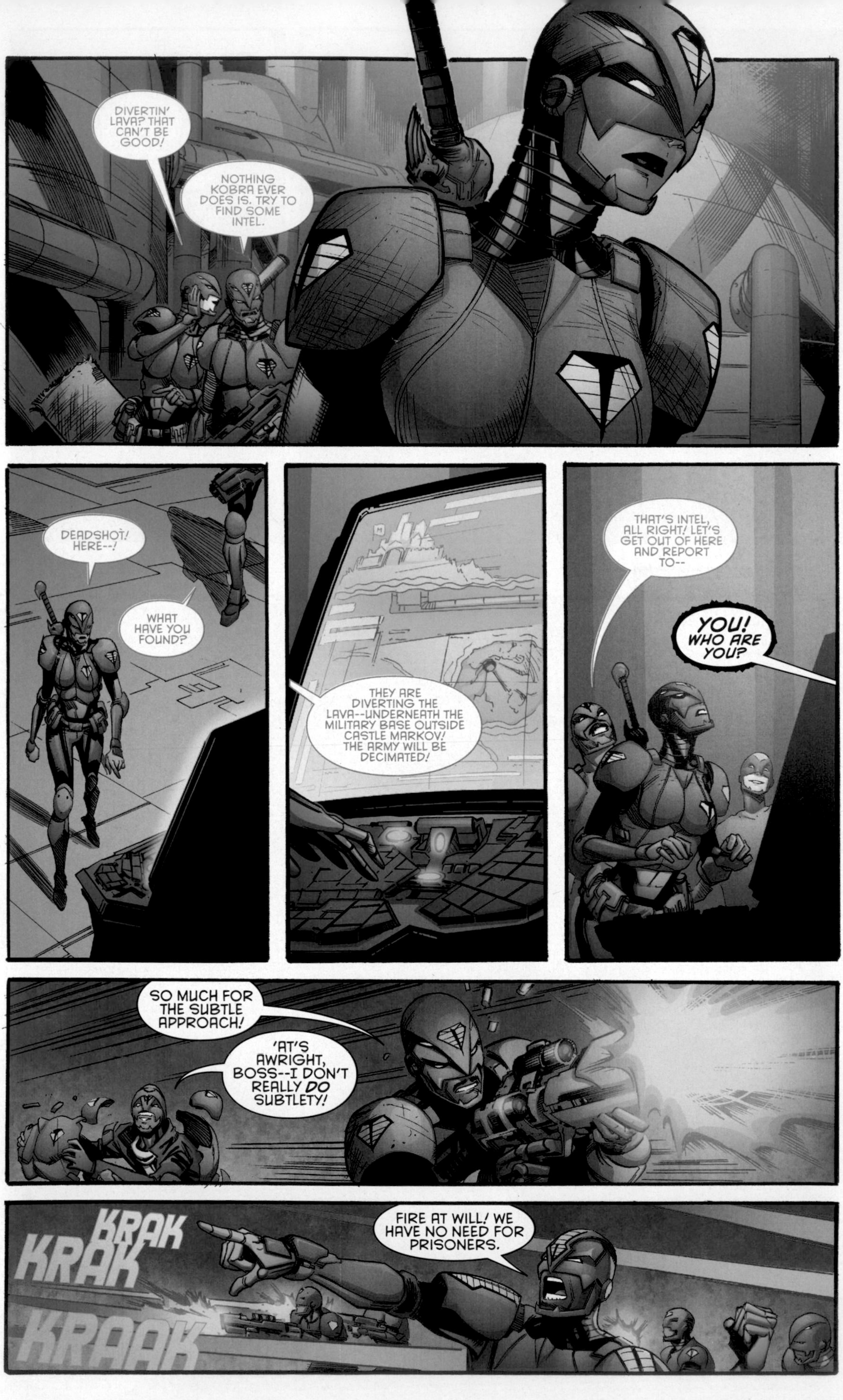
DIVERTIN' LAVA? THAT CAN'T BE GOOD!
NOTHING KOBRA EVER DOES IS. TRY TO FIND SOME INTEL.
DEADSHOT! HERE--!
WHAT HAVE YOU FOUND?
THEY ARE DIVERTING THE LAVA--UNDERNEATH THE MILITARY BASE OUTSIDE CASTLE MARKOV! THE ARMY WILL BE DECIMATED!
THAT'S INTEL, ALL RIGHT! LET'S GET OUT OF HERE AND REPORT TO--
YOU! WHO ARE YOU?
SO MUCH FOR THE SUBTLE APPROACH!
'AT'S AWRIGHT, BOSS--I DON'T REALLY *DO* SUBTLETY!
KRAK
KRAK
KRAAK
FIRE AT WILL! WE HAVE NO NEED FOR PRISONERS.

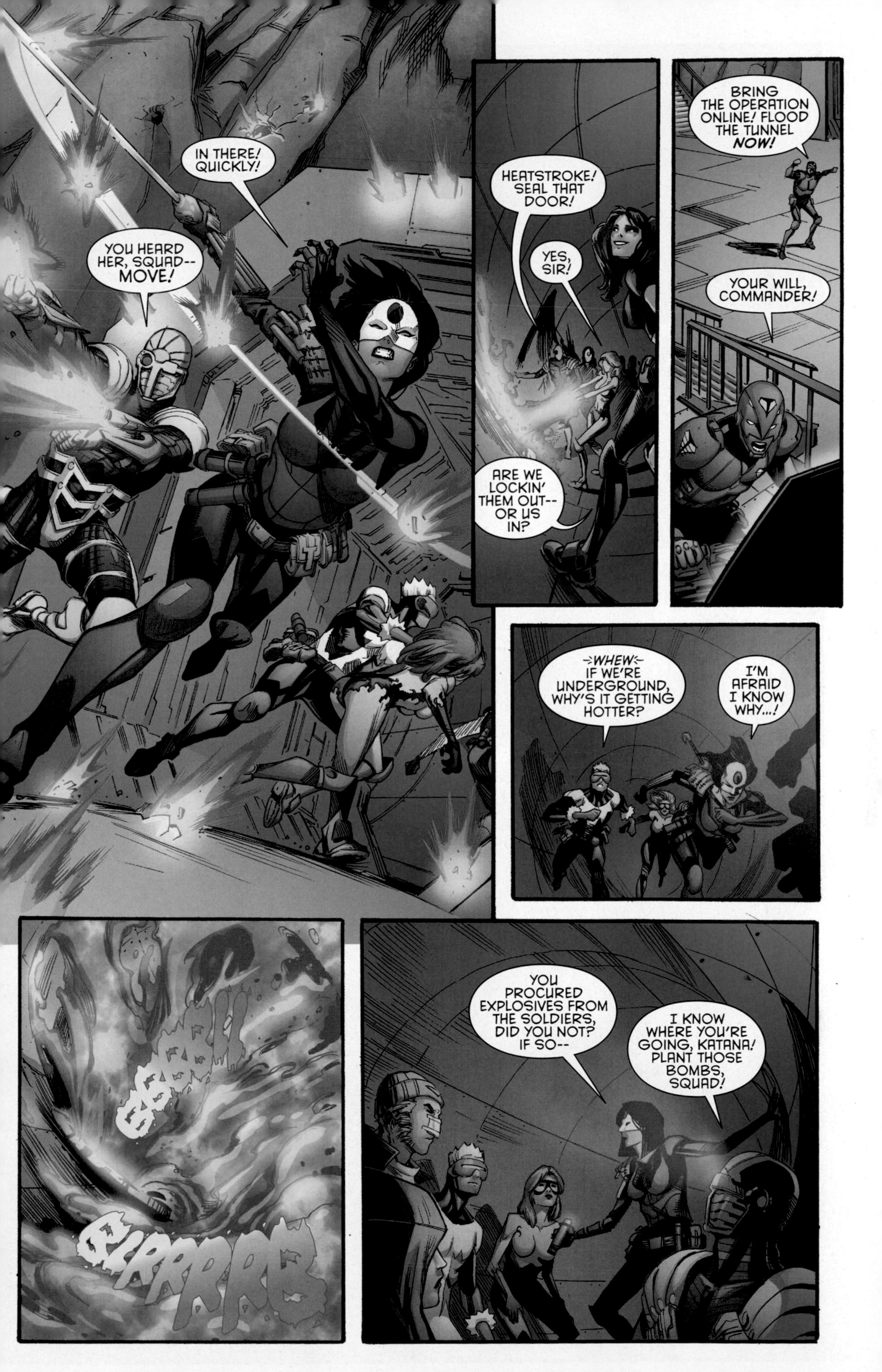

IN THERE! QUICKLY!
YOU HEARD HER, SQUAD-- MOVE!
HEATSTROKE! SEAL THAT DOOR!
YES, SIR!
ARE WE LOCKIN' THEM OUT-- OR US IN?
BRING THE OPERATION ONLINE! FLOOD THE TUNNEL NOW!
YOUR WILL, COMMANDER!
WHEW IF WE'RE UNDERGROUND, WHY'S IT GETTING HOTTER?
I'M AFRAID I KNOW WHY...!
YOU PROCURED EXPLOSIVES FROM THE SOLDIERS, DID YOU NOT? IF SO--
I KNOW WHERE YOU'RE GOING, KATANA! PLANT THOSE BOMBS, SQUAD!

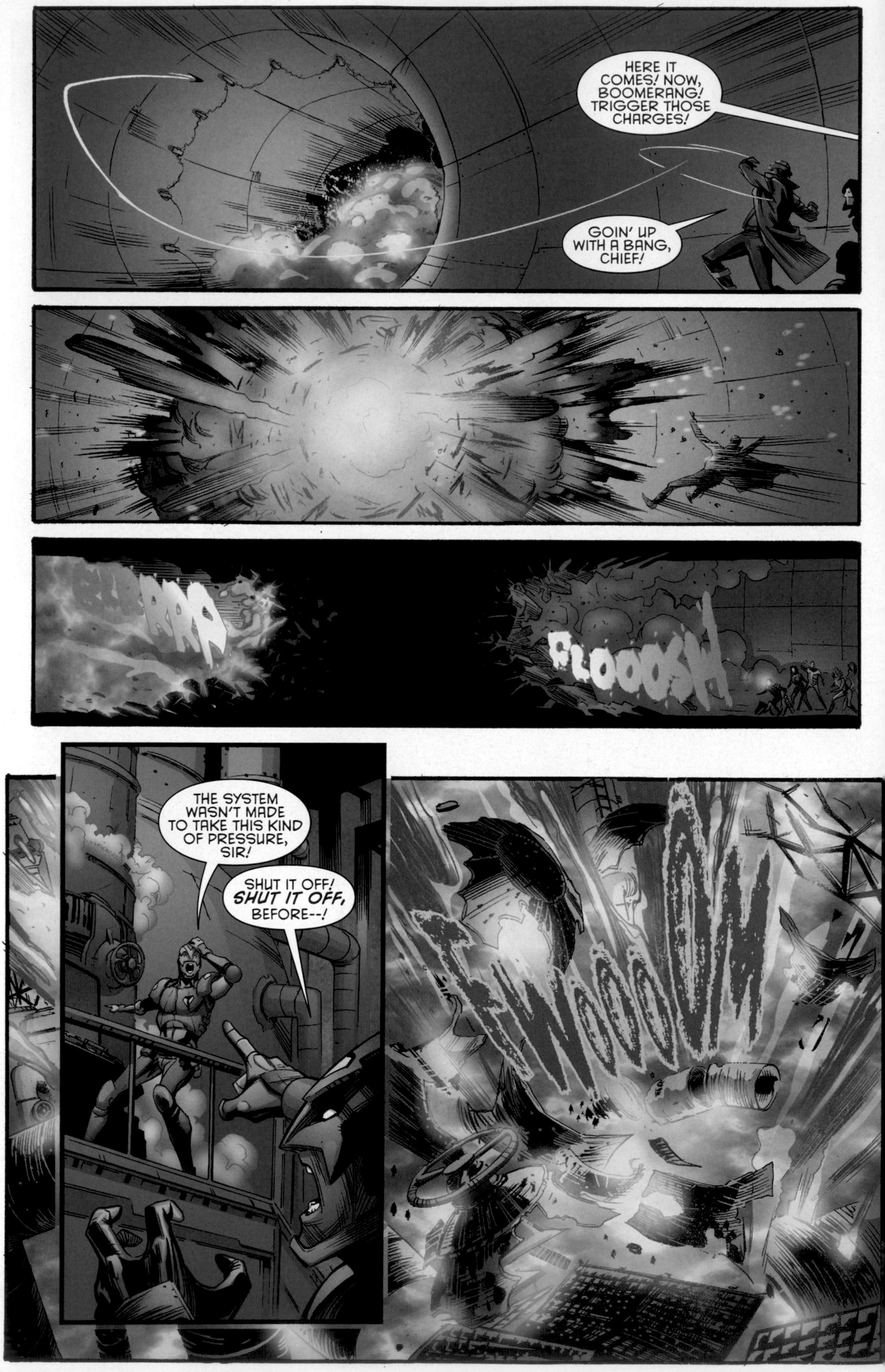
HERE IT COMES! NOW, BOOMERANG! TRIGGER THOSE CHARGES!
GOIN' UP WITH A BANG, CHIEF!
FLOOOSH
THE SYSTEM WASN'T MADE TO TAKE THIS KIND OF PRESSURE, SIR!
SHUT IT OFF! SHUT IT OFF, BEFORE--!
THWOOOOM

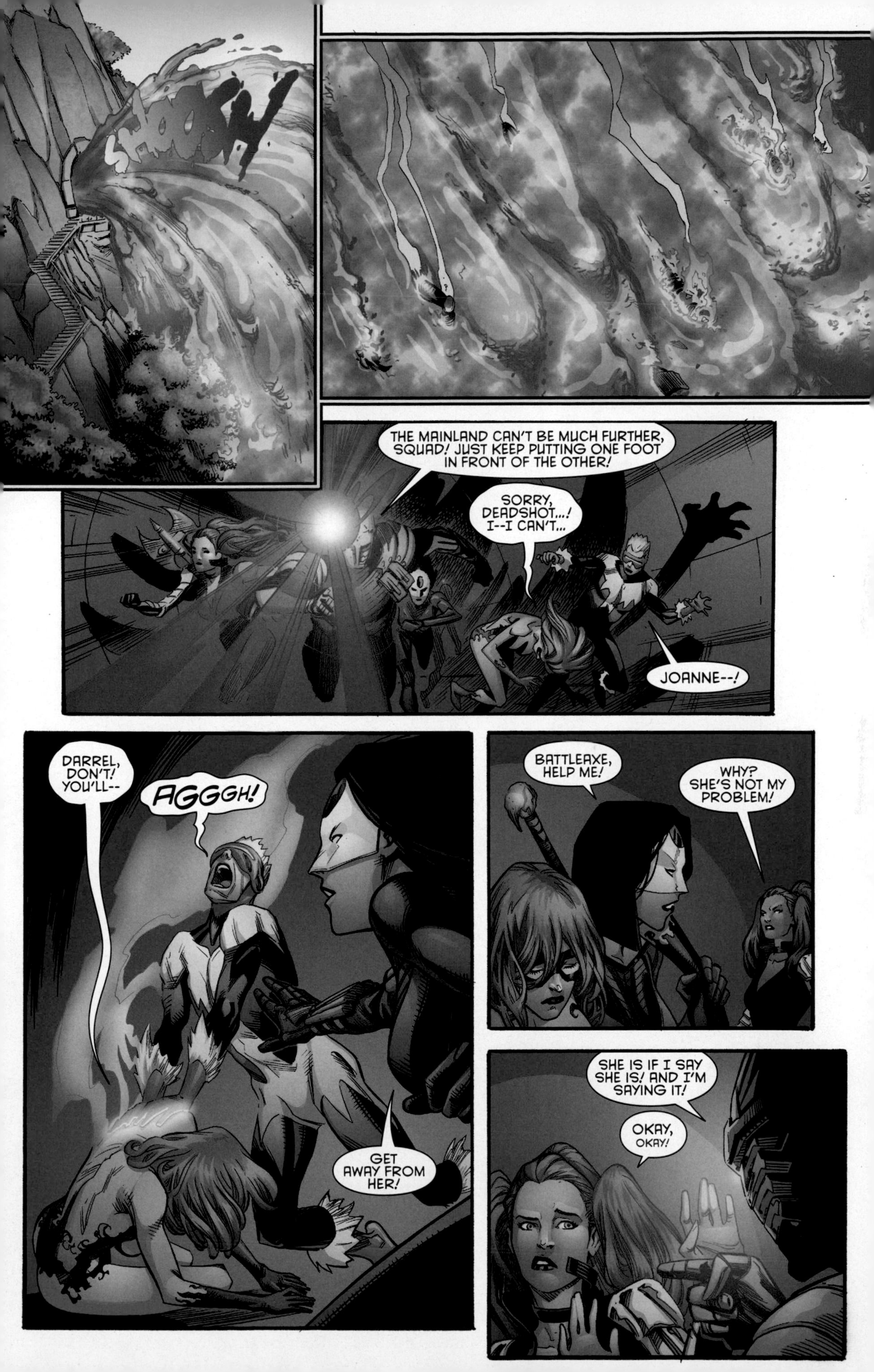
THE MAINLAND CAN'T BE MUCH FURTHER, SQUAD! JUST KEEP PUTTING ONE FOOT IN FRONT OF THE OTHER!
SORRY, DEADSHOT...! I--I CAN'T...
JOANNE--!
DARREL, DON'T! YOU'LL--
AGGGH!
GET AWAY FROM HER!
BATTLEAXE, HELP ME!
WHY? SHE'S NOT MY PROBLEM!
SHE IS IF I SAY SHE IS! AND I'M SAYING IT!
OKAY, OKAY!

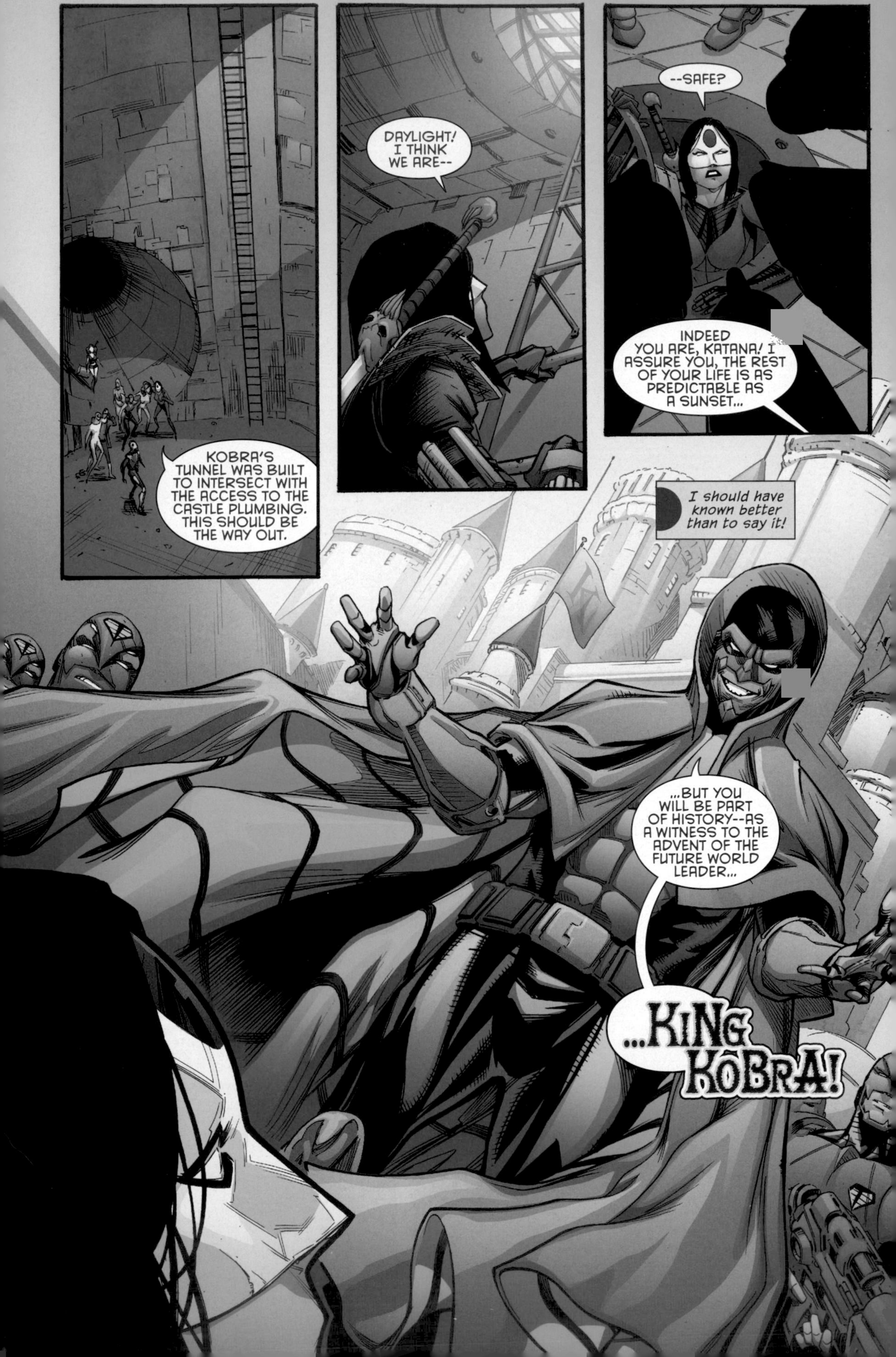
KOBRA'S TUNNEL WAS BUILT TO INTERSECT WITH THE ACCESS TO THE CASTLE PLUMBING. THIS SHOULD BE THE WAY OUT.
DAYLIGHT! I THINK WE ARE--
--SAFE?
INDEED YOU ARE, KATANA! I ASSURE YOU, THE REST OF YOUR LIFE IS AS PREDICTABLE AS A SUNSET...
I should have known better than to say it!
...BUT YOU WILL BE PART OF HISTORY--AS A WITNESS TO THE ADVENT OF THE FUTURE WORLD LEADER...
...KING KOBRA!

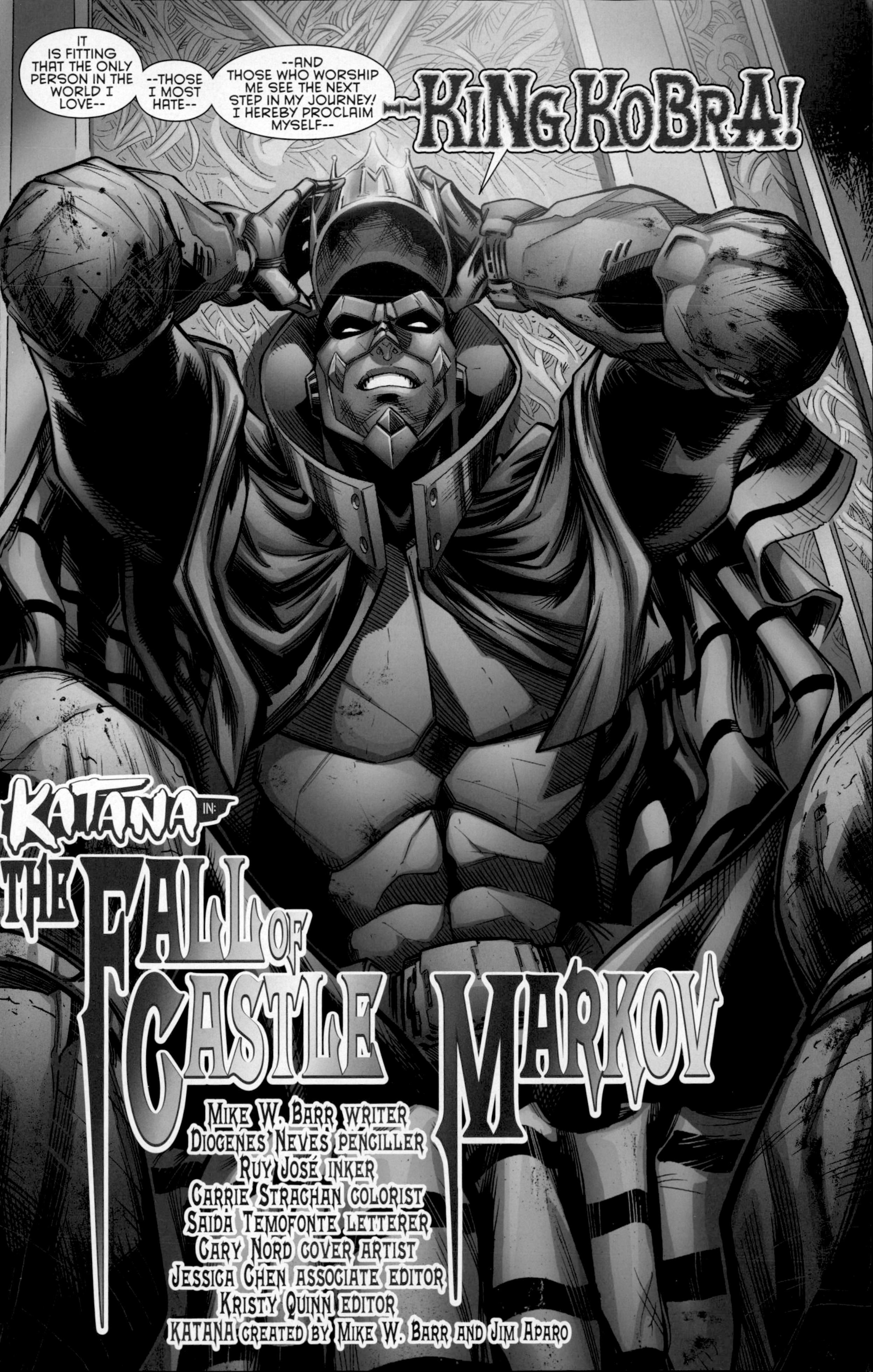
IT IS FITTING THAT THE ONLY PERSON IN THE WORLD I LOVE--
--THOSE I MOST HATE--
--AND THOSE WHO WORSHIP ME SEE THE NEXT STEP IN MY JOURNEY! I HEREBY PROCLAIM MYSELF--
--KING KOBRA!
KATANA IN:
THE FALL OF CASTLE MARKOV
MIKE W. BARR WRITER
DIOGENES NEVES PENCILLER
RUY JOSÉ INKER
CARRIE STRACHAN COLORIST
SAIDA TEMOFONTE LETTERER
CARY NORD COVER ARTIST
JESSICA CHEN ASSOCIATE EDITOR
KRISTY QUINN EDITOR
KATANA CREATED BY MIKE W. BARR AND JIM APARO

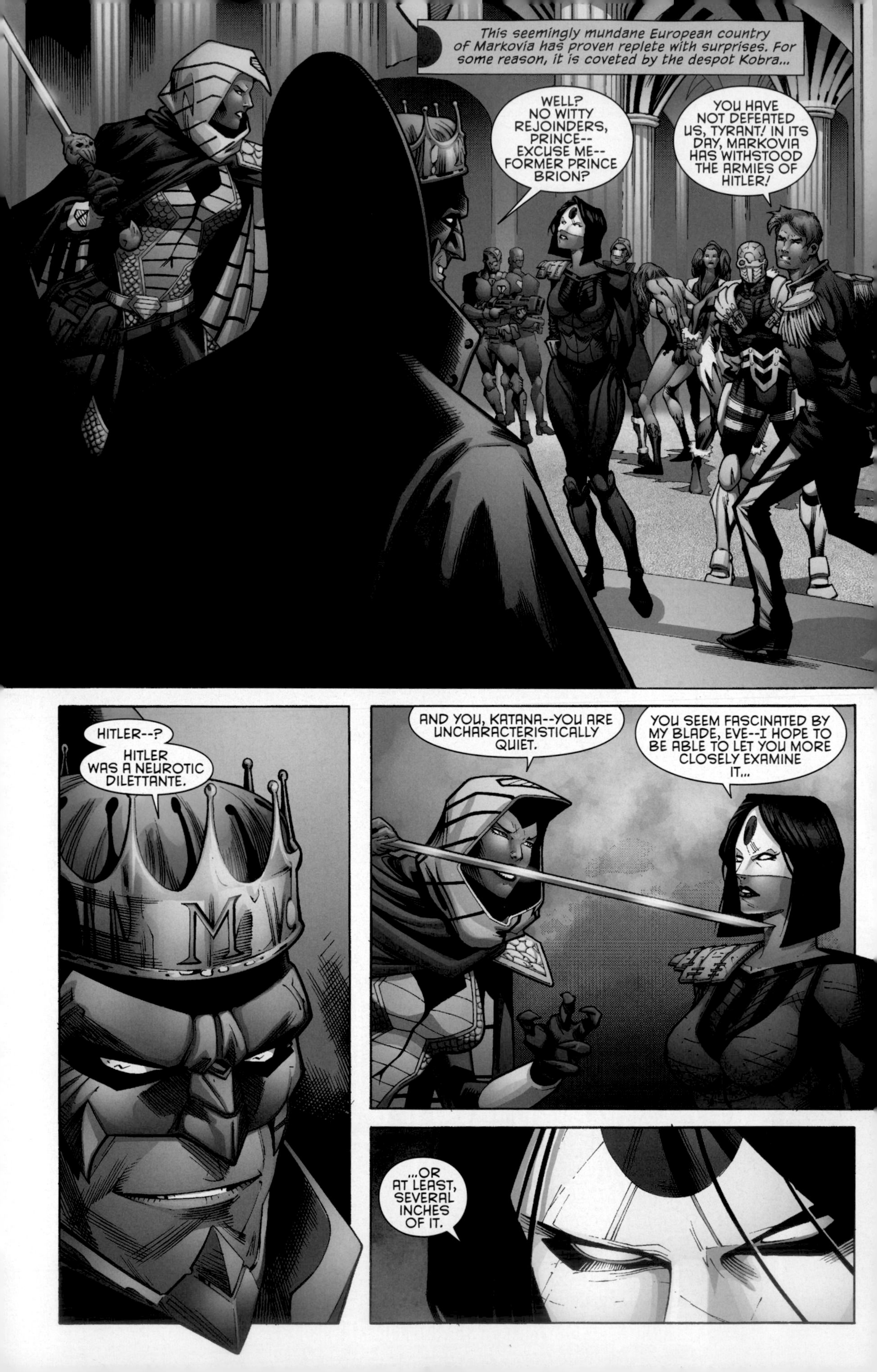
This seemingly mundane European country of Markovia has proven replete with surprises. For some reason, it is coveted by the despot Kobra...
WELL? NO WITTY REJOINDERS, PRINCE--EXCUSE ME--FORMER PRINCE BRION?
YOU HAVE NOT DEFEATED US, TYRANT! IN ITS DAY, MARKOVIA HAS WITHSTOOD THE ARMIES OF HITLER!
HITLER--? HITLER WAS A NEUROTIC DILETTANTE.
AND YOU, KATANA--YOU ARE UNCHARACTERISTICALLY QUIET.
YOU SEEM FASCINATED BY MY BLADE, EVE--I HOPE TO BE ABLE TO LET YOU MORE CLOSELY EXAMINE IT...
...OR AT LEAST, SEVERAL INCHES OF IT.

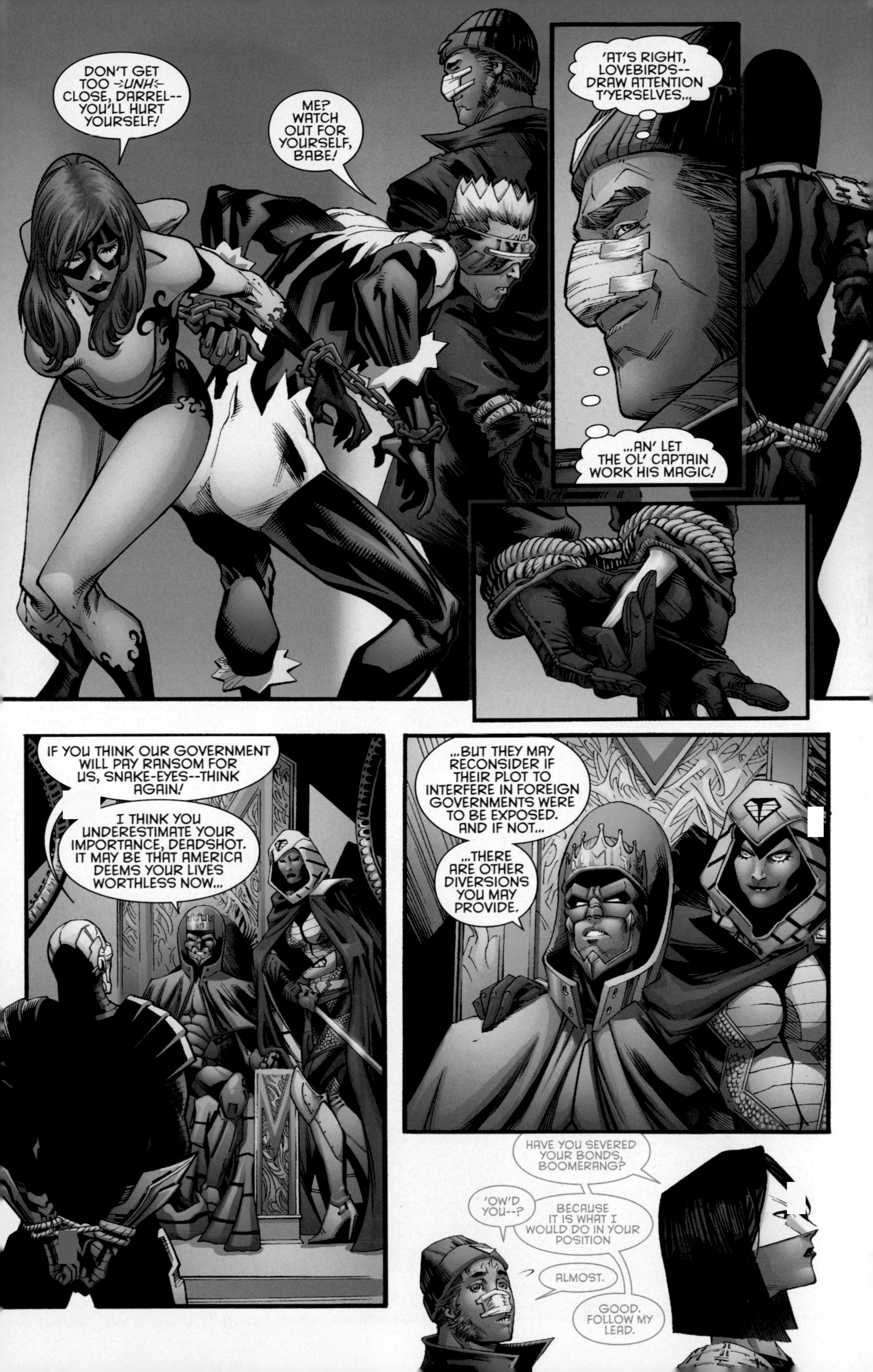
DON'T GET TOO -UNH- CLOSE, DARREL--YOU'LL HURT YOURSELF!
ME? WATCH OUT FOR YOURSELF, BABE!
'AT'S RIGHT, LOVEBIRDS--DRAW ATTENTION T'YERSELVES...
...AN' LET THE OL' CAPTAIN WORK HIS MAGIC!
IF YOU THINK OUR GOVERNMENT WILL PAY RANSOM FOR US, SNAKE-EYES--THINK AGAIN!
I THINK YOU UNDERESTIMATE YOUR IMPORTANCE, DEADSHOT. IT MAY BE THAT AMERICA DEEMS YOUR LIVES WORTHLESS NOW...
...BUT THEY MAY RECONSIDER IF THEIR PLOT TO INTERFERE IN FOREIGN GOVERNMENTS WERE TO BE EXPOSED. AND IF NOT...
...THERE ARE OTHER DIVERSIONS YOU MAY PROVIDE.
HAVE YOU SEVERED YOUR BONDS, BOOMERANG?
'OW'D YOU--?
BECAUSE IT IS WHAT I WOULD DO IN YOUR POSITION
ALMOST.
GOOD. FOLLOW MY LEAD.

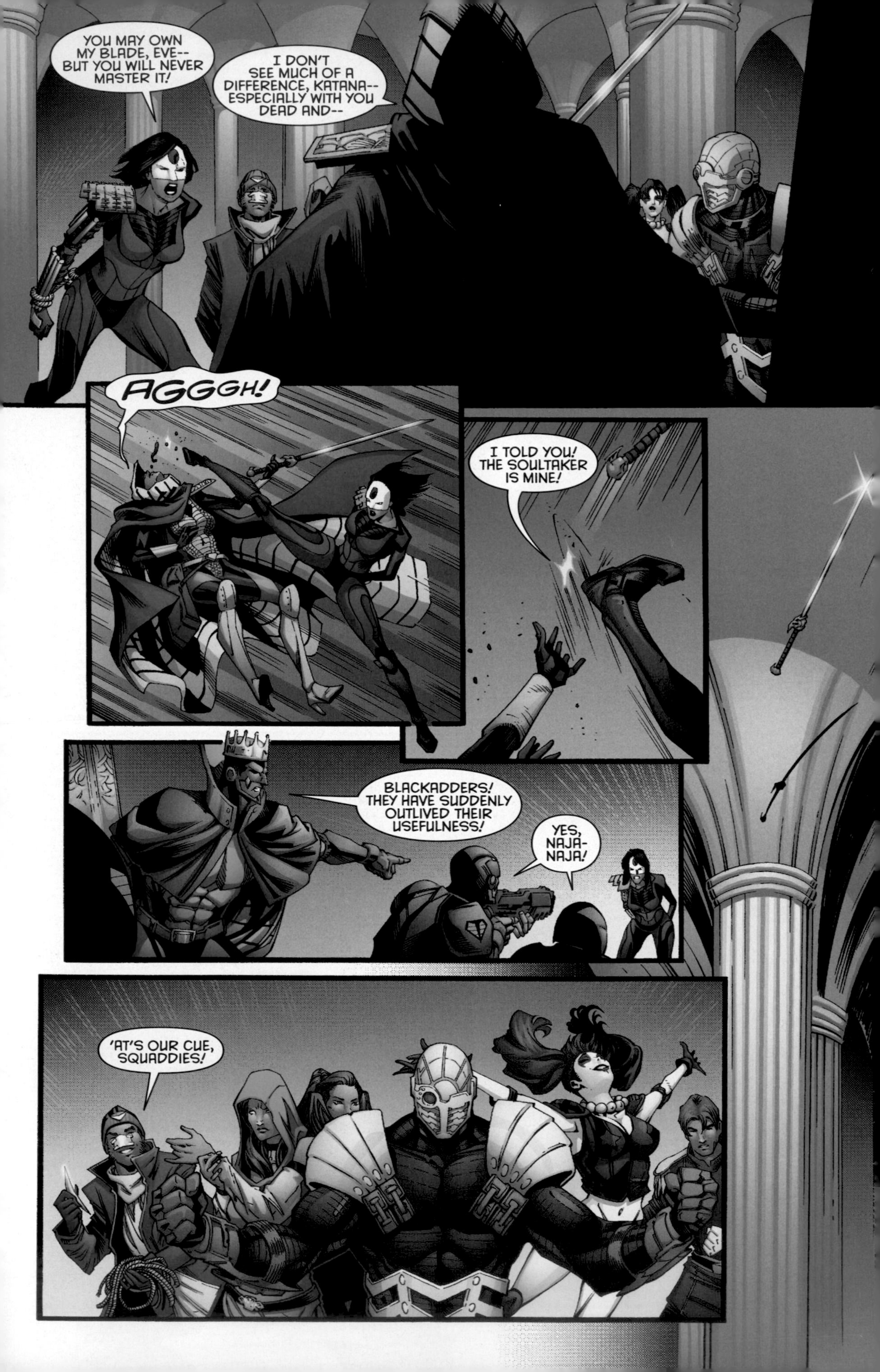
YOU MAY OWN MY BLADE, EVE-- BUT YOU WILL NEVER MASTER IT!
I DON'T SEE MUCH OF A DIFFERENCE, KATANA-- ESPECIALLY WITH YOU DEAD AND--
AGGGH!
I TOLD YOU! THE SOULTAKER IS MINE!
BLACKADDERS! THEY HAVE SUDDENLY OUTLIVED THEIR USEFULNESS!
YES, NAJA-NAJA!
'AT'S OUR CUE, SQUADDIES!

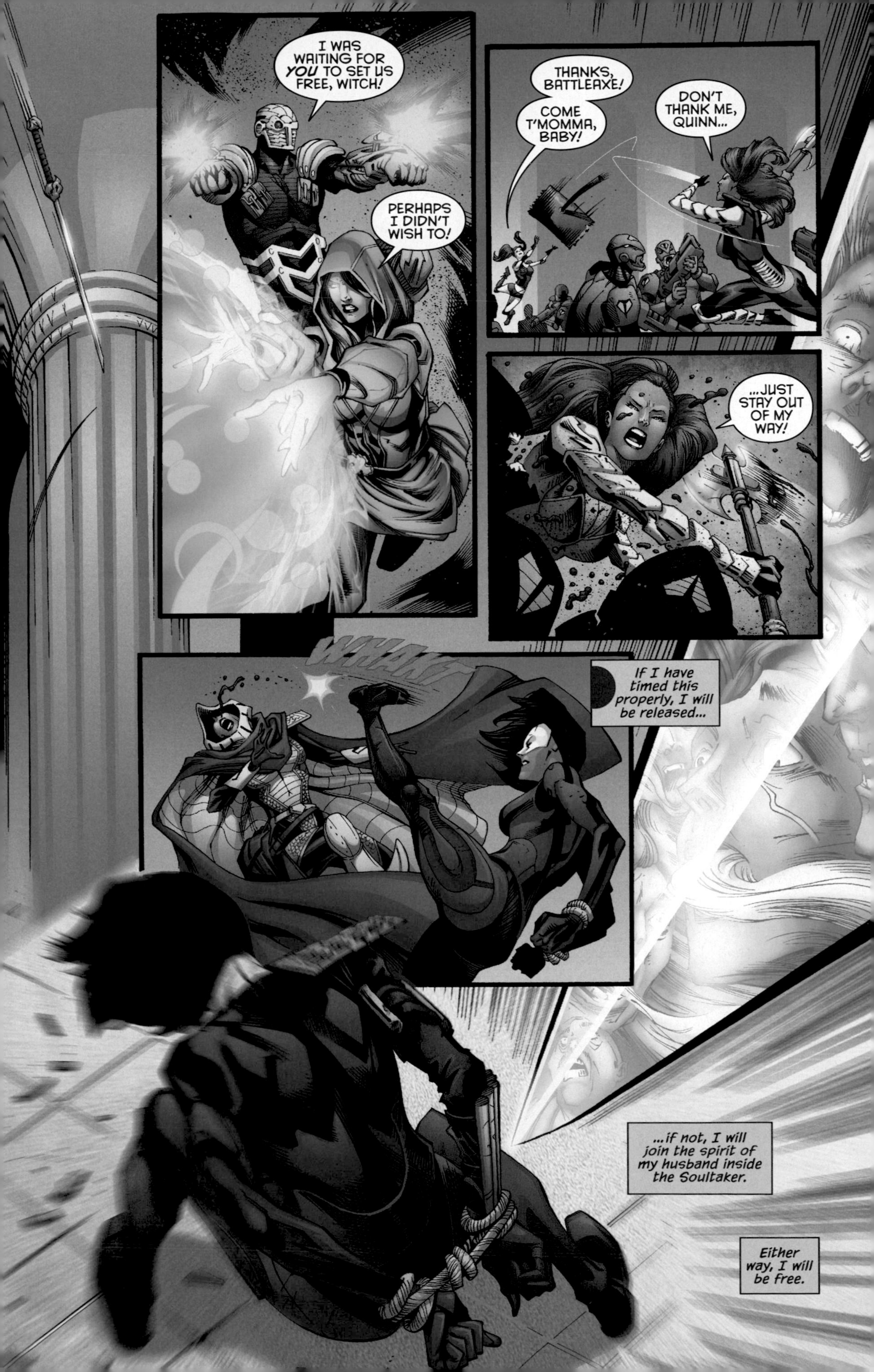
I WAS WAITING FOR YOU TO SET US FREE, WITCH!
PERHAPS I DIDN'T WISH TO!
THANKS, BATTLEAXE!
COME T'MOMMA, BABY!
DON'T THANK ME, QUINN...
...JUST STAY OUT OF MY WAY!
WHAK!
If I have timed this properly, I will be released...
...if not, I will join the spirit of my husband inside the Soultaker.
Either way, I will be free.

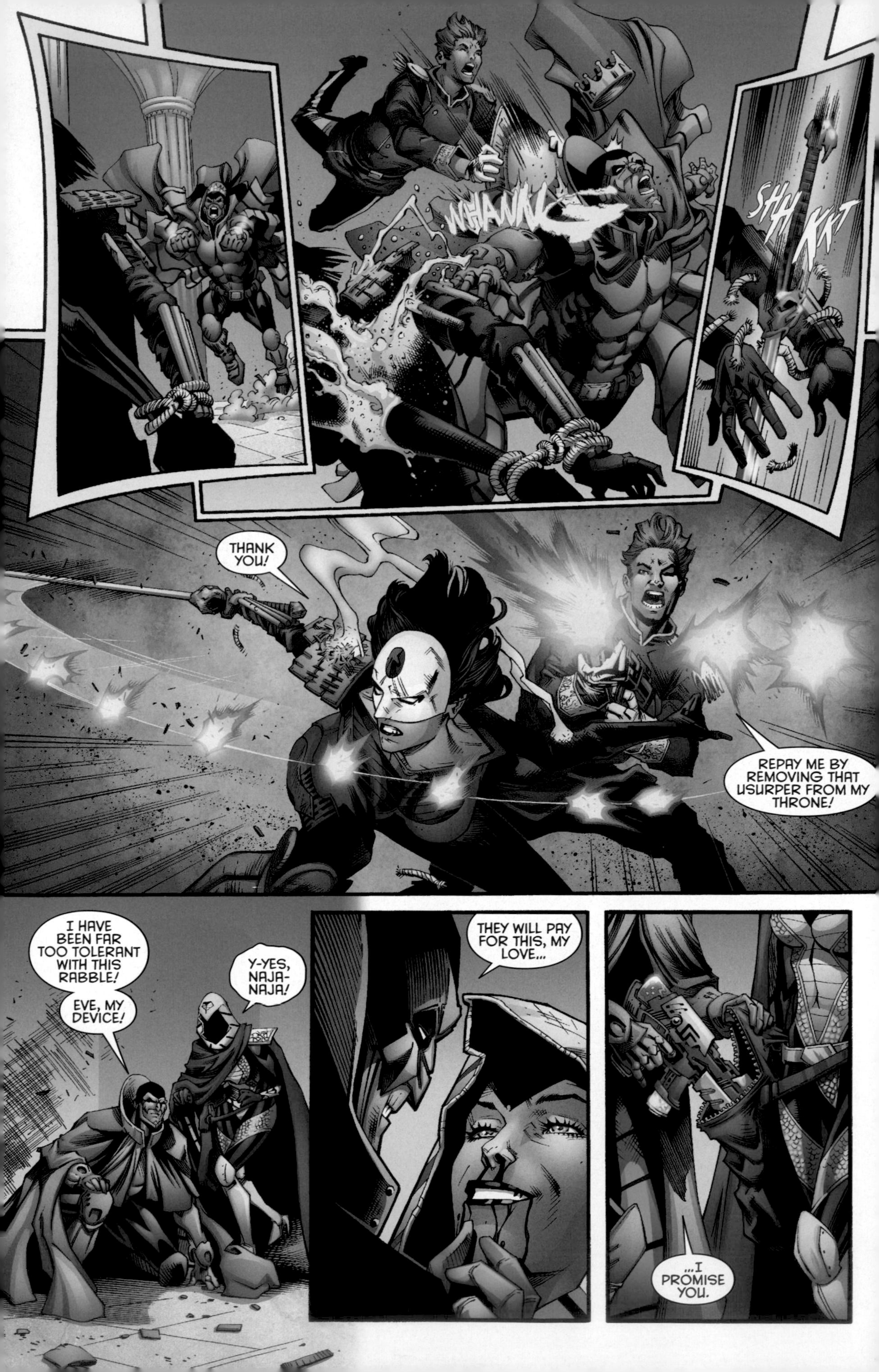
WHANNNG
SHHKKT
THANK YOU!
REPAY ME BY REMOVING THAT USURPER FROM MY THRONE!
I HAVE BEEN FAR TOO TOLERANT WITH THIS RABBLE!
EVE, MY DEVICE!
Y-YES, NAJA-NAJA!
THEY WILL PAY FOR THIS, MY LOVE...
...I PROMISE YOU.

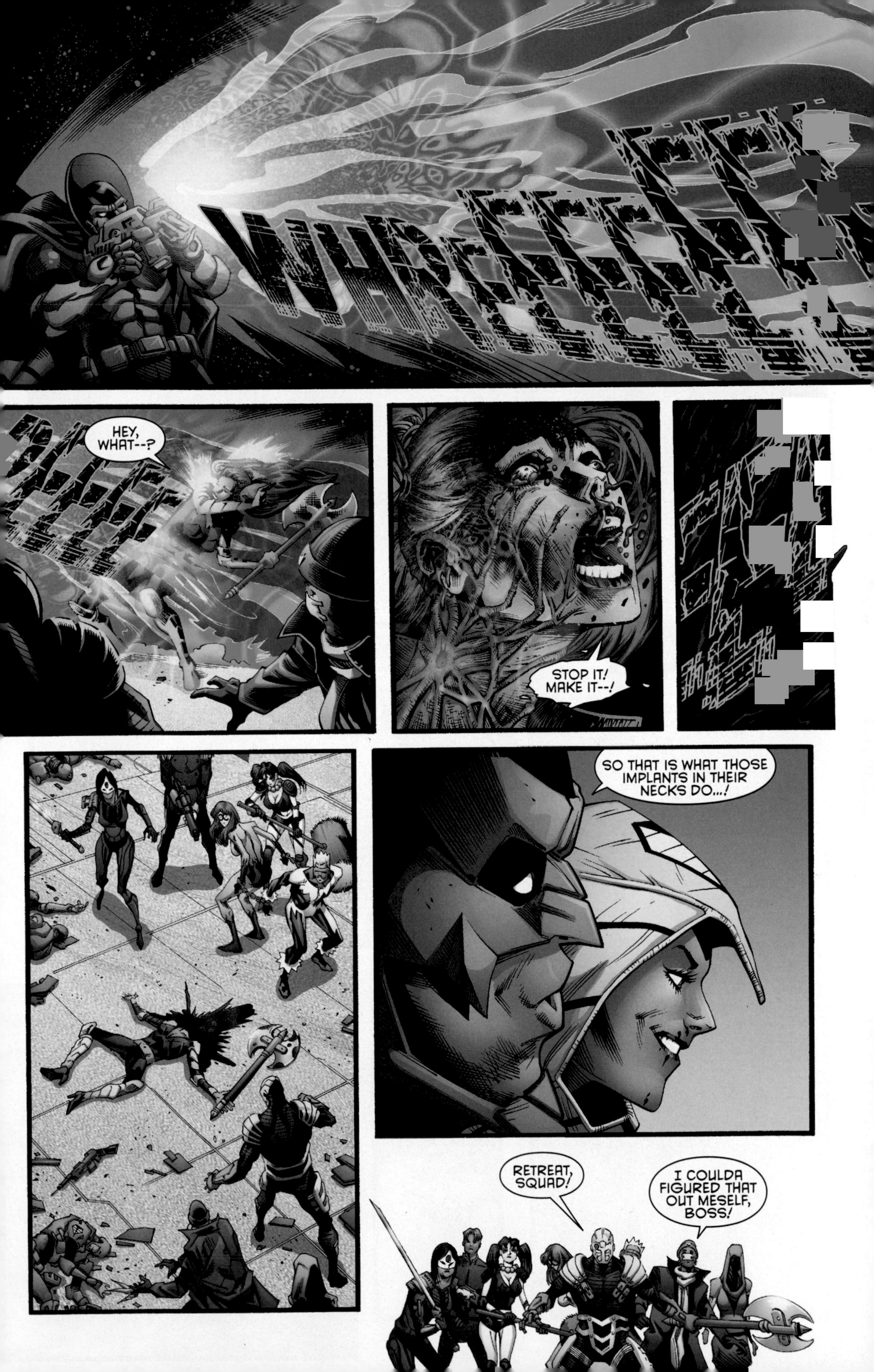
HEY, WHAT--?
STOP IT! MAKE IT--!
SO THAT IS WHAT THOSE IMPLANTS IN THEIR NECKS DO...!
RETREAT, SQUAD!
I COULDA FIGURED THAT OUT MESELF, BOSS!

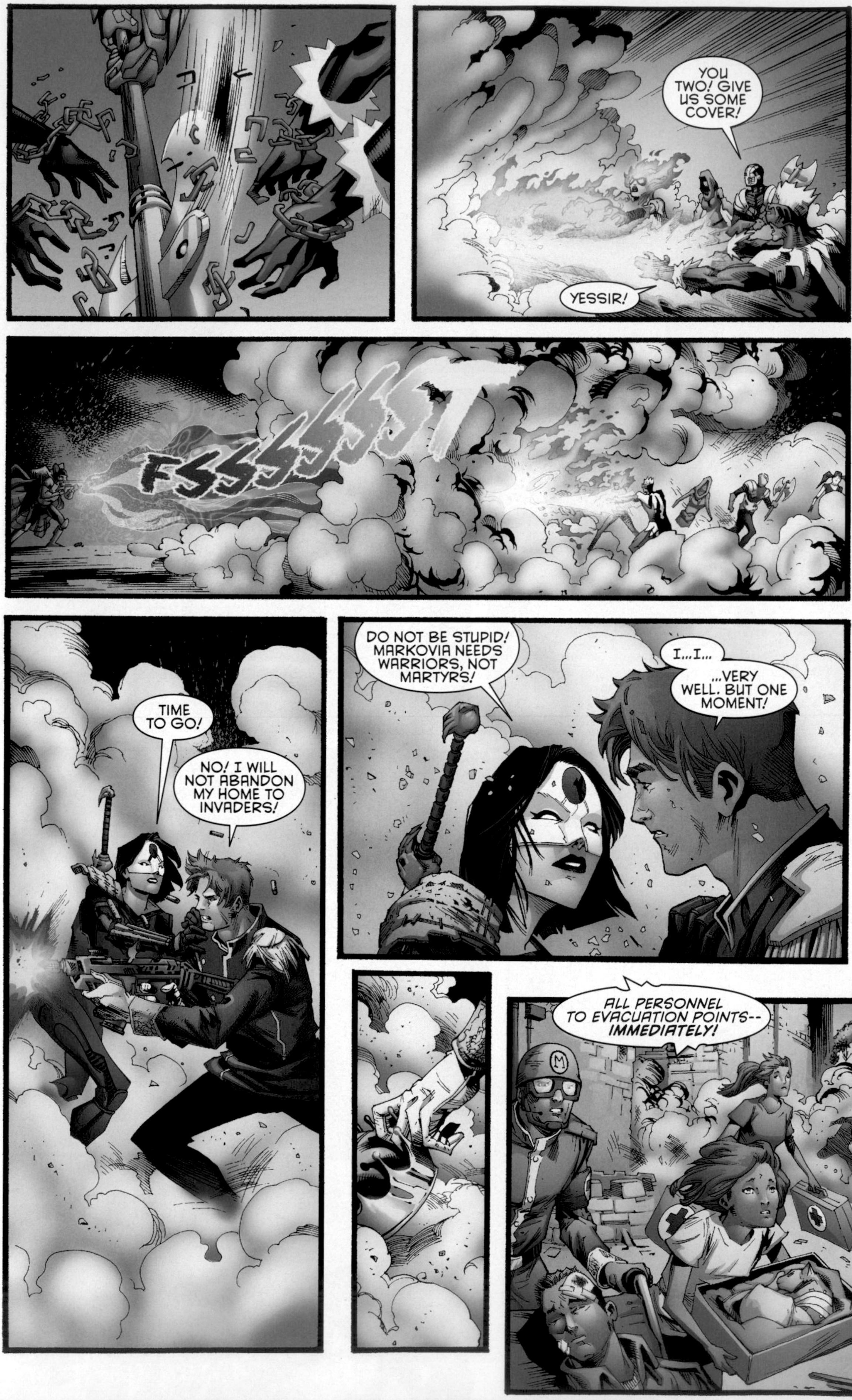

YOU TWO! GIVE US SOME COVER!
YESSIR!
FSSSSSST
TIME TO GO!
NO! I WILL NOT ABANDON MY HOME TO INVADERS!
DO NOT BE STUPID! MARKOVIA NEEDS WARRIORS, NOT MARTYRS!
I...I...
...VERY WELL. BUT ONE MOMENT!
ALL PERSONNEL TO EVACUATION POINTS-- IMMEDIATELY!

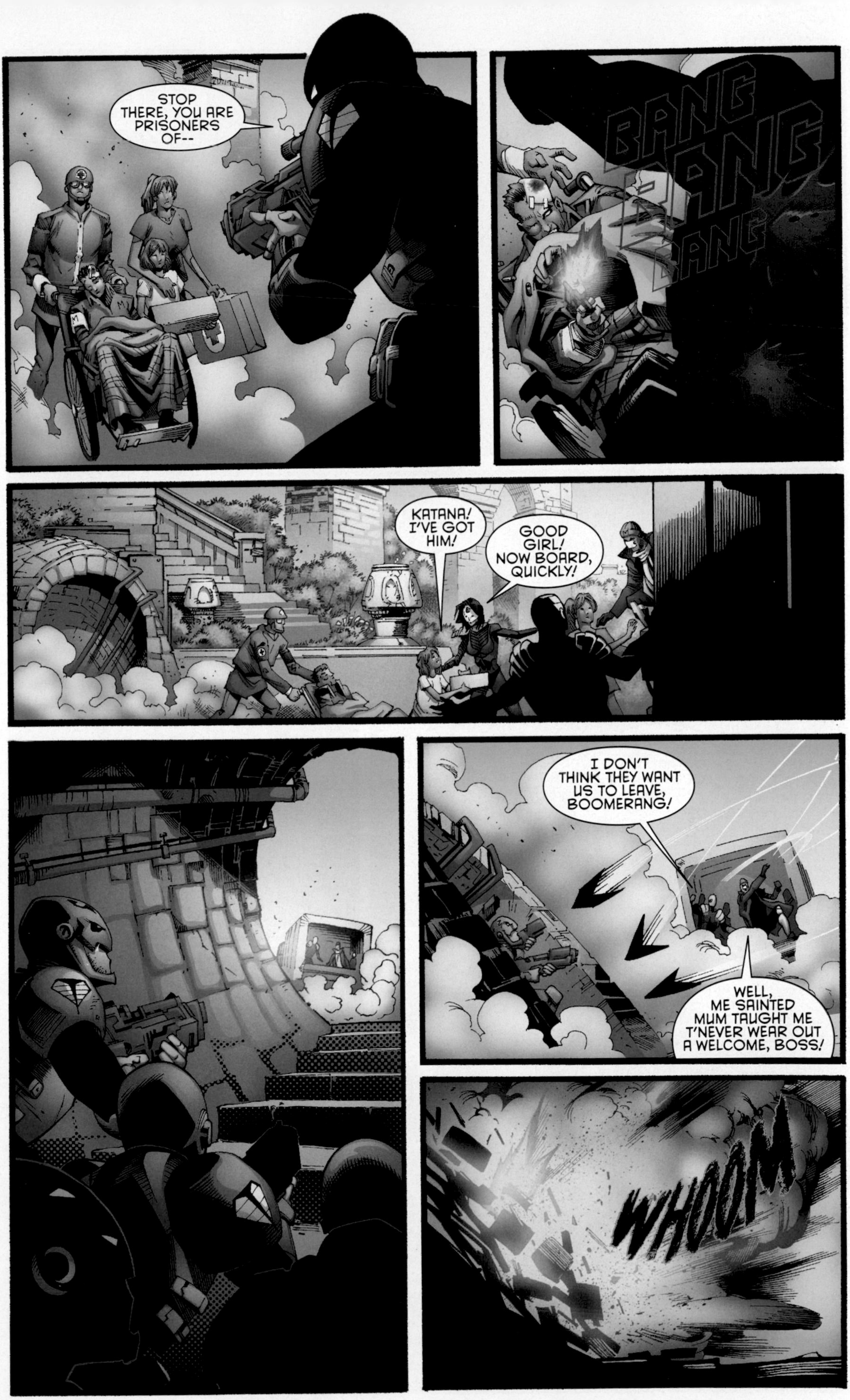
STOP THERE, YOU ARE PRISONERS OF--
BANG BANG BANG
KATANA! I'VE GOT HIM!
GOOD GIRL! NOW BOARD, QUICKLY!
I DON'T THINK THEY WANT US TO LEAVE, BOOMERANG!
WELL, ME SAINTED MUM TAUGHT ME T'NEVER WEAR OUT A WELCOME, BOSS!
WHOOM

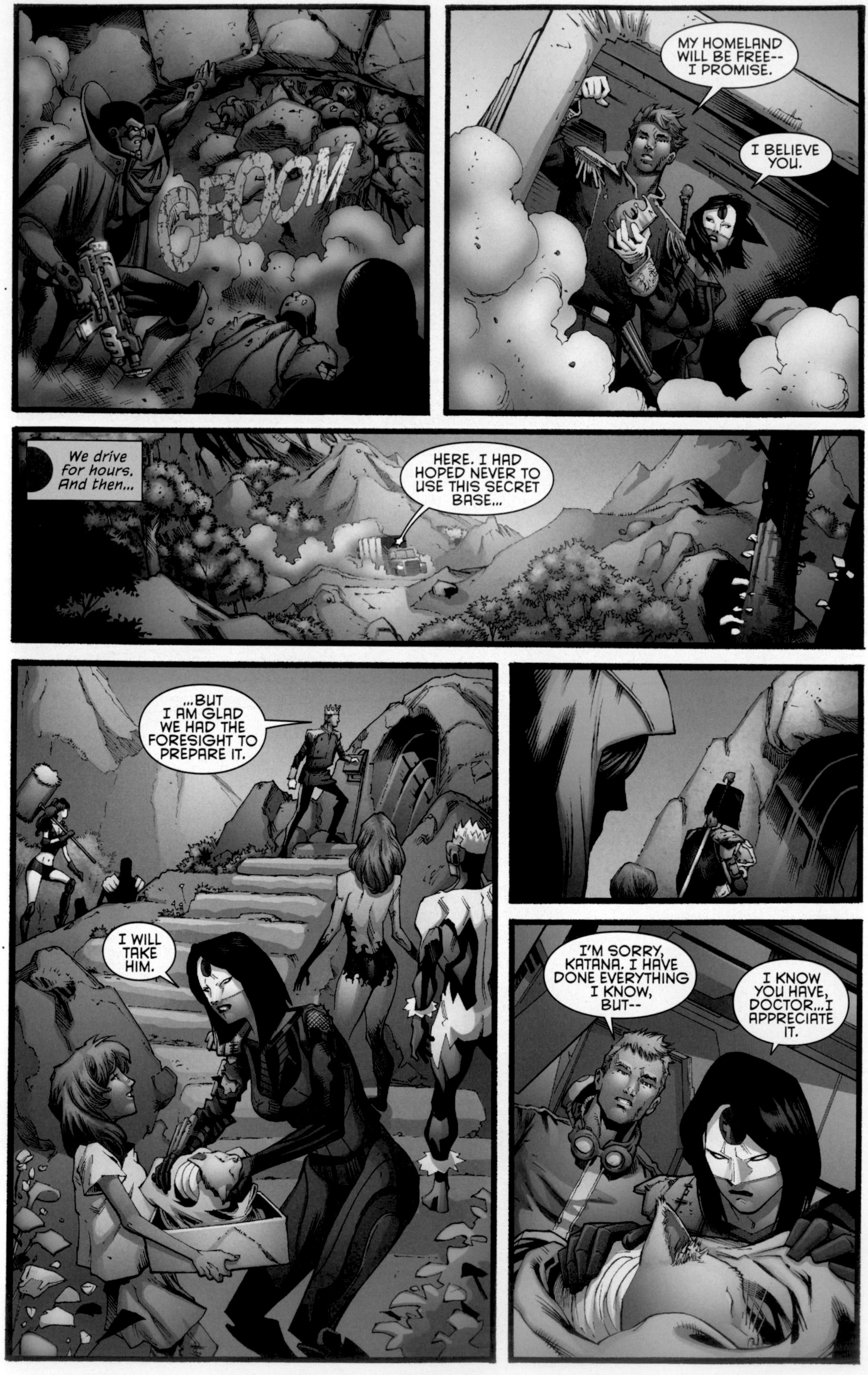
CROOM
MY HOMELAND WILL BE FREE-- I PROMISE.
I BELIEVE YOU.
We drive for hours. And then...
HERE. I HAD HOPED NEVER TO USE THIS SECRET BASE...
...BUT I AM GLAD WE HAD THE FORESIGHT TO PREPARE IT.
I WILL TAKE HIM.
I'M SORRY, KATANA. I HAVE DONE EVERYTHING I KNOW, BUT--
I KNOW YOU HAVE, DOCTOR...I APPRECIATE IT.

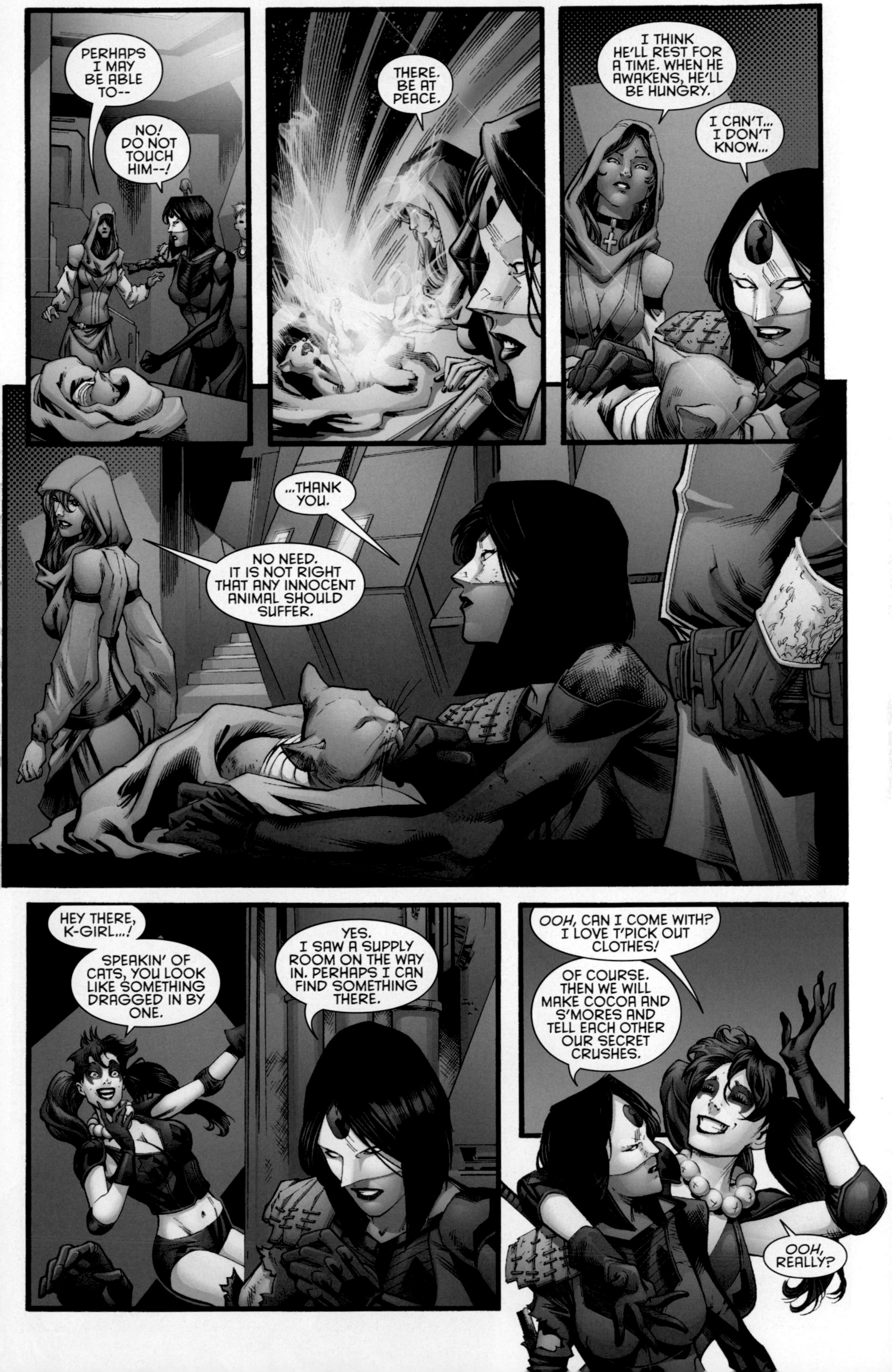
PERHAPS I MAY BE ABLE TO--
NO! DO NOT TOUCH HIM--!
THERE. BE AT PEACE.
I THINK HE'LL REST FOR A TIME. WHEN HE AWAKENS, HE'LL BE HUNGRY.
I CAN'T... I DON'T KNOW...
...THANK YOU.
NO NEED. IT IS NOT RIGHT THAT ANY INNOCENT ANIMAL SHOULD SUFFER.
HEY THERE, K-GIRL...!
SPEAKIN' OF CATS, YOU LOOK LIKE SOMETHING DRAGGED IN BY ONE.
YES. I SAW A SUPPLY ROOM ON THE WAY IN. PERHAPS I CAN FIND SOMETHING THERE.
OOH, CAN I COME WITH? I LOVE T'PICK OUT CLOTHES!
OF COURSE. THEN WE WILL MAKE COCOA AND S'MORES AND TELL EACH OTHER OUR SECRET CRUSHES.
OOH, REALLY?

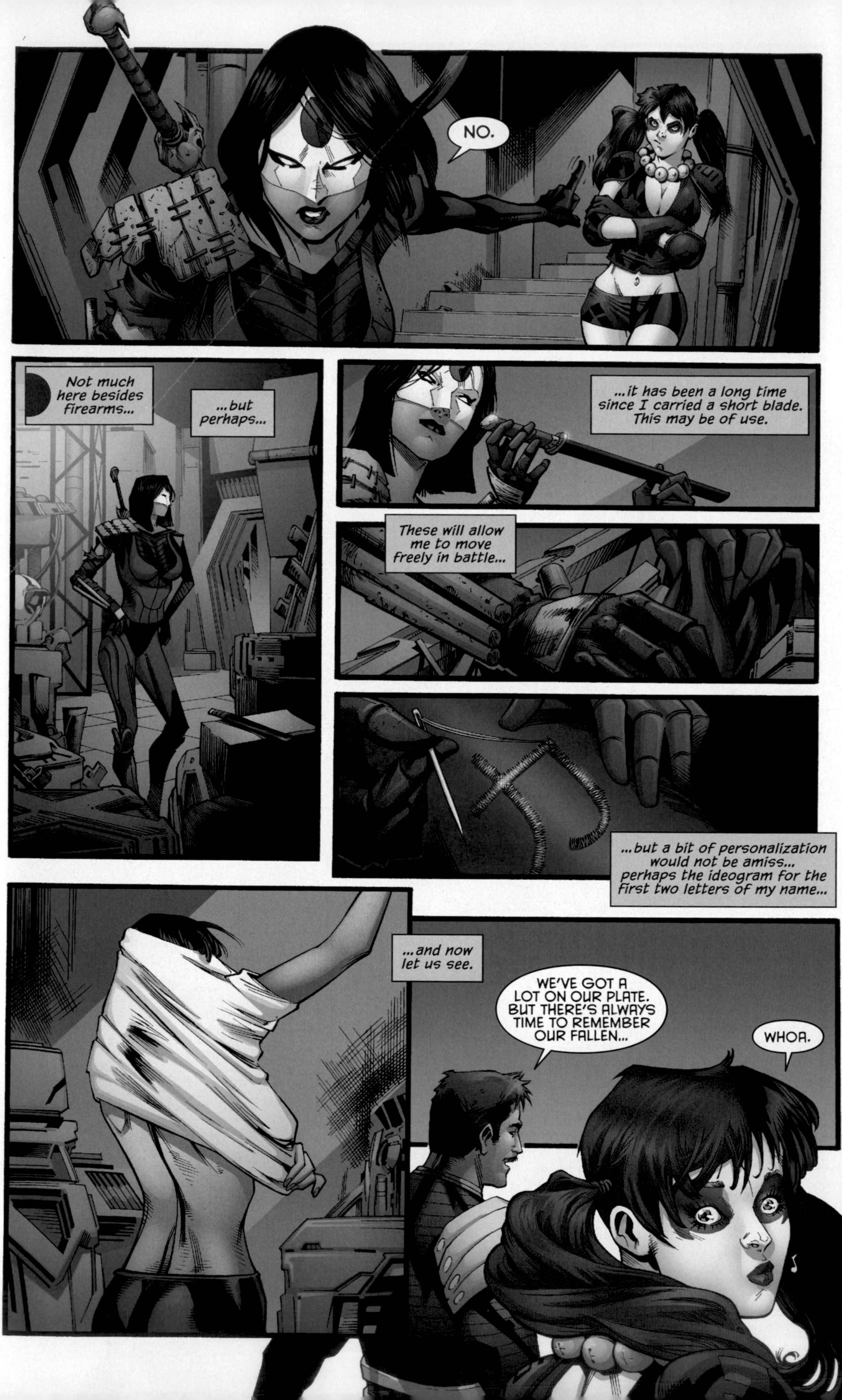

NO.
Not much here besides firearms...
...but perhaps...
...it has been a long time since I carried a short blade. This may be of use.
These will allow me to move freely in battle...
...but a bit of personalization would not be amiss... perhaps the ideogram for the first two letters of my name...
...and now let us see.
WE'VE GOT A LOT ON OUR PLATE. BUT THERE'S ALWAYS TIME TO REMEMBER OUR FALLEN...
WHOA.

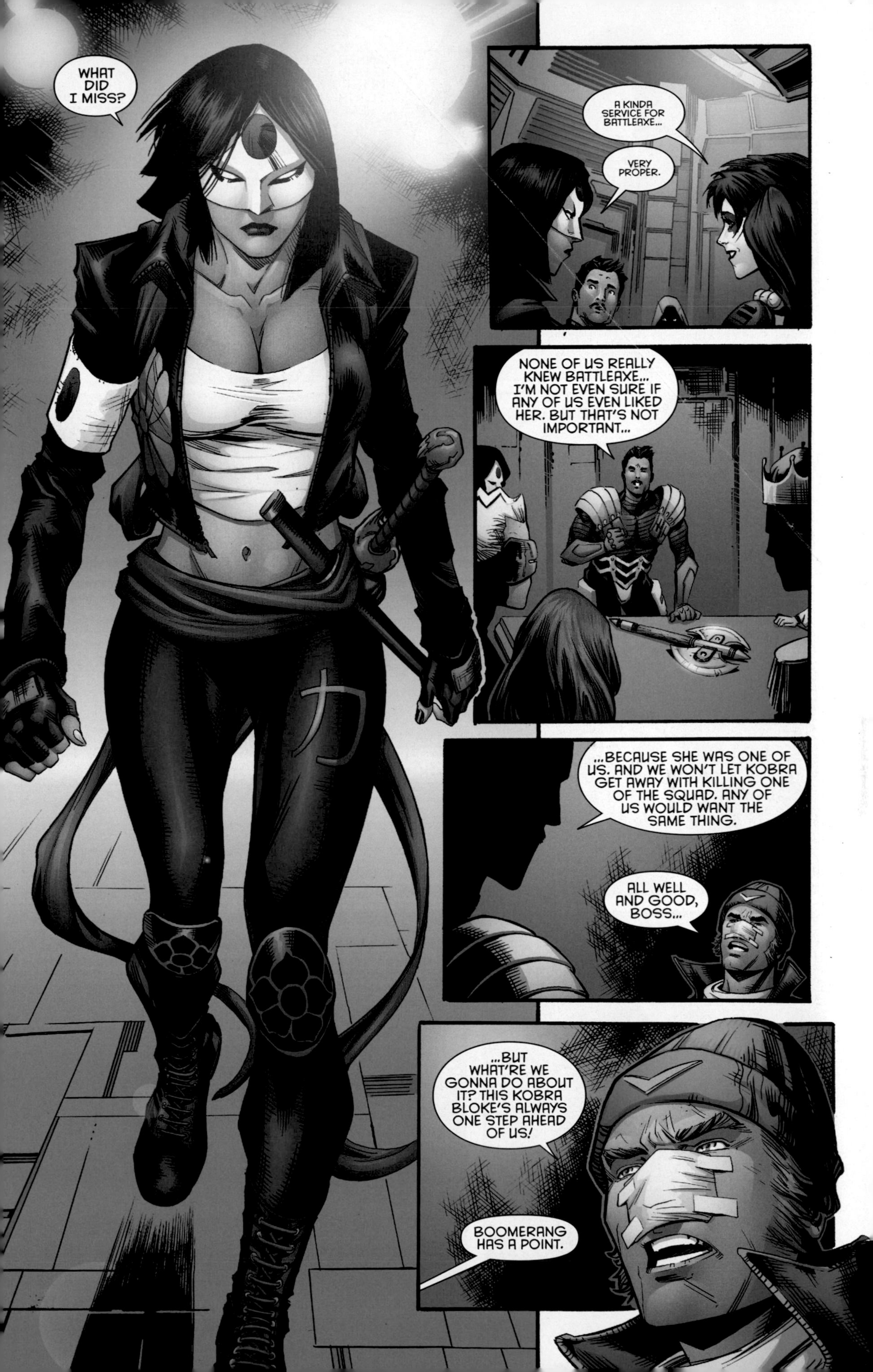
WHAT DID I MISS?
A KINDA SERVICE FOR BATTLEAXE...
VERY PROPER.
NONE OF US REALLY KNEW BATTLEAXE... I'M NOT EVEN SURE IF ANY OF US EVEN LIKED HER. BUT THAT'S NOT IMPORTANT...
...BECAUSE SHE WAS ONE OF US. AND WE WON'T LET KOBRA GET AWAY WITH KILLING ONE OF THE SQUAD. ANY OF US WOULD WANT THE SAME THING.
ALL WELL AND GOOD, BOSS...
...BUT WHAT'RE WE GONNA DO ABOUT IT? THIS KOBRA BLOKE'S ALWAYS ONE STEP AHEAD OF US!
BOOMERANG HAS A POINT.

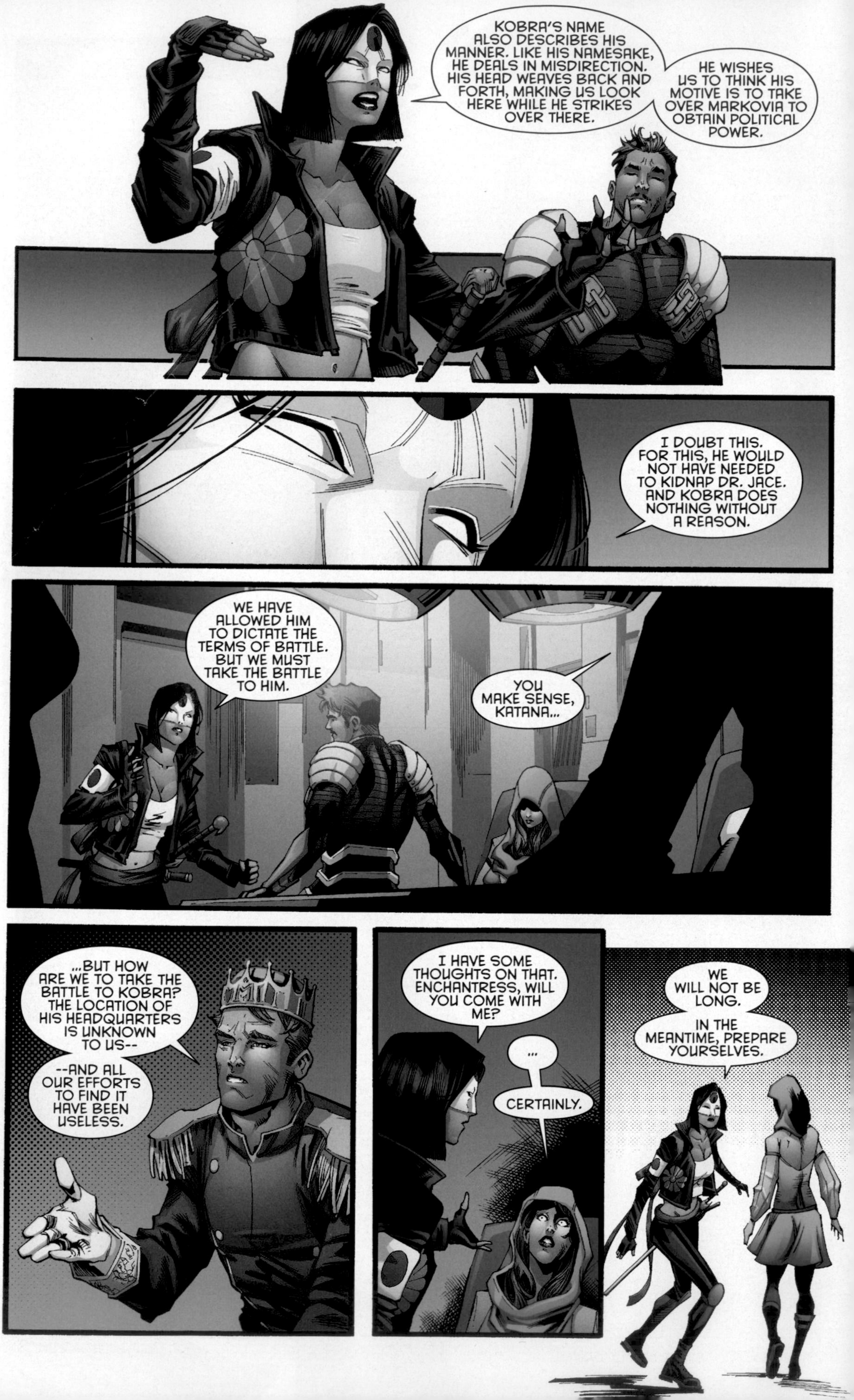
KOBRA'S NAME ALSO DESCRIBES HIS MANNER. LIKE HIS NAMESAKE, HE DEALS IN MISDIRECTION. HIS HEAD WEAVES BACK AND FORTH, MAKING US LOOK HERE WHILE HE STRIKES OVER THERE.
HE WISHES US TO THINK HIS MOTIVE IS TO TAKE OVER MARKOVIA TO OBTAIN POLITICAL POWER.
I DOUBT THIS. FOR THIS, HE WOULD NOT HAVE NEEDED TO KIDNAP DR. JACE. AND KOBRA DOES NOTHING WITHOUT A REASON.
WE HAVE ALLOWED HIM TO DICTATE THE TERMS OF BATTLE. BUT WE MUST TAKE THE BATTLE TO HIM.
YOU MAKE SENSE, KATANA...
...BUT HOW ARE WE TO TAKE THE BATTLE TO KOBRA? THE LOCATION OF HIS HEADQUARTERS IS UNKNOWN TO US--
--AND ALL OUR EFFORTS TO FIND IT HAVE BEEN USELESS.
I HAVE SOME THOUGHTS ON THAT. ENCHANTRESS, WILL YOU COME WITH ME?
...
CERTAINLY.
WE WILL NOT BE LONG.
IN THE MEANTIME, PREPARE YOURSELVES.

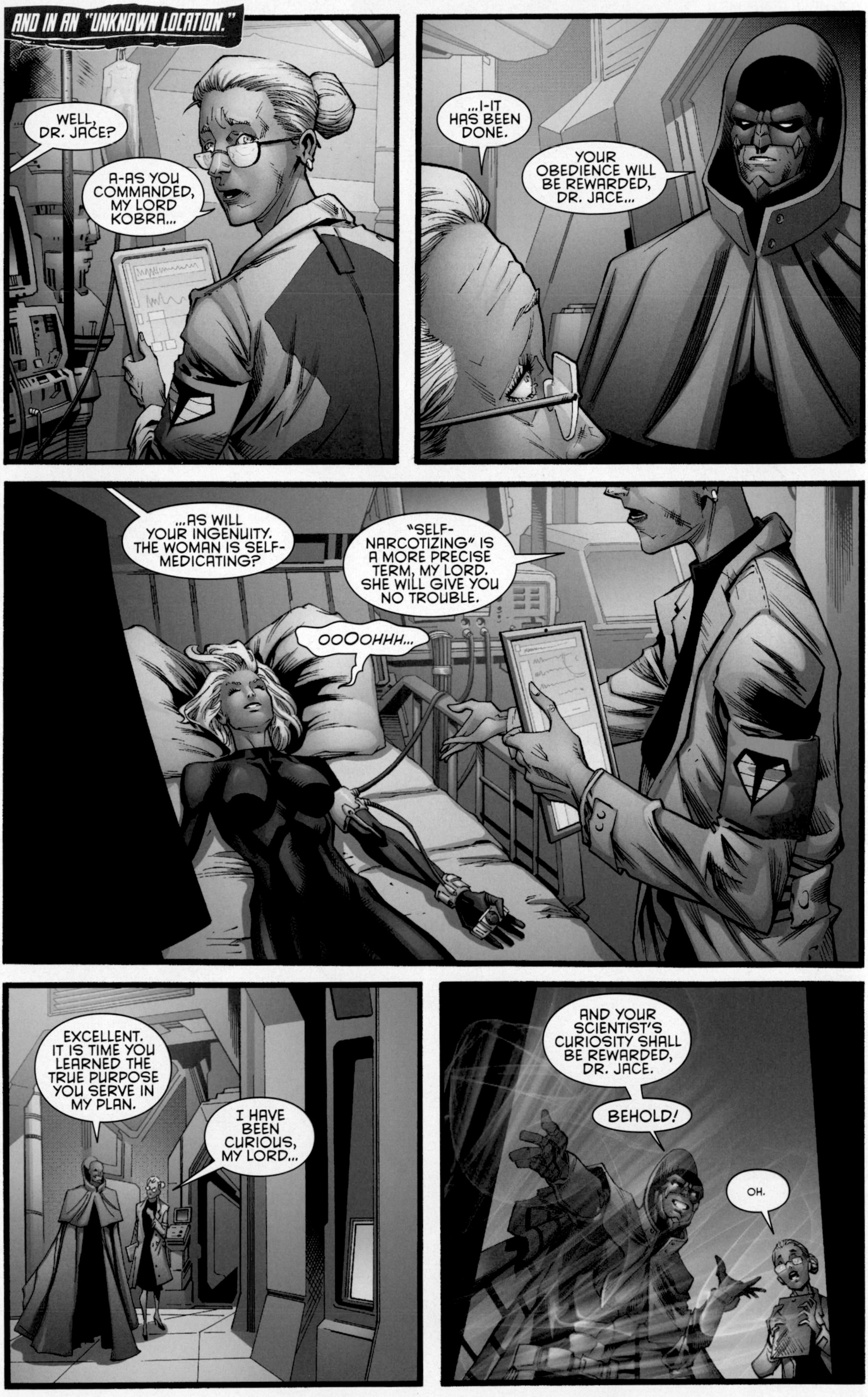
AND IN AN "UNKNOWN LOCATION."
WELL, DR. JACE?
A-AS YOU COMMANDED, MY LORD KOBRA...
...I-IT HAS BEEN DONE.
YOUR OBEDIENCE WILL BE REWARDED, DR. JACE...
...AS WILL YOUR INGENUITY. THE WOMAN IS SELF-MEDICATING?
"SELF-NARCOTIZING" IS A MORE PRECISE TERM, MY LORD. SHE WILL GIVE YOU NO TROUBLE.
OOOOHHH...
EXCELLENT. IT IS TIME YOU LEARNED THE TRUE PURPOSE YOU SERVE IN MY PLAN.
I HAVE BEEN CURIOUS, MY LORD...
AND YOUR SCIENTIST'S CURIOSITY SHALL BE REWARDED, DR. JACE.
BEHOLD!
OH.

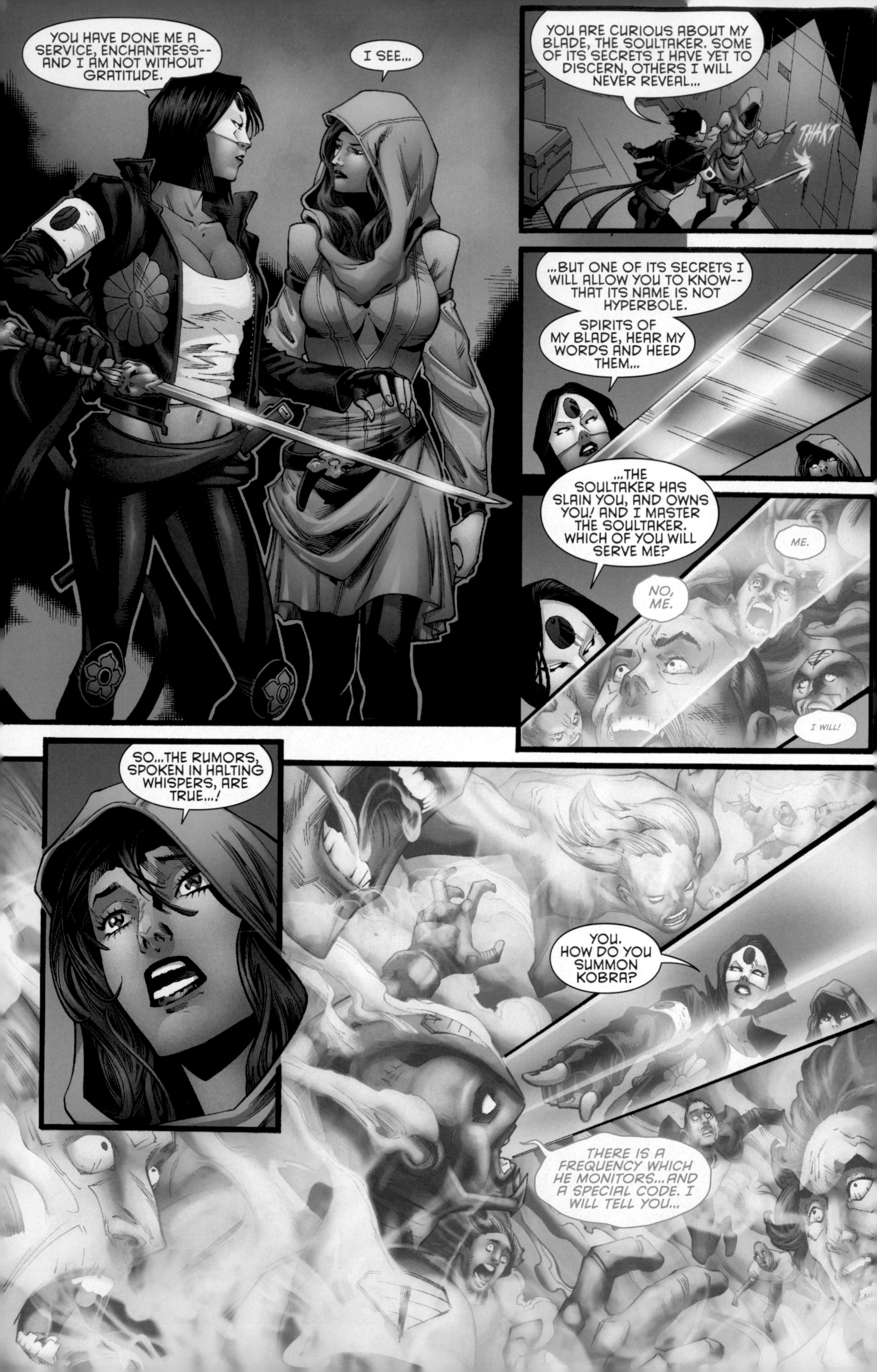
YOU HAVE DONE ME A SERVICE, ENCHANTRESS-- AND I AM NOT WITHOUT GRATITUDE.
I SEE...
YOU ARE CURIOUS ABOUT MY BLADE, THE SOULTAKER. SOME OF ITS SECRETS I HAVE YET TO DISCERN, OTHERS I WILL NEVER REVEAL...
THAKT
...BUT ONE OF ITS SECRETS I WILL ALLOW YOU TO KNOW-- THAT ITS NAME IS NOT HYPERBOLE.
SPIRITS OF MY BLADE, HEAR MY WORDS AND HEED THEM...
...THE SOULTAKER HAS SLAIN YOU, AND OWNS YOU! AND I MASTER THE SOULTAKER. WHICH OF YOU WILL SERVE ME?
ME.
NO, ME.
I WILL!
SO...THE RUMORS, SPOKEN IN HALTING WHISPERS, ARE TRUE...!
YOU. HOW DO YOU SUMMON KOBRA?
THERE IS A FREQUENCY WHICH HE MONITORS...AND A SPECIAL CODE. I WILL TELL YOU...

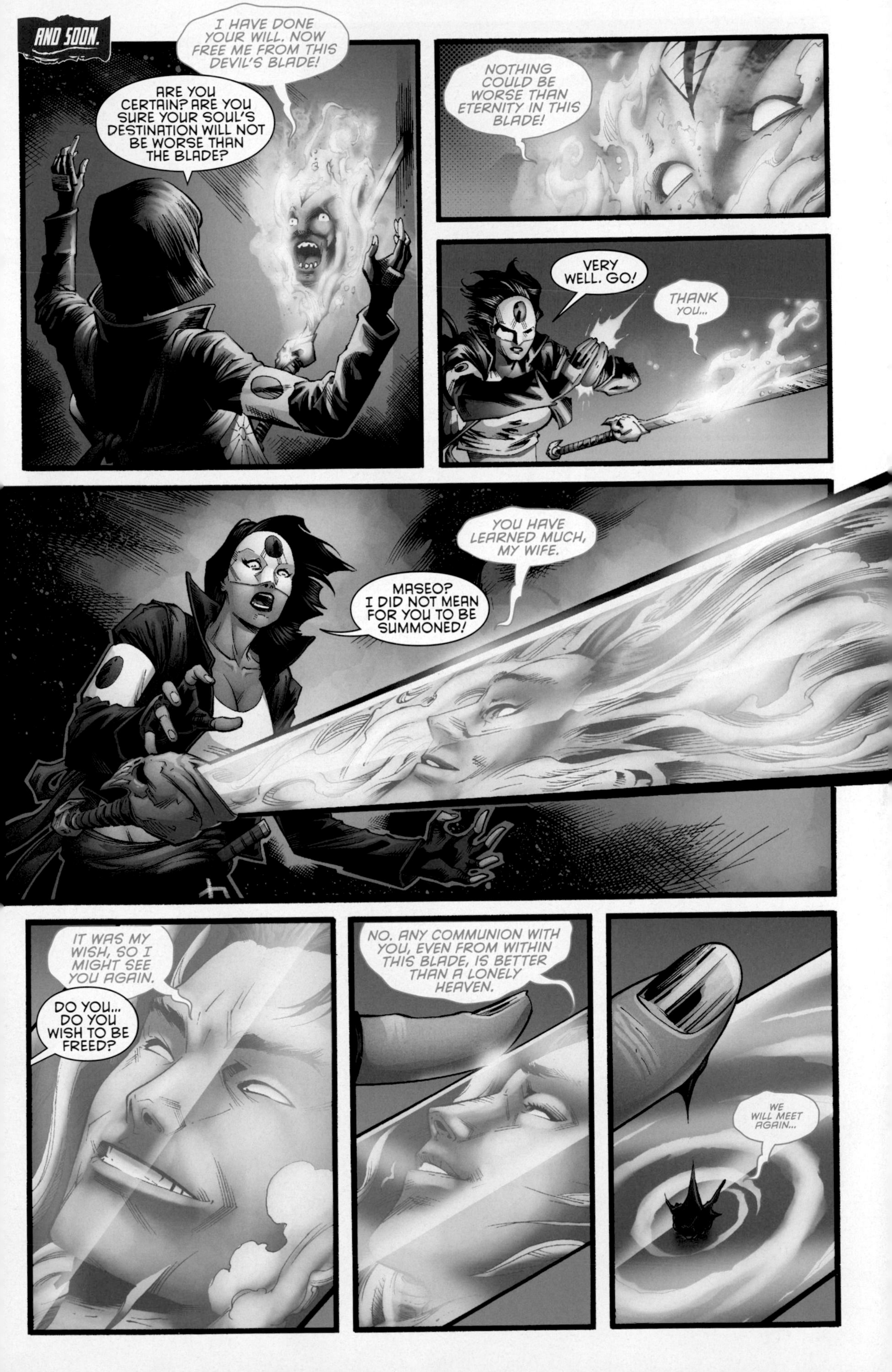

AND SOON.
I HAVE DONE YOUR WILL. NOW FREE ME FROM THIS DEVIL'S BLADE!
ARE YOU CERTAIN? ARE YOU SURE YOUR SOUL'S DESTINATION WILL NOT BE WORSE THAN THE BLADE?
NOTHING COULD BE WORSE THAN ETERNITY IN THIS BLADE!
VERY WELL. GO!
THANK YOU...
YOU HAVE LEARNED MUCH, MY WIFE.
MASEO? I DID NOT MEAN FOR YOU TO BE SUMMONED!
IT WAS MY WISH, SO I MIGHT SEE YOU AGAIN.
DO YOU... DO YOU WISH TO BE FREED?
NO. ANY COMMUNION WITH YOU, EVEN FROM WITHIN THIS BLADE, IS BETTER THAN A LONELY HEAVEN.
WE WILL MEET AGAIN...

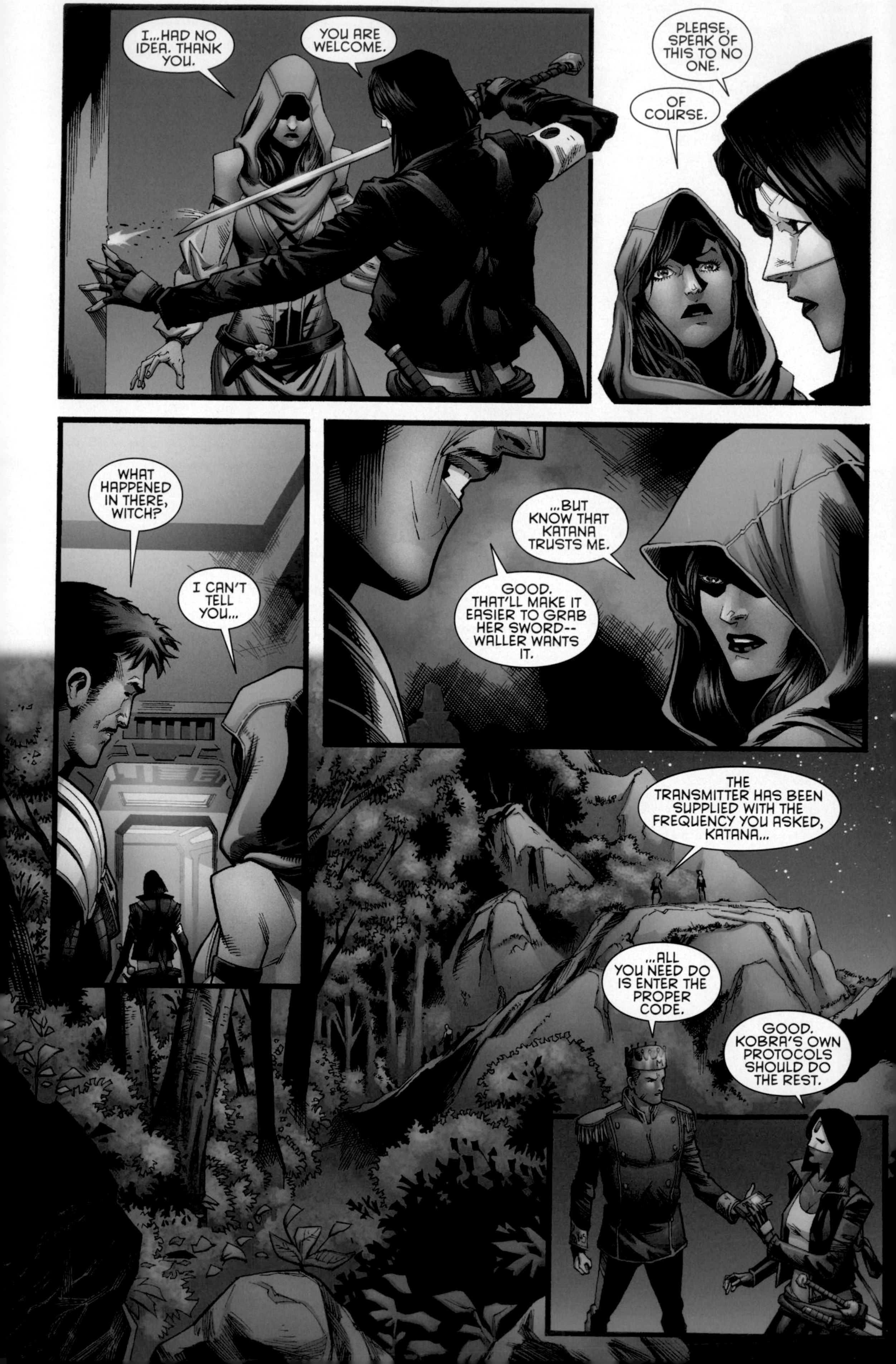
I...HAD NO IDEA. THANK YOU.
YOU ARE WELCOME.
PLEASE, SPEAK OF THIS TO NO ONE.
OF COURSE.
WHAT HAPPENED IN THERE, WITCH?
I CAN'T TELL YOU...
...BUT KNOW THAT KATANA TRUSTS ME.
GOOD. THAT'LL MAKE IT EASIER TO GRAB HER SWORD--WALLER WANTS IT.
THE TRANSMITTER HAS BEEN SUPPLIED WITH THE FREQUENCY YOU ASKED, KATANA...
...ALL YOU NEED DO IS ENTER THE PROPER CODE.
GOOD. KOBRA'S OWN PROTOCOLS SHOULD DO THE REST.

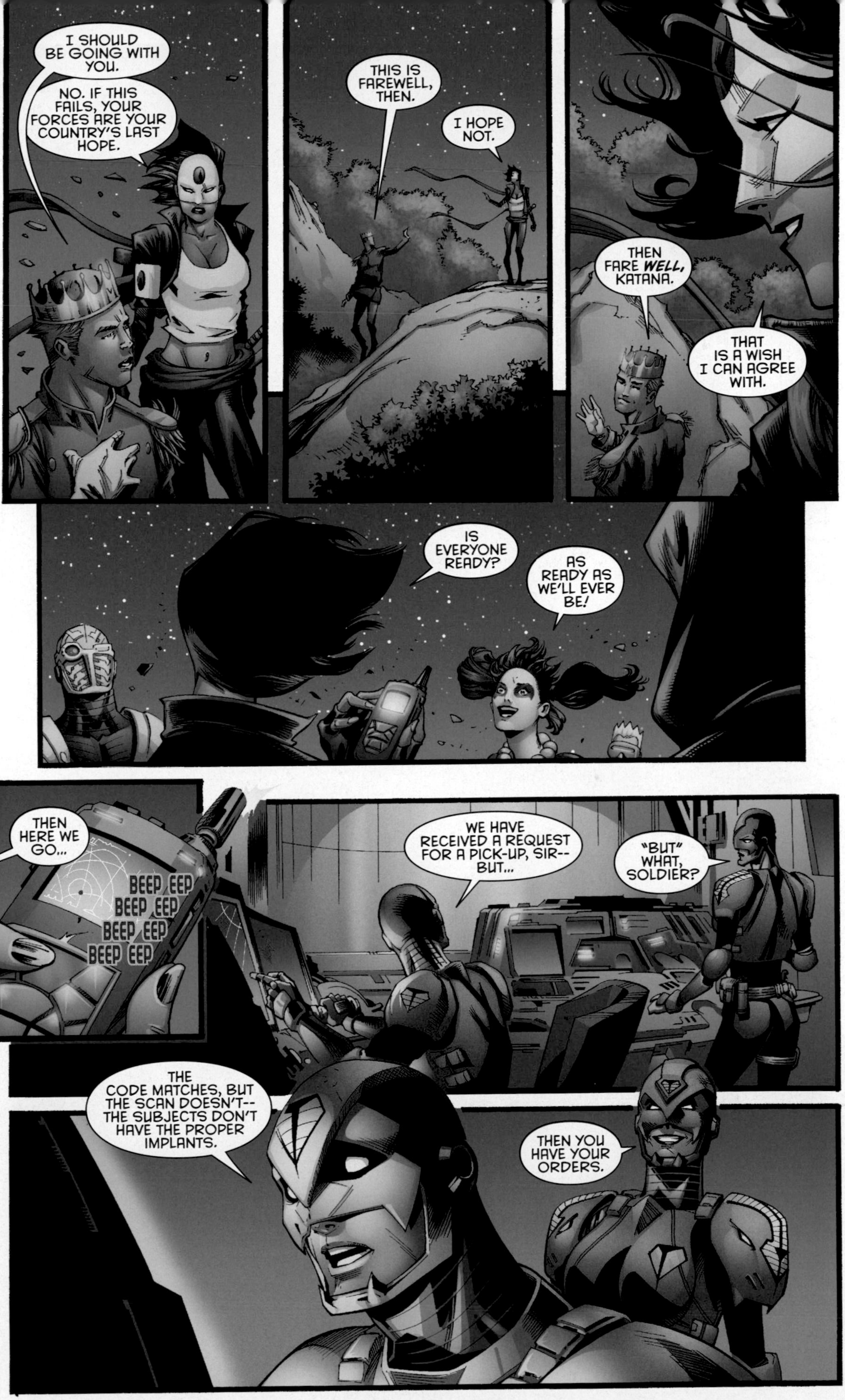
I SHOULD BE GOING WITH YOU.
NO. IF THIS FAILS, YOUR FORCES ARE YOUR COUNTRY'S LAST HOPE.
THIS IS FAREWELL, THEN.
I HOPE NOT.
THEN FARE WELL, KATANA.
THAT IS A WISH I CAN AGREE WITH.
IS EVERYONE READY?
AS READY AS WE'LL EVER BE!
THEN HERE WE GO...
BEEP EEP
BEEP EEP
BEEP EEP
BEEP EEP
WE HAVE RECEIVED A REQUEST FOR A PICK-UP, SIR-- BUT...
"BUT" WHAT, SOLDIER?
THE CODE MATCHES, BUT THE SCAN DOESN'T-- THE SUBJECTS DON'T HAVE THE PROPER IMPLANTS.
THEN YOU HAVE YOUR ORDERS.

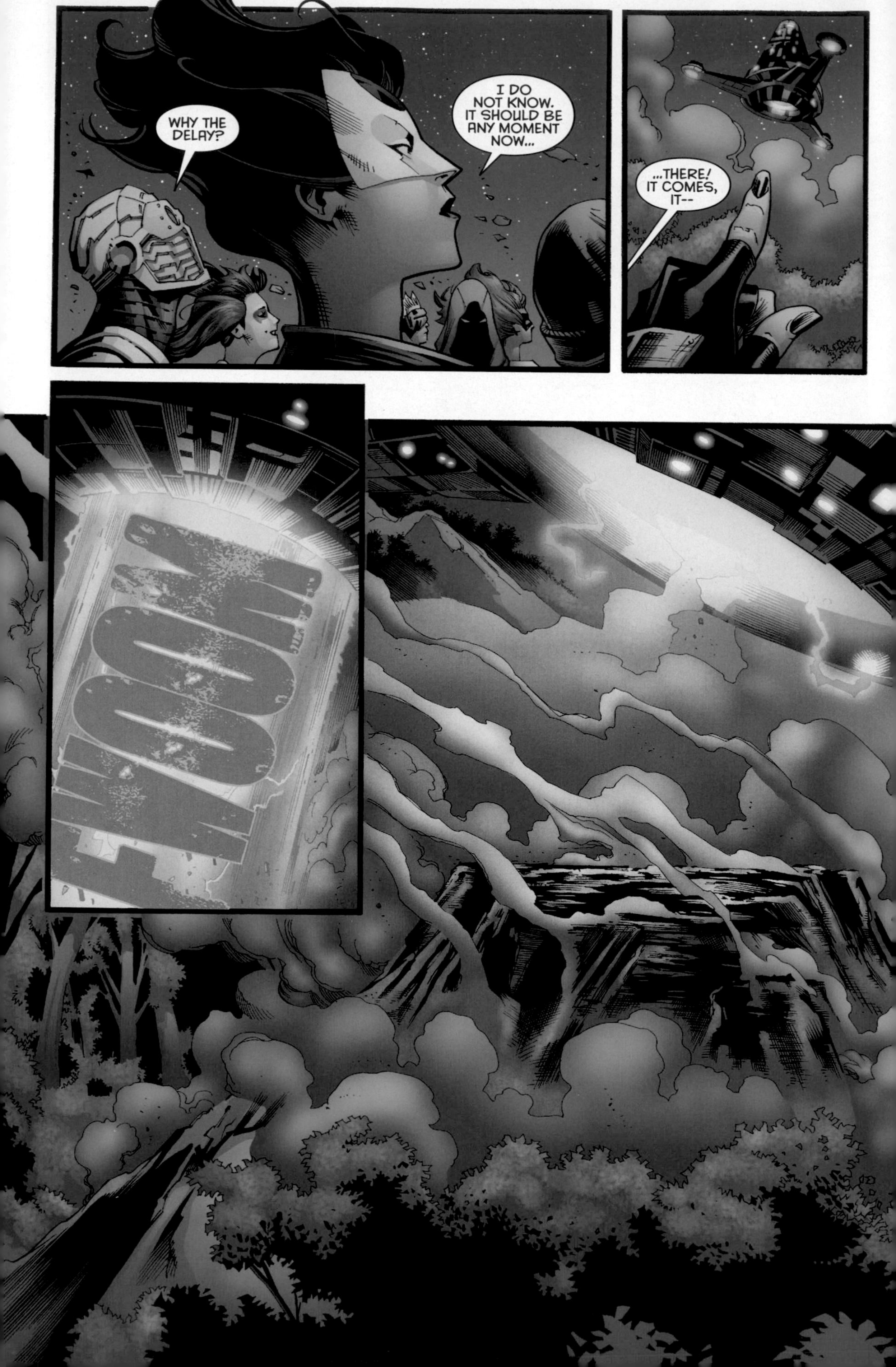
WHY THE DELAY?
I DO NOT KNOW. IT SHOULD BE ANY MOMENT NOW...
...THERE! IT COMES, IT--
FOOM!

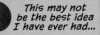

This may not be the best idea I have ever had...

KATANA in: Call her... Halo

MIKE W. BARR writer
DIOGENES NEVES penciller
RUY JOSE inker
CARRIE STRACHAN colorist
SAIDA TEMOFONTE letterer
CARY NORD cover artist
JESSICA CHEN assistant editor
KRISTY QUINN editor
Katana created by Mike W. Barr and Jim Aparo

...but it may be our last chance to bring Kobra to justice!

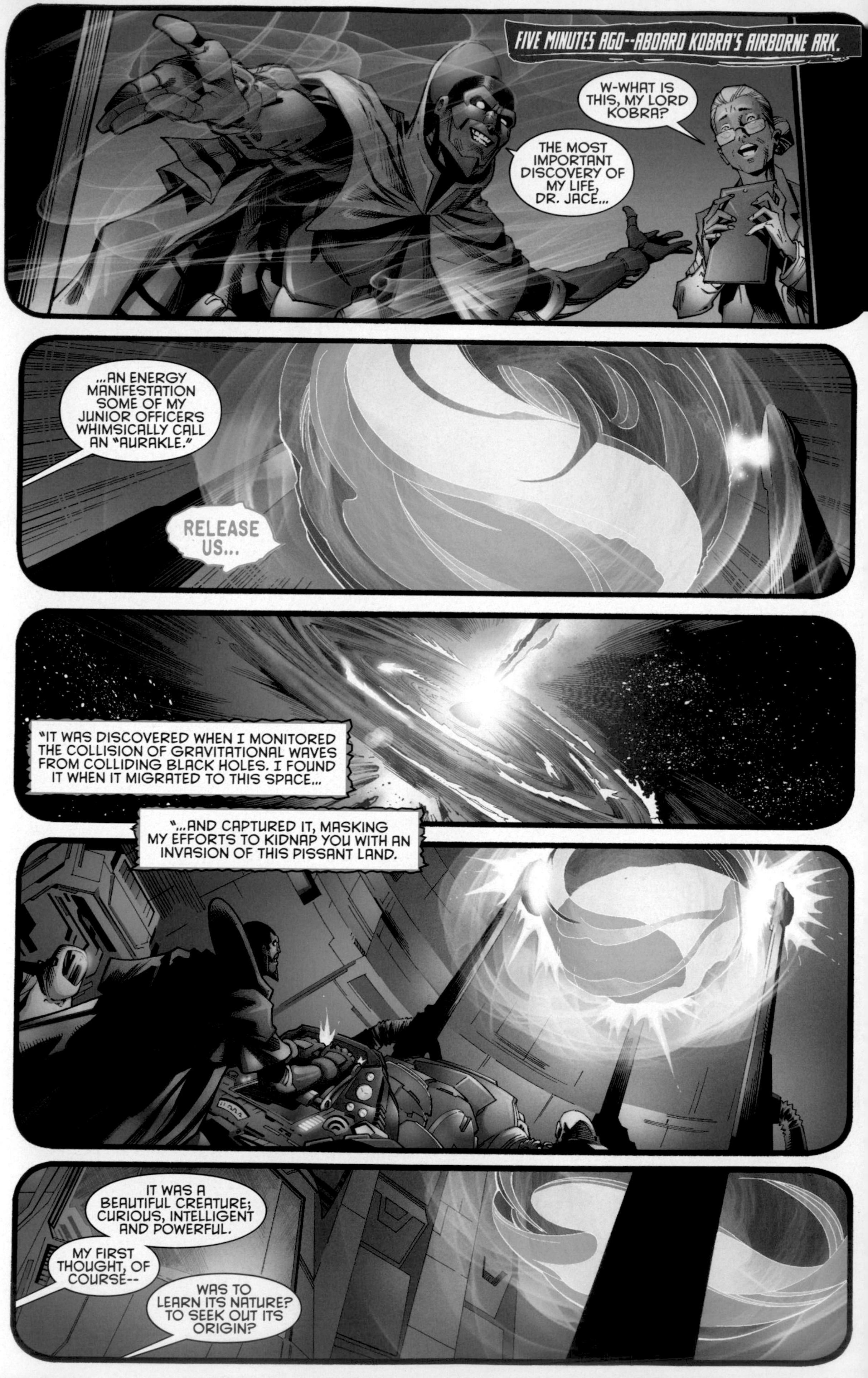
FIVE MINUTES AGO--ABOARD KOBRA'S AIRBORNE ARK.
W-WHAT IS THIS, MY LORD KOBRA?
THE MOST IMPORTANT DISCOVERY OF MY LIFE, DR. JACE...
...AN ENERGY MANIFESTATION SOME OF MY JUNIOR OFFICERS WHIMSICALLY CALL AN "AURAKLE."
RELEASE US...
"IT WAS DISCOVERED WHEN I MONITORED THE COLLISION OF GRAVITATIONAL WAVES FROM COLLIDING BLACK HOLES. I FOUND IT WHEN IT MIGRATED TO THIS SPACE...
"...AND CAPTURED IT, MASKING MY EFFORTS TO KIDNAP YOU WITH AN INVASION OF THIS PISSANT LAND.
IT WAS A BEAUTIFUL CREATURE; CURIOUS, INTELLIGENT AND POWERFUL.
MY FIRST THOUGHT, OF COURSE--
WAS TO LEARN ITS NATURE? TO SEEK OUT ITS ORIGIN?

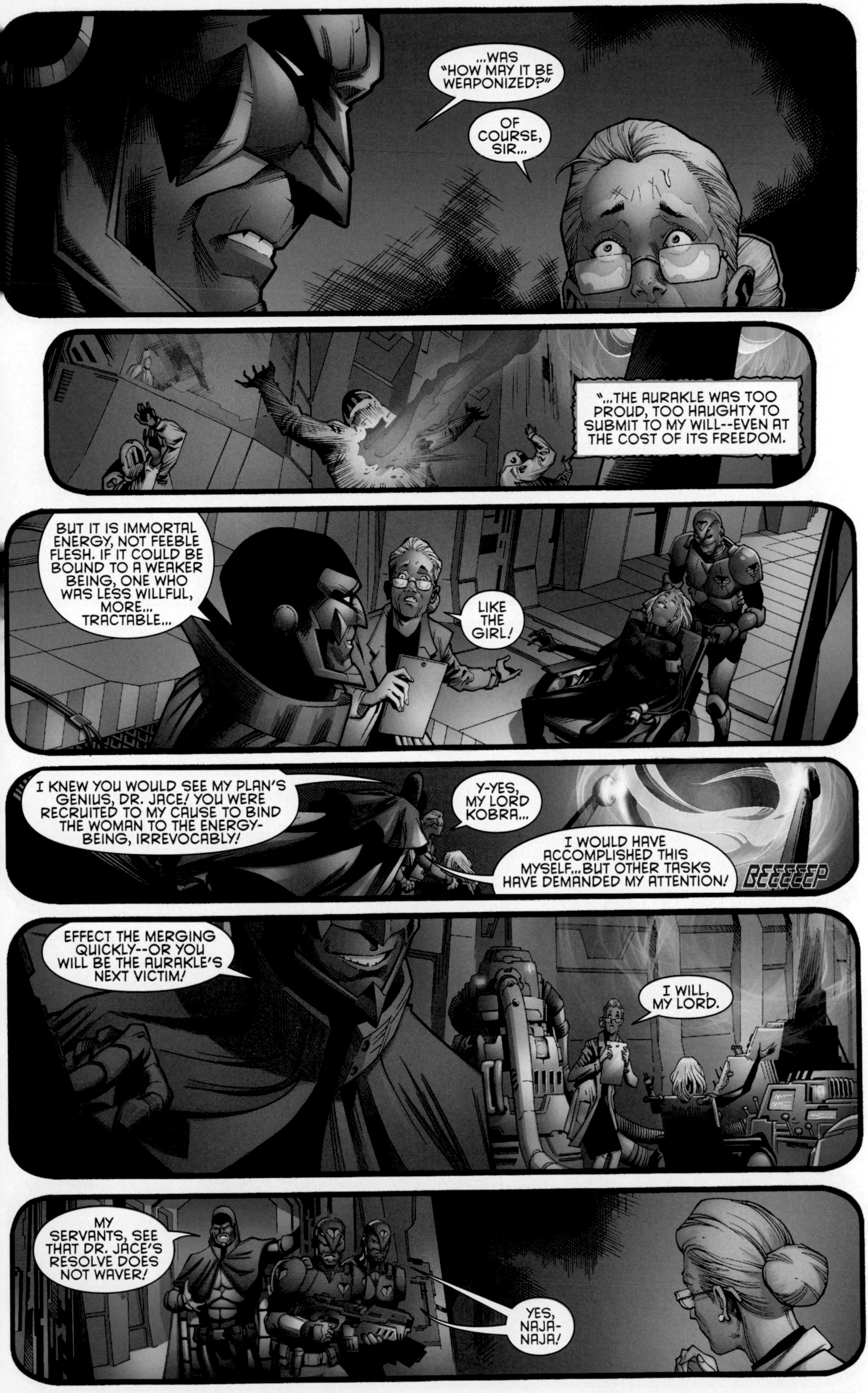
...WAS "HOW MAY IT BE WEAPONIZED?"
OF COURSE, SIR...
"...THE AURAKLE WAS TOO PROUD, TOO HAUGHTY TO SUBMIT TO MY WILL--EVEN AT THE COST OF ITS FREEDOM.
BUT IT IS IMMORTAL ENERGY, NOT FEEBLE FLESH. IF IT COULD BE BOUND TO A WEAKER BEING, ONE WHO WAS LESS WILLFUL, MORE... TRACTABLE...
LIKE THE GIRL!
I KNEW YOU WOULD SEE MY PLAN'S GENIUS, DR. JACE! YOU WERE RECRUITED TO MY CAUSE TO BIND THE WOMAN TO THE ENERGY-BEING, IRREVOCABLY!
Y-YES, MY LORD KOBRA...
I WOULD HAVE ACCOMPLISHED THIS MYSELF...BUT OTHER TASKS HAVE DEMANDED MY ATTENTION!
BEEEEEP
EFFECT THE MERGING QUICKLY--OR YOU WILL BE THE AURAKLE'S NEXT VICTIM!
I WILL, MY LORD.
MY SERVANTS, SEE THAT DR. JACE'S RESOLVE DOES NOT WAVER!
YES, NAJA-NAJA!

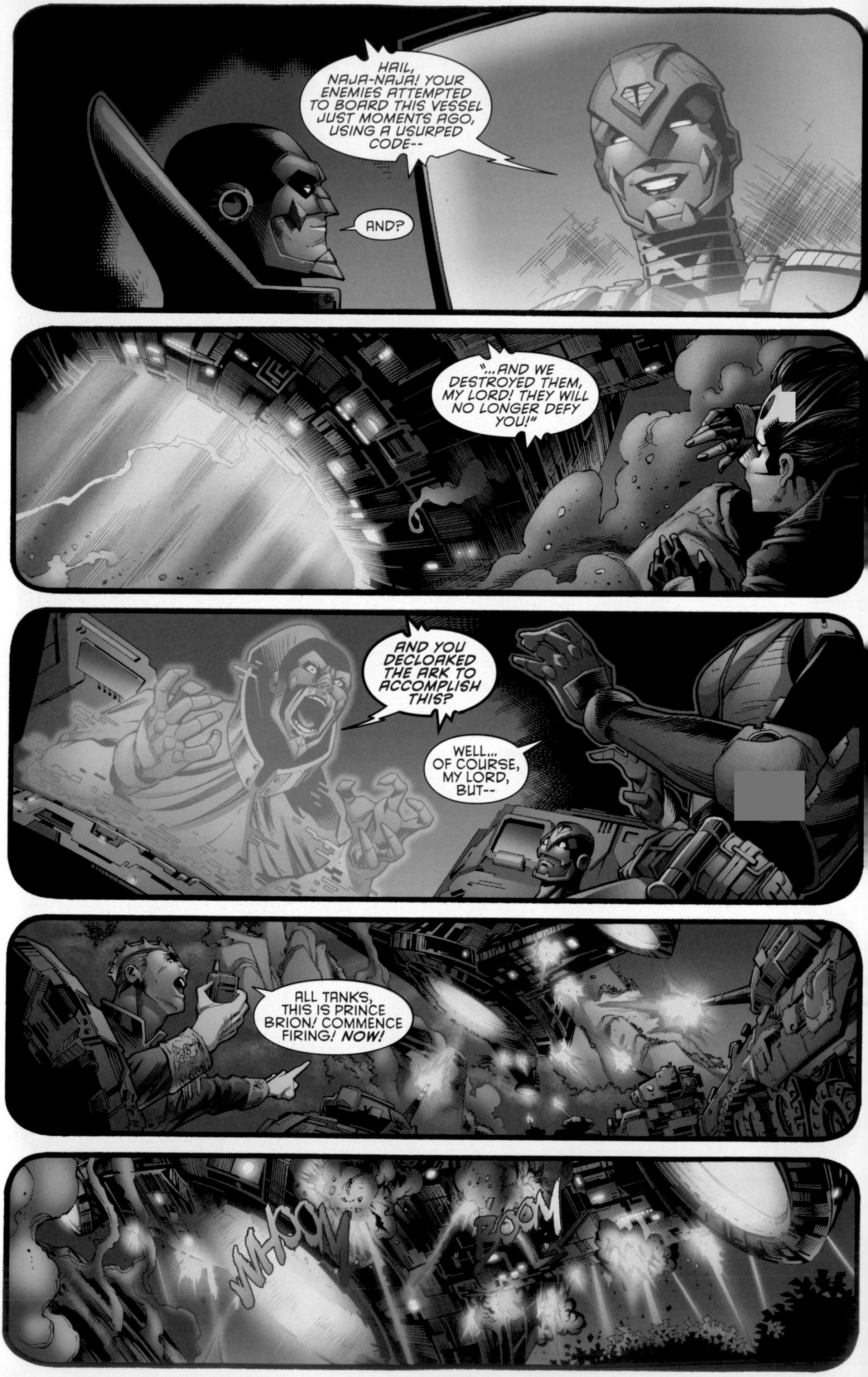
HAIL, NAJA-NAJA! YOUR ENEMIES ATTEMPTED TO BOARD THIS VESSEL JUST MOMENTS AGO, USING A USURPED CODE--
AND?
"...AND WE DESTROYED THEM, MY LORD! THEY WILL NO LONGER DEFY YOU!"
AND YOU DECLOAKED THE ARK TO ACCOMPLISH THIS?
WELL... OF COURSE, MY LORD, BUT--
ALL TANKS, THIS IS PRINCE BRION! COMMENCE FIRING! NOW!
WHOOM
BOOM

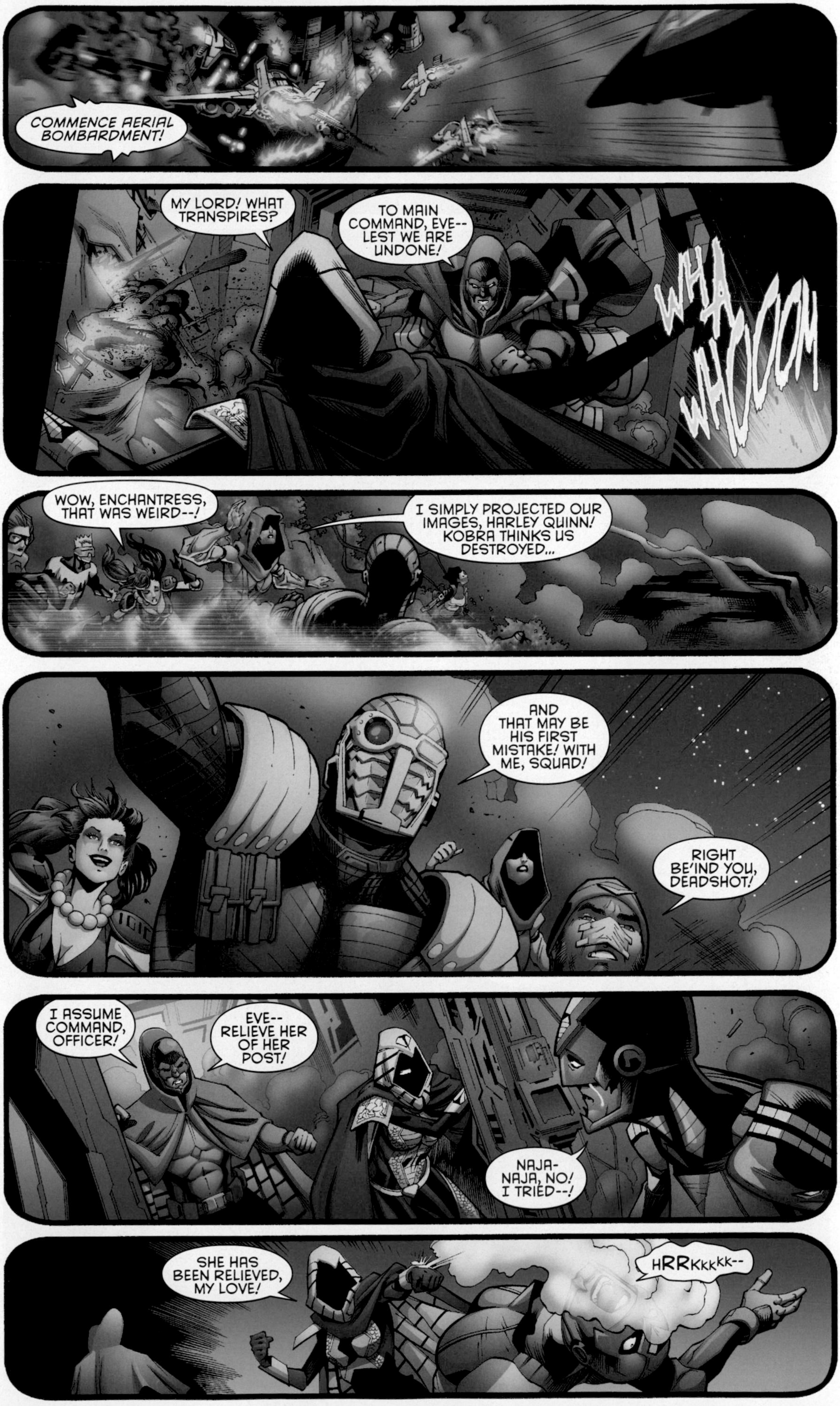
COMMENCE AERIAL BOMBARDMENT!
MY LORD! WHAT TRANSPIRES?
TO MAIN COMMAND, EVE-- LEST WE ARE UNDONE!
WHA WHOOOM
WOW, ENCHANTRESS, THAT WAS WEIRD--!
I SIMPLY PROJECTED OUR IMAGES, HARLEY QUINN! KOBRA THINKS US DESTROYED...
AND THAT MAY BE HIS FIRST MISTAKE! WITH ME, SQUAD!
RIGHT BE'IND YOU, DEADSHOT!
I ASSUME COMMAND, OFFICER!
EVE-- RELIEVE HER OF HER POST!
NAJA-NAJA, NO! I TRIED--!
SHE HAS BEEN RELIEVED, MY LOVE!
HRRKKKKK--

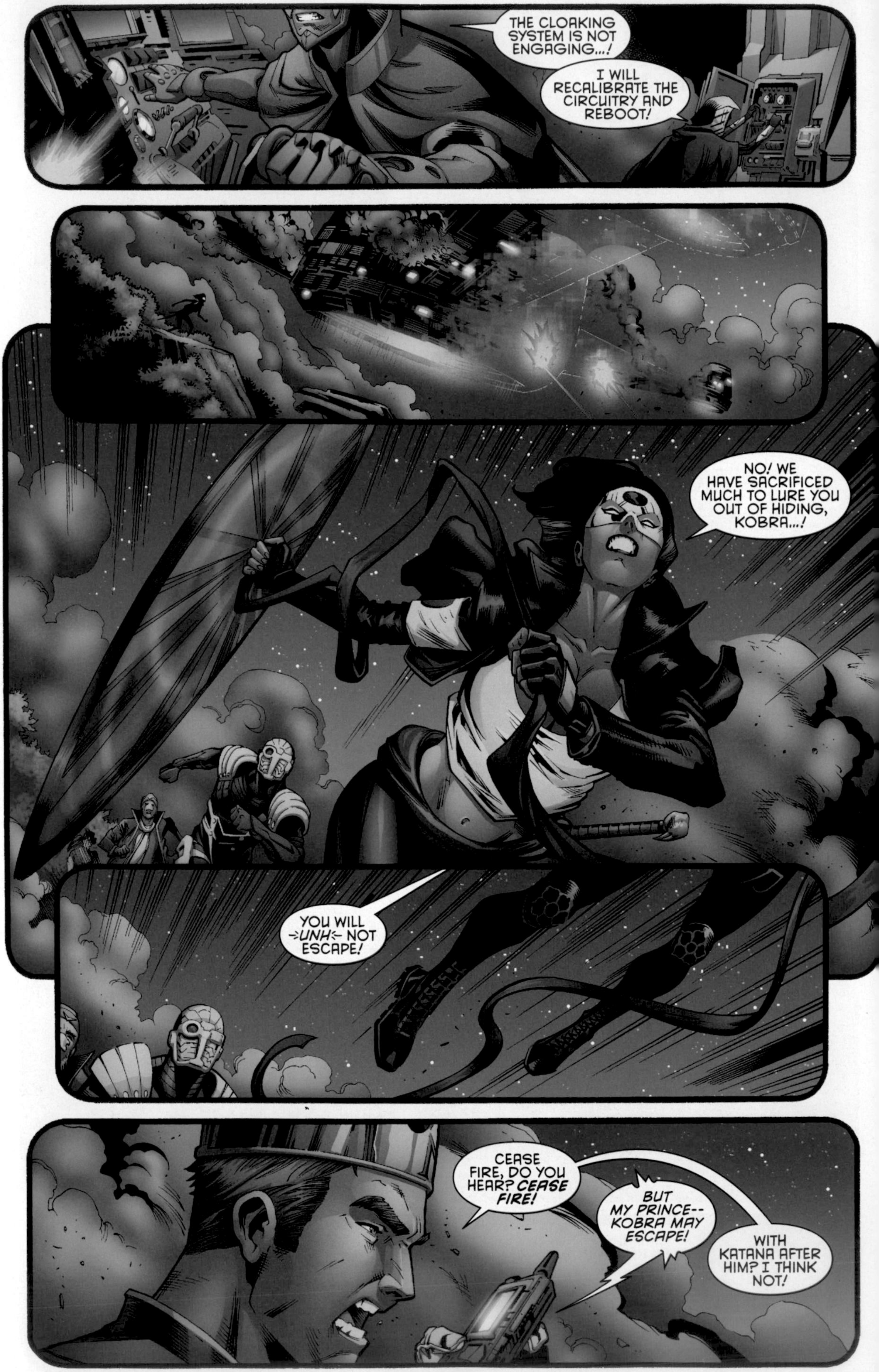
THE CLOAKING SYSTEM IS NOT ENGAGING...!
I WILL RECALIBRATE THE CIRCUITRY AND REBOOT!
NO! WE HAVE SACRIFICED MUCH TO LURE YOU OUT OF HIDING, KOBRA...!
YOU WILL -UNH- NOT ESCAPE!
CEASE FIRE, DO YOU HEAR? CEASE FIRE!
BUT MY PRINCE-- KOBRA MAY ESCAPE!
WITH KATANA AFTER HIM? I THINK NOT!

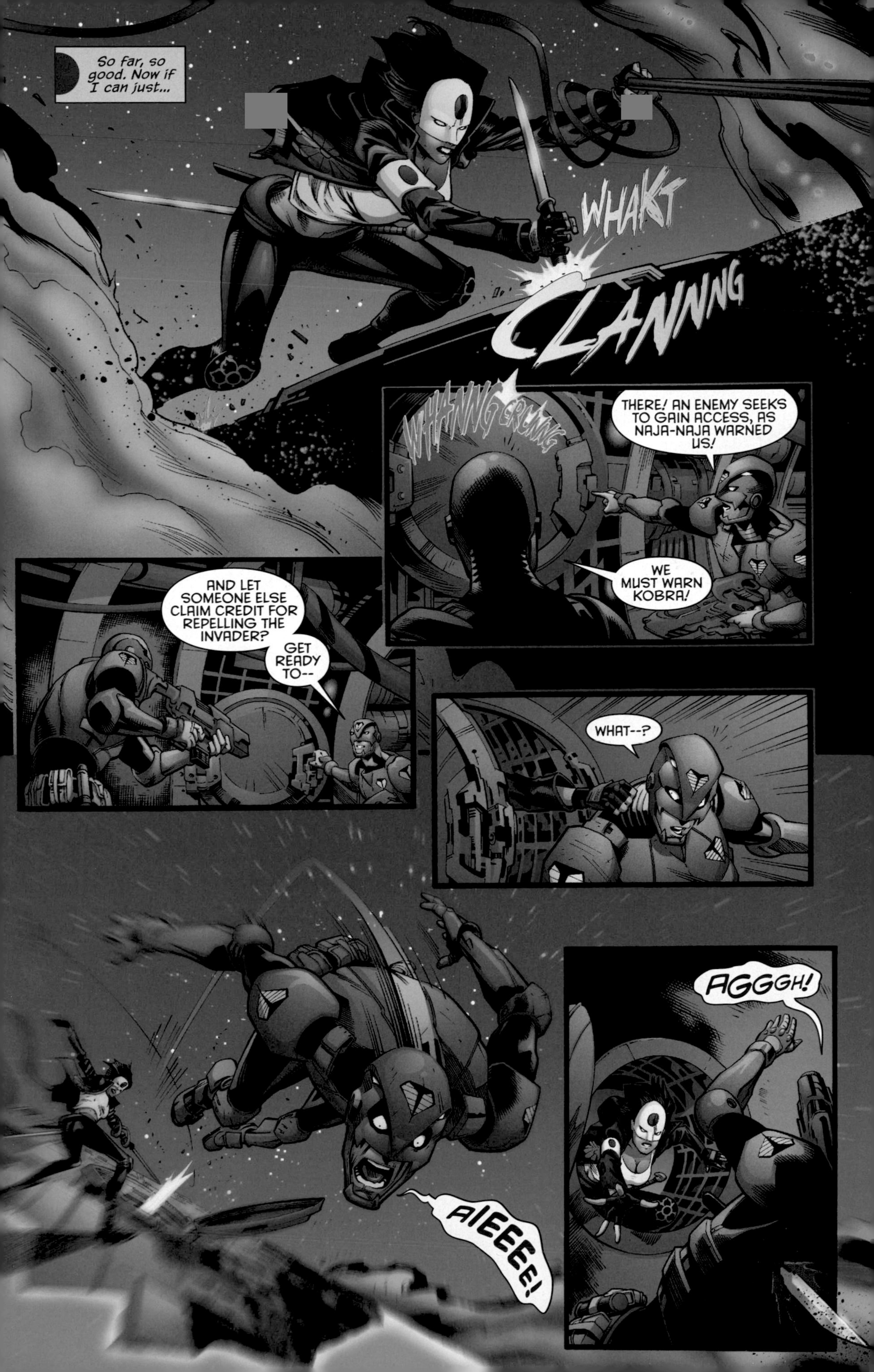
So far, so good. Now if I can just...
WHAKT
CLANNNG
WHANNG ERLNNG
THERE! AN ENEMY SEEKS TO GAIN ACCESS, AS NAJA-NAJA WARNED US!
WE MUST WARN KOBRA!
AND LET SOMEONE ELSE CLAIM CREDIT FOR REPELLING THE INVADER?
GET READY TO--
WHAT--?
AIEEEE!
AGGGH!

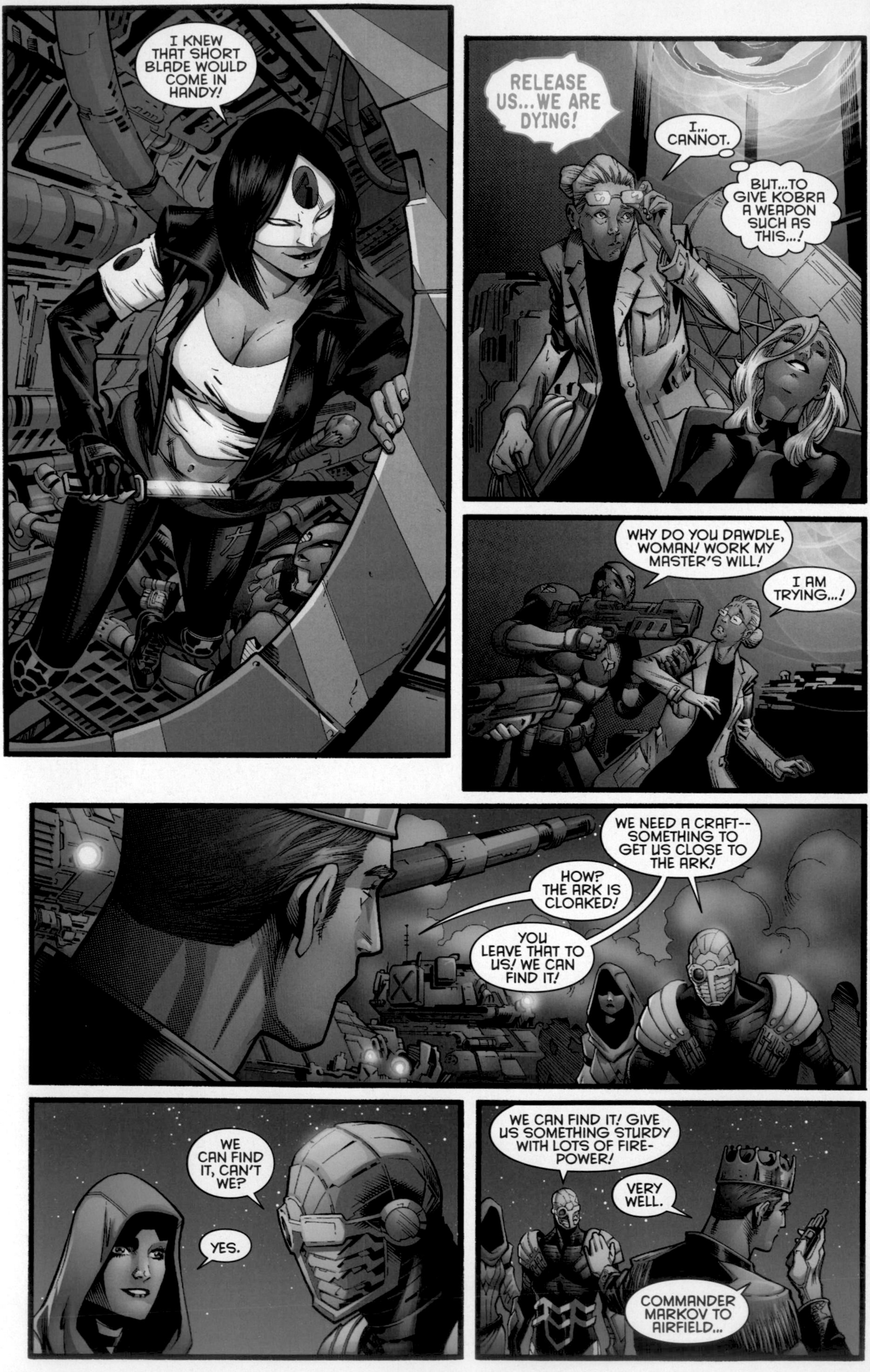
I KNEW THAT SHORT BLADE WOULD COME IN HANDY!
RELEASE US...WE ARE DYING!
I... CANNOT.
BUT...TO GIVE KOBRA A WEAPON SUCH AS THIS...!
WHY DO YOU DAWDLE, WOMAN! WORK MY MASTER'S WILL!
I AM TRYING...!
WE NEED A CRAFT-- SOMETHING TO GET US CLOSE TO THE ARK!
HOW? THE ARK IS CLOAKED!
YOU LEAVE THAT TO US! WE CAN FIND IT!
WE CAN FIND IT, CAN'T WE?
YES.
WE CAN FIND IT! GIVE US SOMETHING STURDY WITH LOTS OF FIRE-POWER!
VERY WELL.
COMMANDER MARKOV TO AIRFIELD...

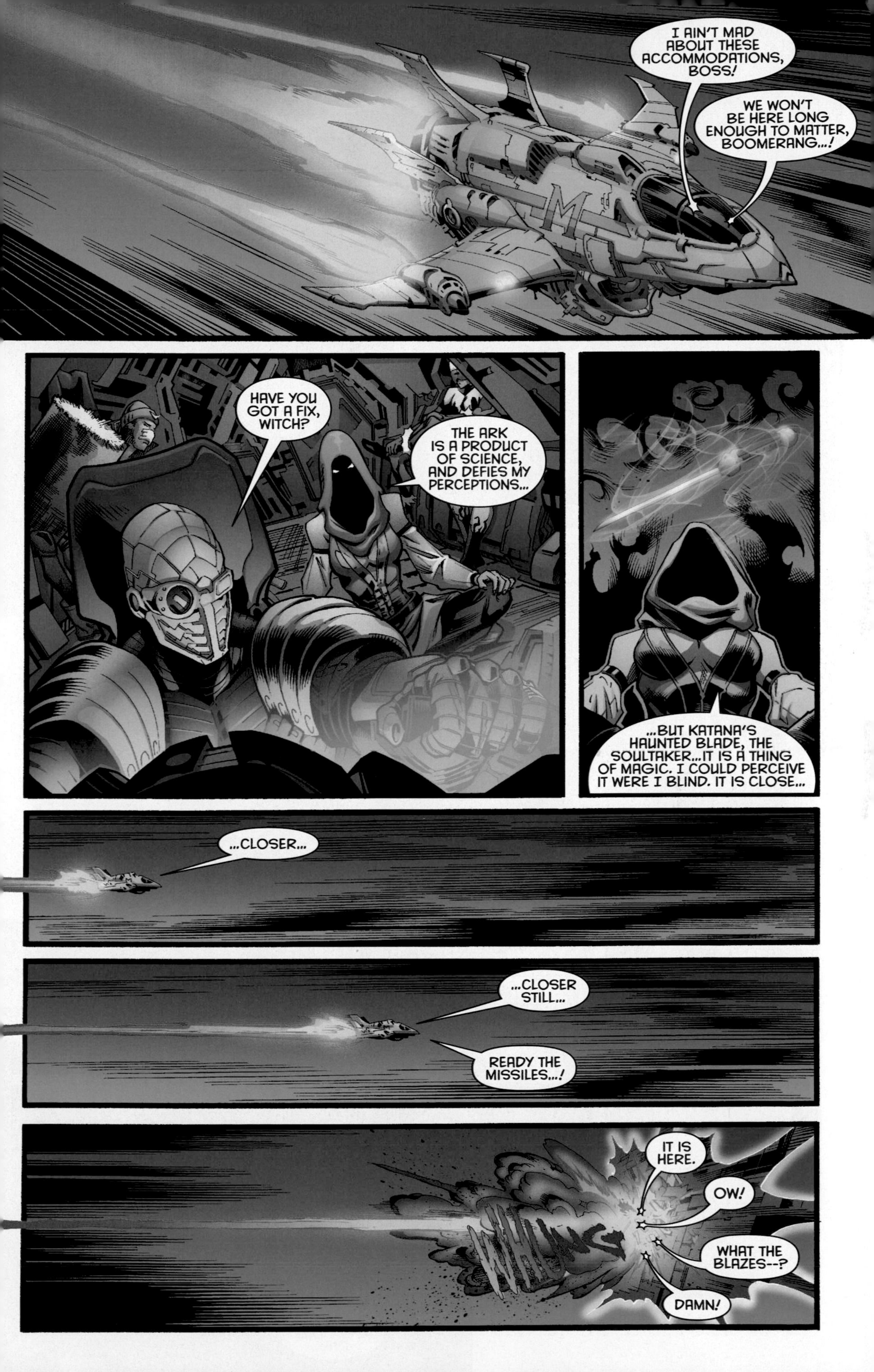
I AIN'T MAD ABOUT THESE ACCOMMODATIONS, BOSS!
WE WON'T BE HERE LONG ENOUGH TO MATTER, BOOMERANG...!
HAVE YOU GOT A FIX, WITCH?
THE ARK IS A PRODUCT OF SCIENCE, AND DEFIES MY PERCEPTIONS...
...BUT KATANA'S HAUNTED BLADE, THE SOULTAKER...IT IS A THING OF MAGIC. I COULD PERCEIVE IT WERE I BLIND. IT IS CLOSE...
...CLOSER...
...CLOSER STILL...
READY THE MISSILES...!
IT IS HERE.
OW!
WHAT THE BLAZES--?
DAMN!
WHUNG

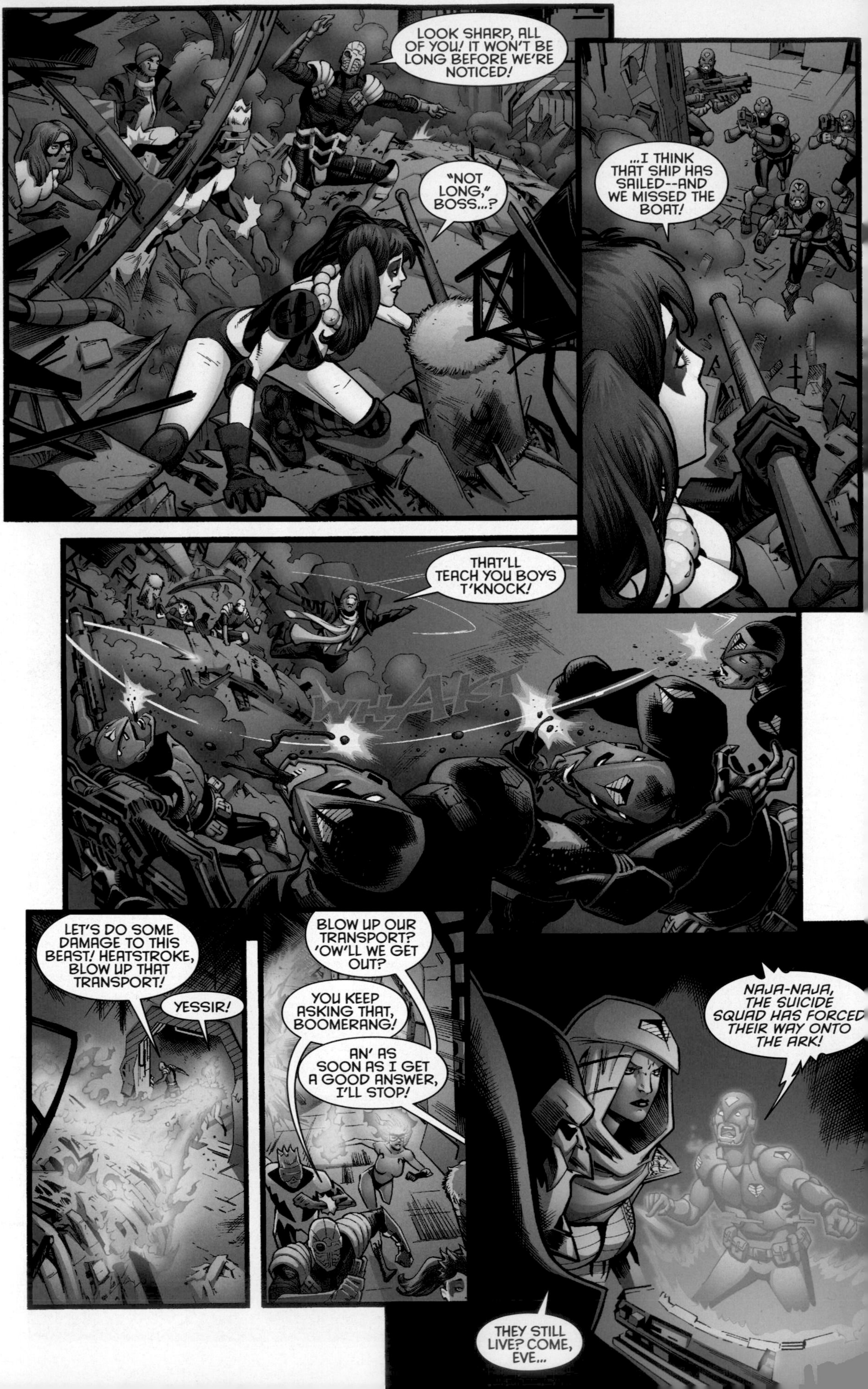
LOOK SHARP, ALL OF YOU! IT WON'T BE LONG BEFORE WE'RE NOTICED!
"NOT LONG," BOSS...?
...I THINK THAT SHIP HAS SAILED--AND WE MISSED THE BOAT!
THAT'LL TEACH YOU BOYS T'KNOCK!
WHAK!
LET'S DO SOME DAMAGE TO THIS BEAST! HEATSTROKE, BLOW UP THAT TRANSPORT!
YESSIR!
BLOW UP OUR TRANSPORT? 'OW'LL WE GET OUT?
YOU KEEP ASKING THAT, BOOMERANG!
AN' AS SOON AS I GET A GOOD ANSWER, I'LL STOP!
NAJA-NAJA, THE SUICIDE SQUAD HAS FORCED THEIR WAY ONTO THE ARK!
THEY STILL LIVE? COME, EVE...

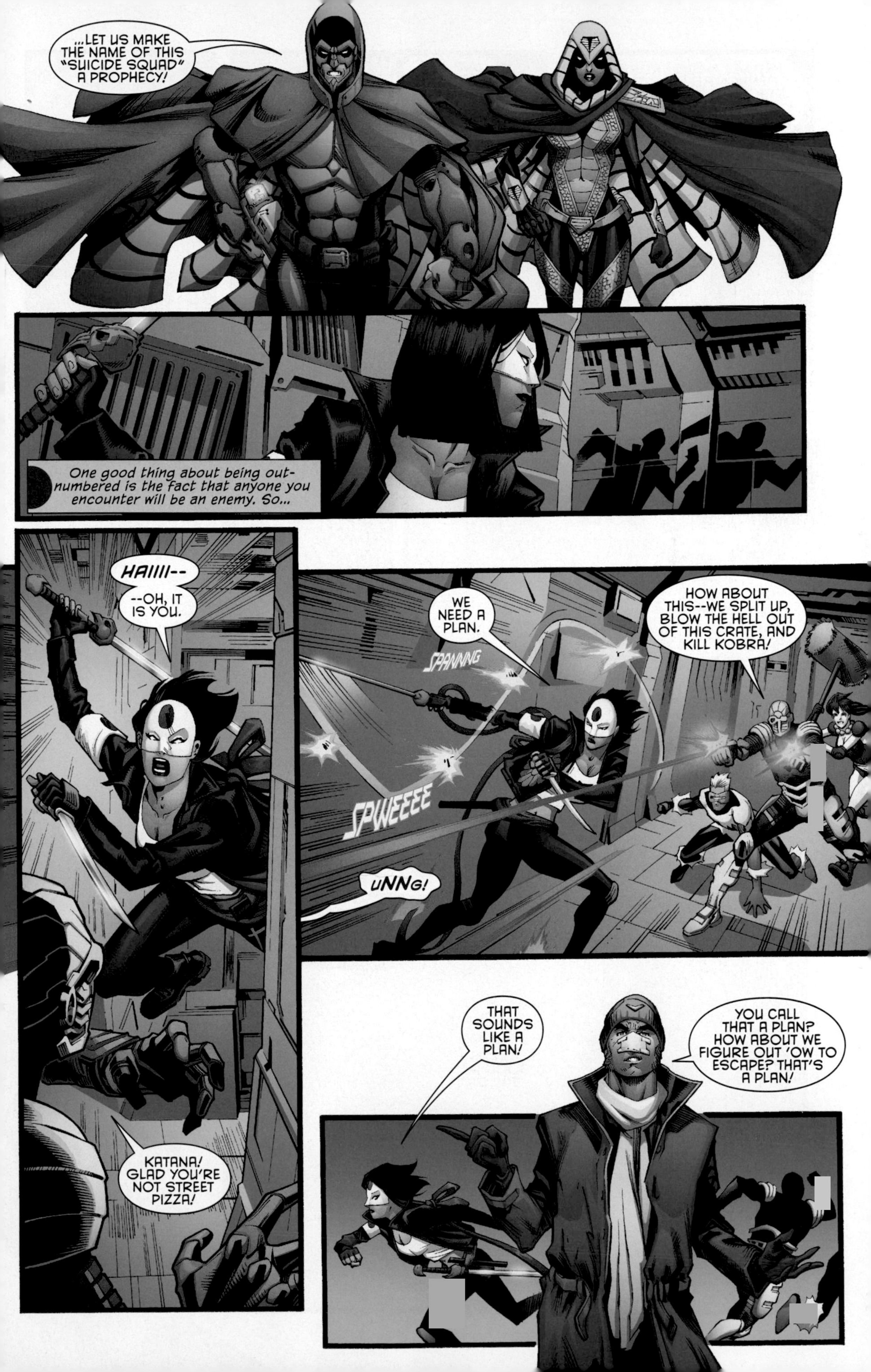
...LET US MAKE THE NAME OF THIS "SUICIDE SQUAD" A PROPHECY!
One good thing about being outnumbered is the fact that anyone you encounter will be an enemy. So...
HAIIII--
--OH, IT IS YOU.
KATANA! GLAD YOU'RE NOT STREET PIZZA!
WE NEED A PLAN.
SPANNNG
HOW ABOUT THIS--WE SPLIT UP, BLOW THE HELL OUT OF THIS CRATE, AND KILL KOBRA!
SPWEEEE
UNNG!
THAT SOUNDS LIKE A PLAN!
YOU CALL THAT A PLAN? HOW ABOUT WE FIGURE OUT 'OW TO ESCAPE? THAT'S A PLAN!

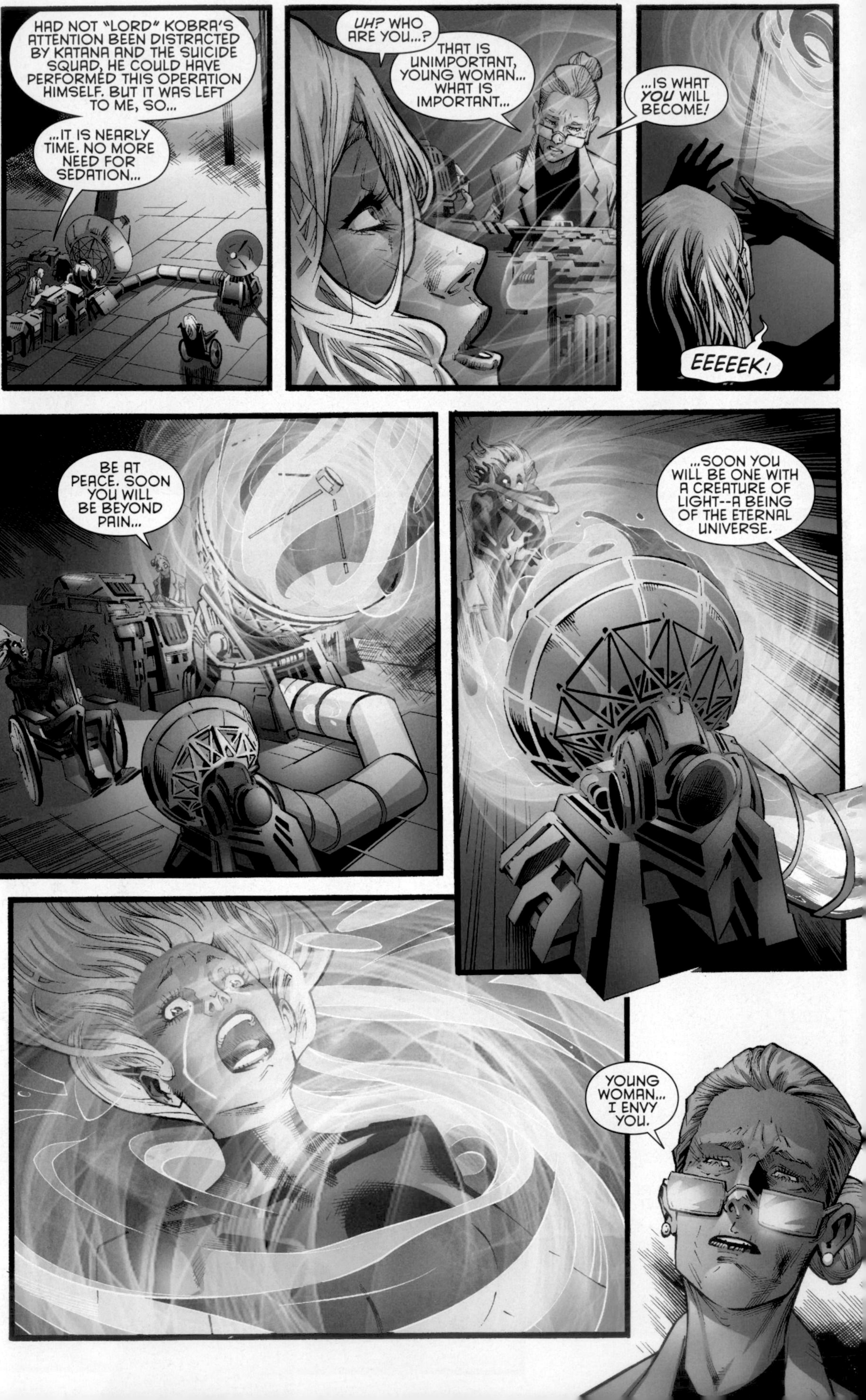
HAD NOT "LORD" KOBRA'S ATTENTION BEEN DISTRACTED BY KATANA AND THE SUICIDE SQUAD, HE COULD HAVE PERFORMED THIS OPERATION HIMSELF. BUT IT WAS LEFT TO ME, SO...
...IT IS NEARLY TIME. NO MORE NEED FOR SEDATION...
UH? WHO ARE YOU...?
THAT IS UNIMPORTANT, YOUNG WOMAN... WHAT IS IMPORTANT...
...IS WHAT YOU WILL BECOME!
EEEEEK!
BE AT PEACE. SOON YOU WILL BE BEYOND PAIN...
...SOON YOU WILL BE ONE WITH A CREATURE OF LIGHT--A BEING OF THE ETERNAL UNIVERSE.
YOUNG WOMAN... I ENVY YOU.

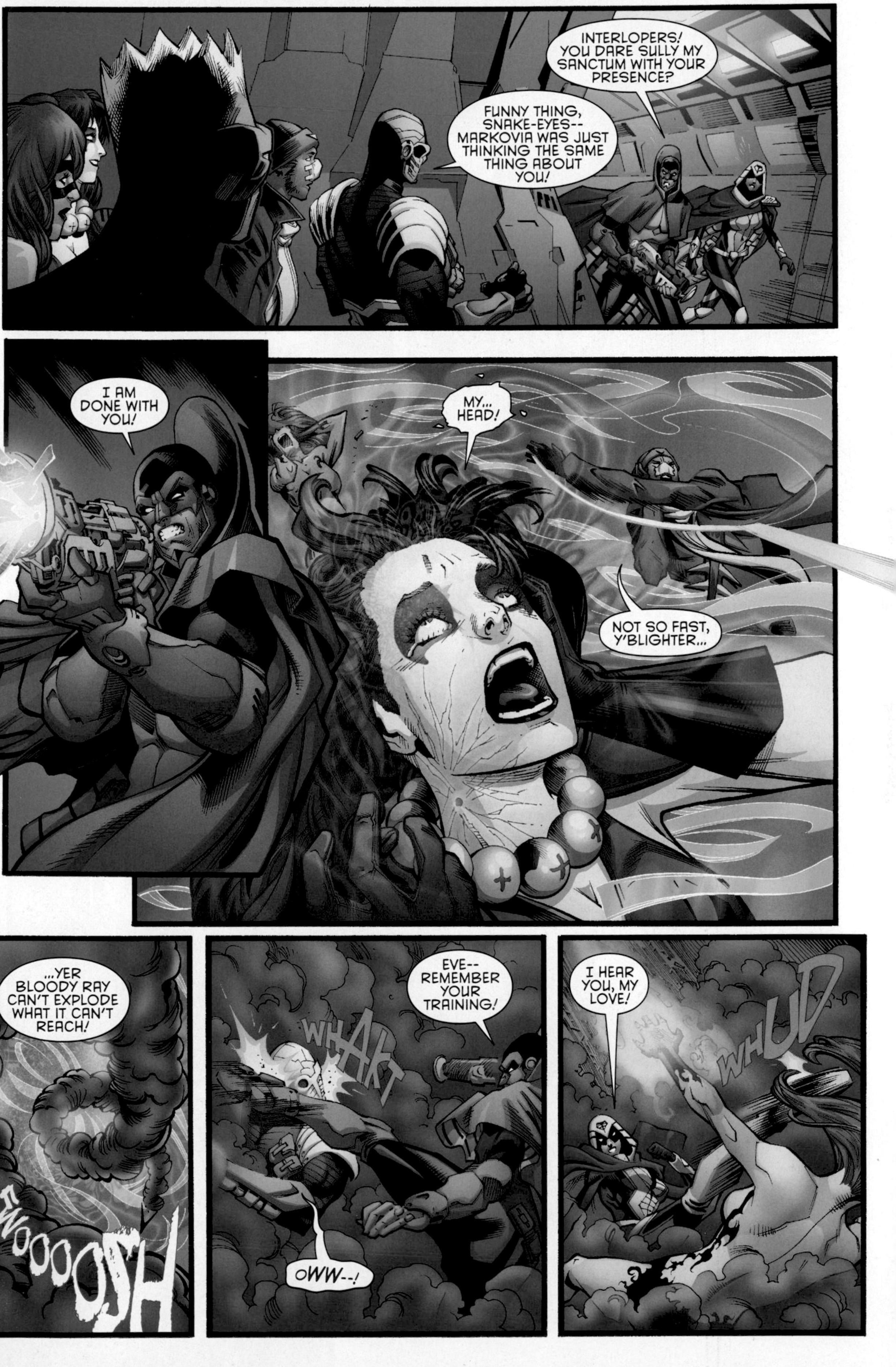
INTERLOPERS! YOU DARE SULLY MY SANCTUM WITH YOUR PRESENCE?
FUNNY THING, SNAKE-EYES-- MARKOVIA WAS JUST THINKING THE SAME THING ABOUT YOU!
I AM DONE WITH YOU!
MY... HEAD!
NOT SO FAST, Y'BLIGHTER...
...YER BLOODY RAY CAN'T EXPLODE WHAT IT CAN'T REACH!
FWOOOOSH
EVE-- REMEMBER YOUR TRAINING!
WHAKT
OWW--!
I HEAR YOU, MY LOVE!
WHUD

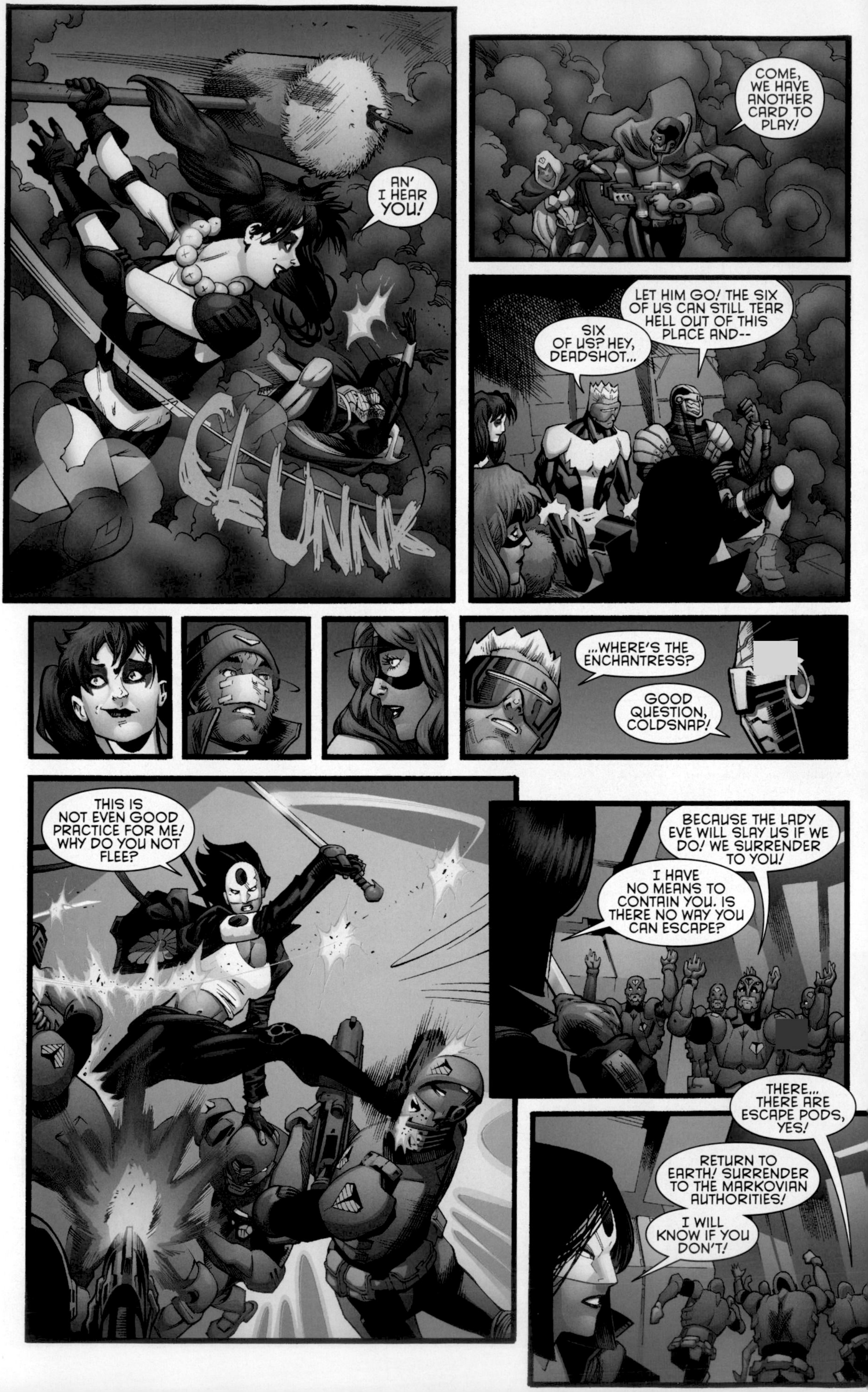
AN' I HEAR YOU!
CLUNNK
COME, WE HAVE ANOTHER CARD TO PLAY!
LET HIM GO! THE SIX OF US CAN STILL TEAR HELL OUT OF THIS PLACE AND--
SIX OF US? HEY, DEADSHOT...
...WHERE'S THE ENCHANTRESS?
GOOD QUESTION, COLDSNAP!
THIS IS NOT EVEN GOOD PRACTICE FOR ME! WHY DO YOU NOT FLEE?
BECAUSE THE LADY EVE WILL SLAY US IF WE DO! WE SURRENDER TO YOU!
I HAVE NO MEANS TO CONTAIN YOU. IS THERE NO WAY YOU CAN ESCAPE?
THERE... THERE ARE ESCAPE PODS, YES!
RETURN TO EARTH! SURRENDER TO THE MARKOVIAN AUTHORITIES!
I WILL KNOW IF YOU DON'T!

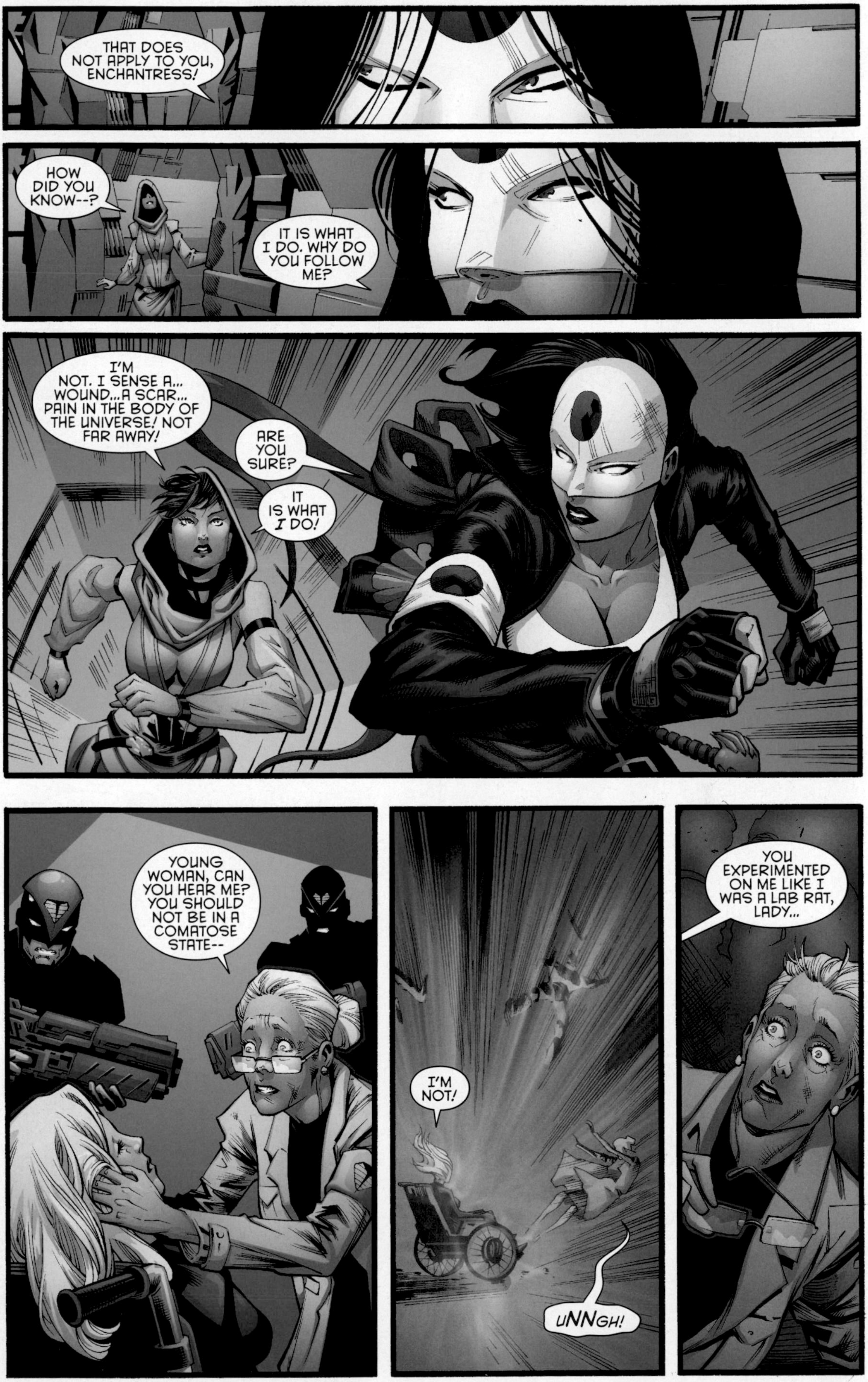
THAT DOES NOT APPLY TO YOU, ENCHANTRESS!
HOW DID YOU KNOW--?
IT IS WHAT I DO. WHY DO YOU FOLLOW ME?
I'M NOT. I SENSE A... WOUND...A SCAR... PAIN IN THE BODY OF THE UNIVERSE! NOT FAR AWAY!
ARE YOU SURE?
IT IS WHAT *I* DO!
YOUNG WOMAN, CAN YOU HEAR ME? YOU SHOULD NOT BE IN A COMATOSE STATE--
I'M NOT!
UNNGH!
YOU EXPERIMENTED ON ME LIKE I WAS A LAB RAT, LADY...

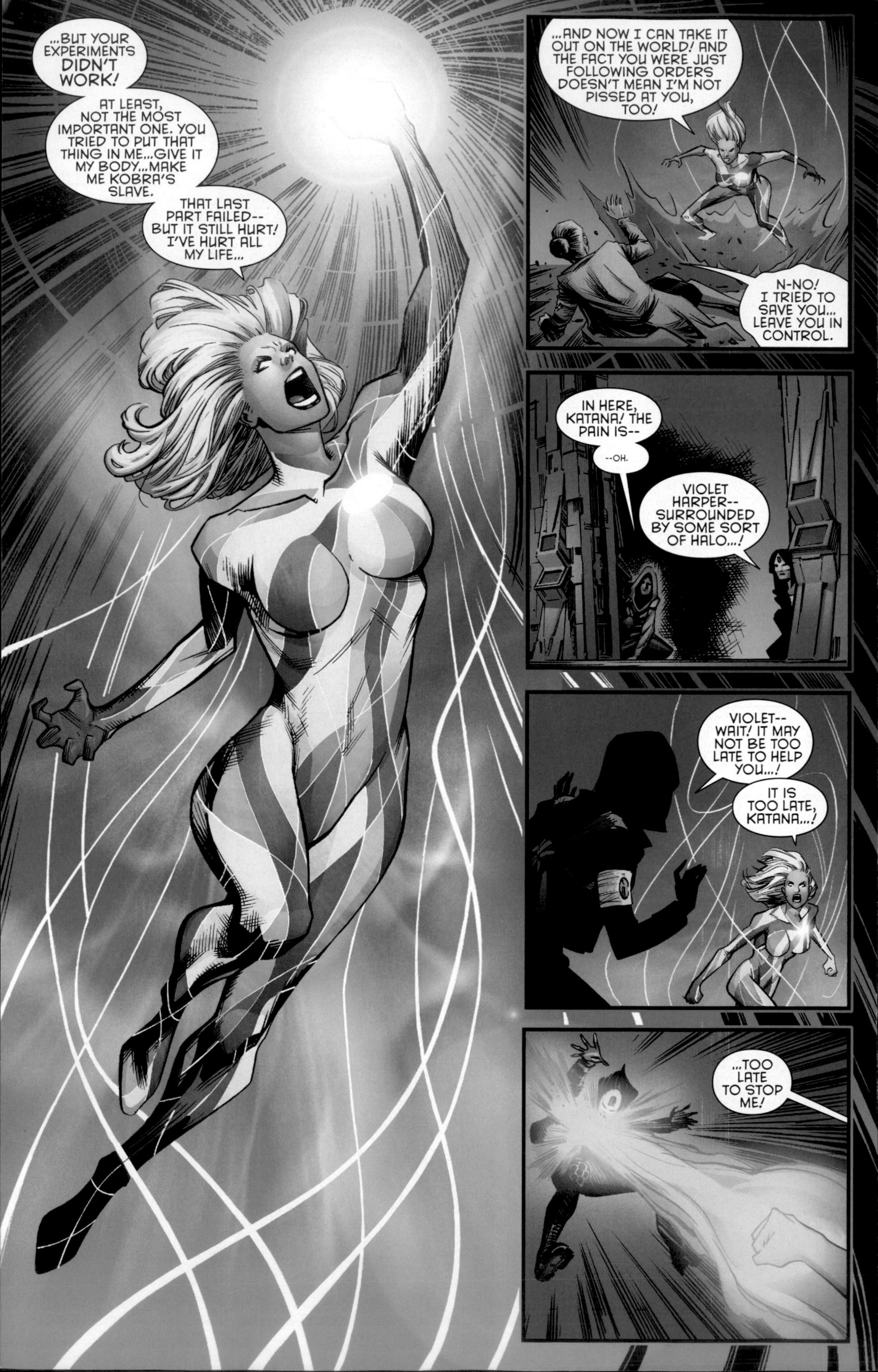
...BUT YOUR EXPERIMENTS DIDN'T WORK!
AT LEAST, NOT THE MOST IMPORTANT ONE. YOU TRIED TO PUT THAT THING IN ME...GIVE IT MY BODY...MAKE ME KOBRA'S SLAVE.
THAT LAST PART FAILED-- BUT IT STILL HURT! I'VE HURT ALL MY LIFE...
...AND NOW I CAN TAKE IT OUT ON THE WORLD! AND THE FACT YOU WERE JUST FOLLOWING ORDERS DOESN'T MEAN I'M NOT PISSED AT YOU, TOO!
N-NO! I TRIED TO SAVE YOU... LEAVE YOU IN CONTROL.
IN HERE, KATANA! THE PAIN IS--
--OH.
VIOLET HARPER-- SURROUNDED BY SOME SORT OF HALO...!
VIOLET-- WAIT! IT MAY NOT BE TOO LATE TO HELP YOU...!
IT IS TOO LATE, KATANA...!
...TOO LATE TO STOP ME!

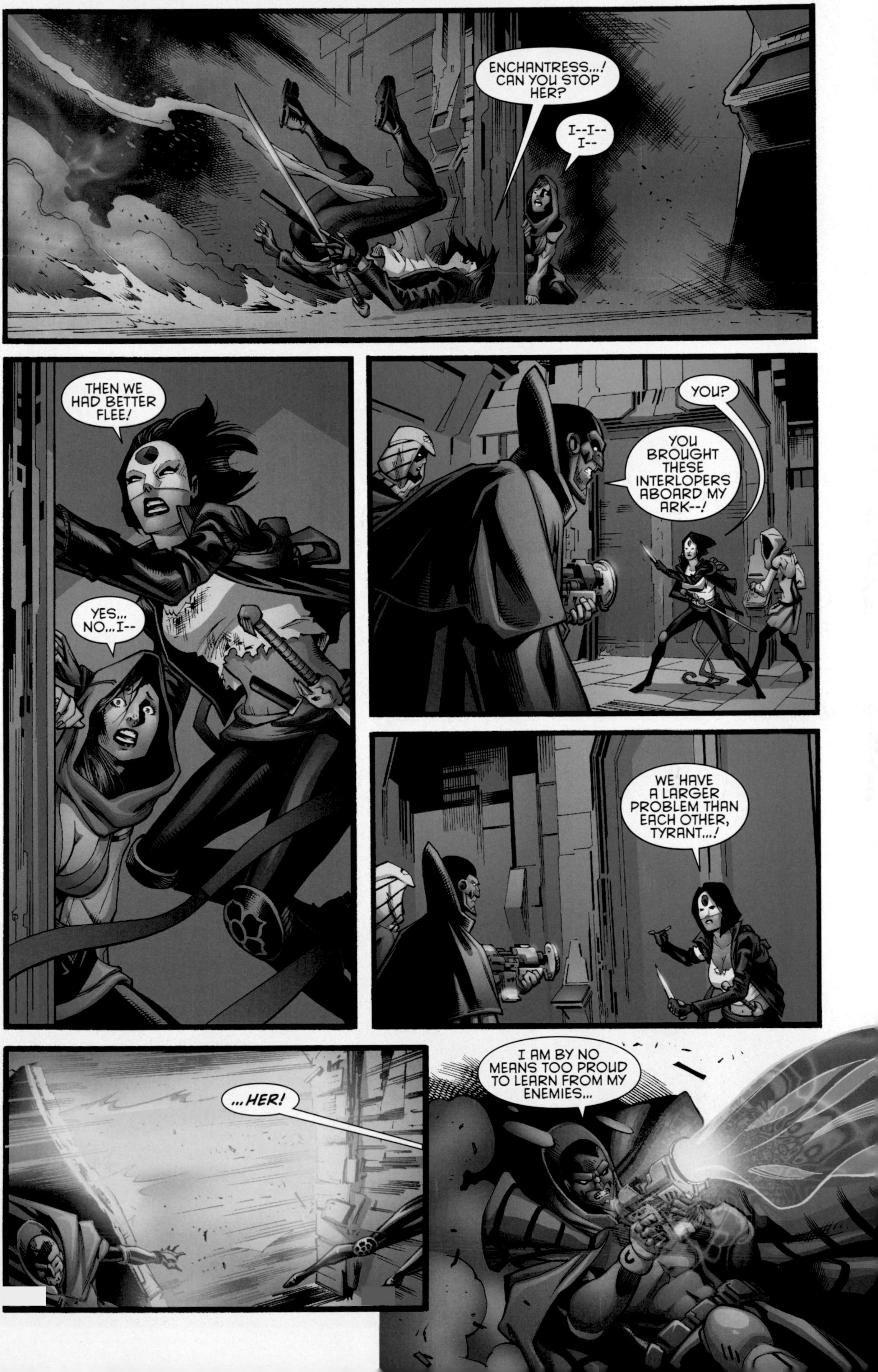
ENCHANTRESS...! CAN YOU STOP HER?
I--I-- I--
THEN WE HAD BETTER FLEE!
YES... NO...I--
YOU?
YOU BROUGHT THESE INTERLOPERS ABOARD MY ARK--!
WE HAVE A LARGER PROBLEM THAN EACH OTHER, TYRANT...!
...HER!
I AM BY NO MEANS TOO PROUD TO LEARN FROM MY ENEMIES...

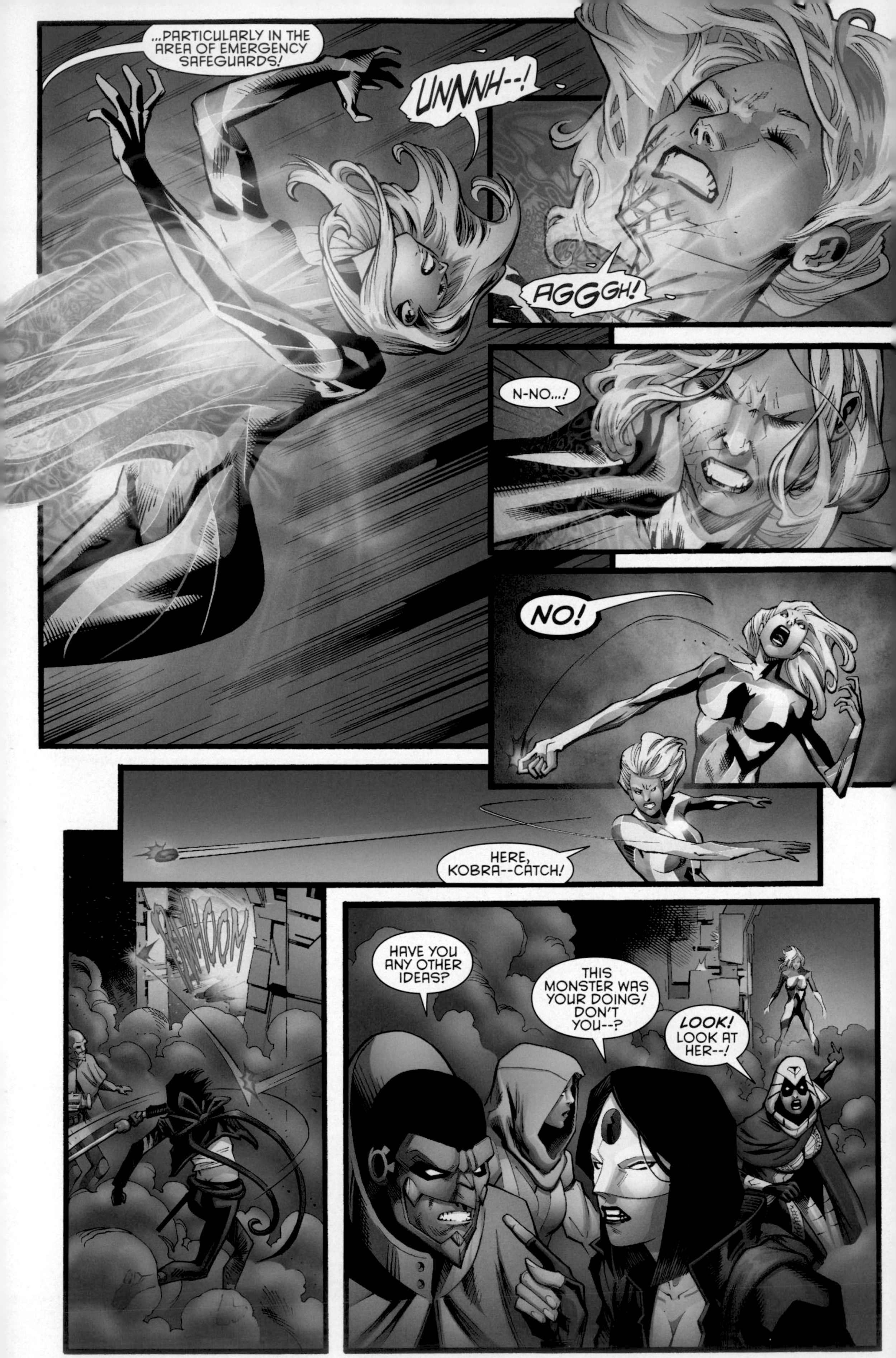
...PARTICULARLY IN THE AREA OF EMERGENCY SAFEGUARDS!
UNNNH--!
AGGGH!
N-NO...!
NO!
HERE, KOBRA--CATCH!
SHWHOOM
HAVE YOU ANY OTHER IDEAS?
THIS MONSTER WAS YOUR DOING! DON'T YOU--?
LOOK! LOOK AT HER--!

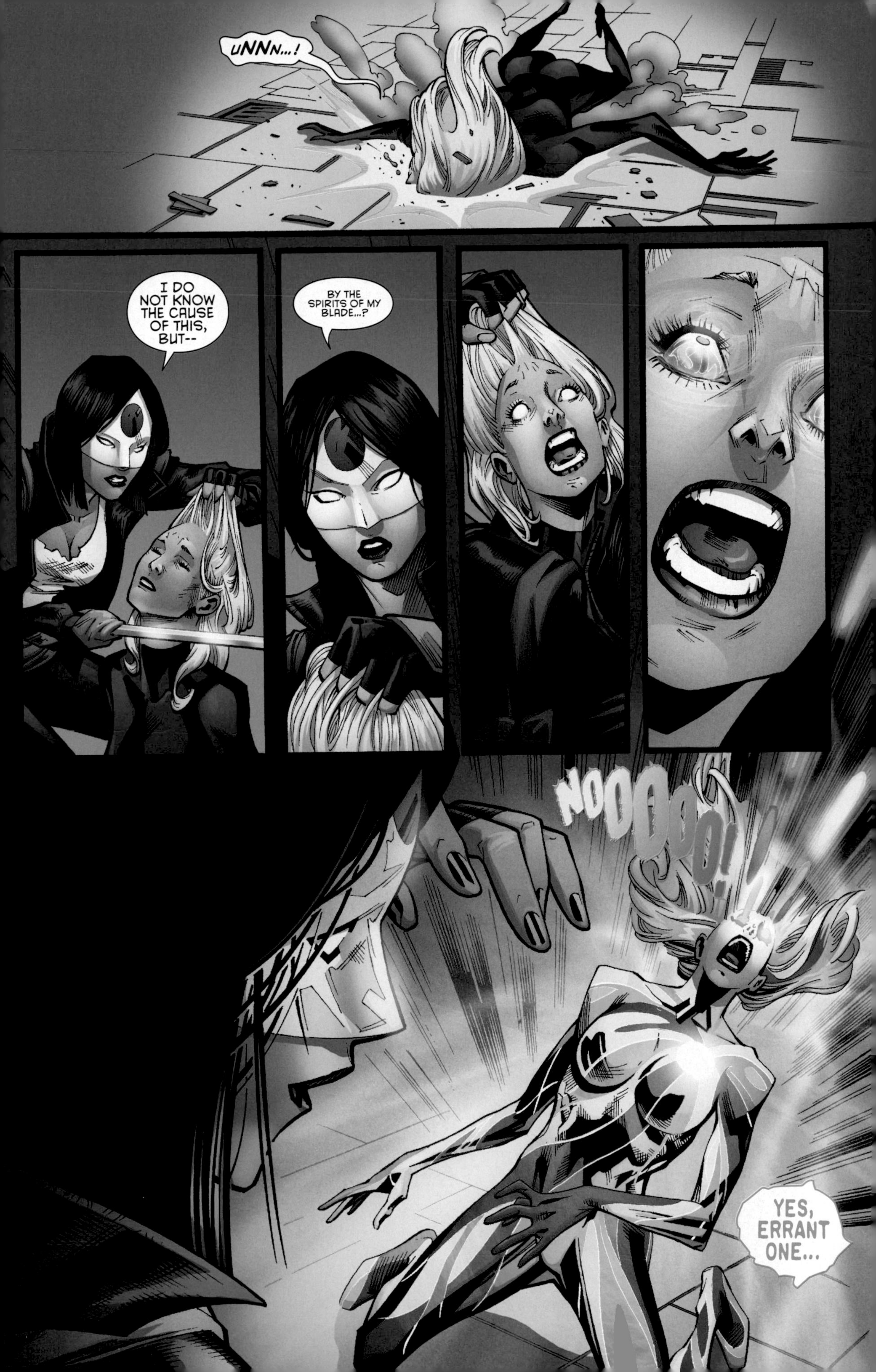
UNNN...!
I DO NOT KNOW THE CAUSE OF THIS, BUT--
BY THE SPIRITS OF MY BLADE...?
NOOOOO!
YES, ERRANT ONE...

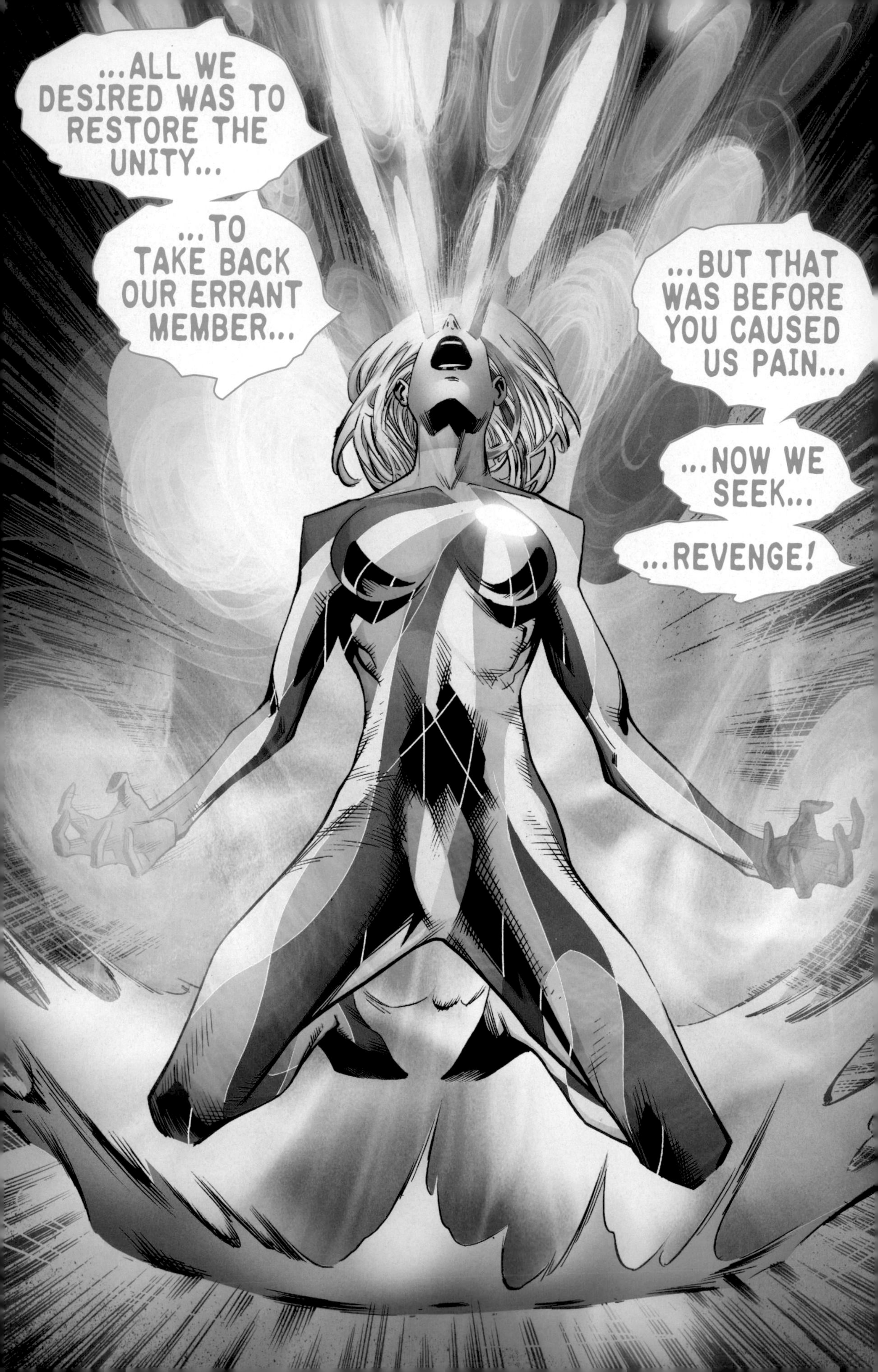
...ALL WE DESIRED WAS TO RESTORE THE UNITY...
...TO TAKE BACK OUR ERRANT MEMBER...
...BUT THAT WAS BEFORE YOU CAUSED US PAIN...
...NOW WE SEEK...
...REVENGE!

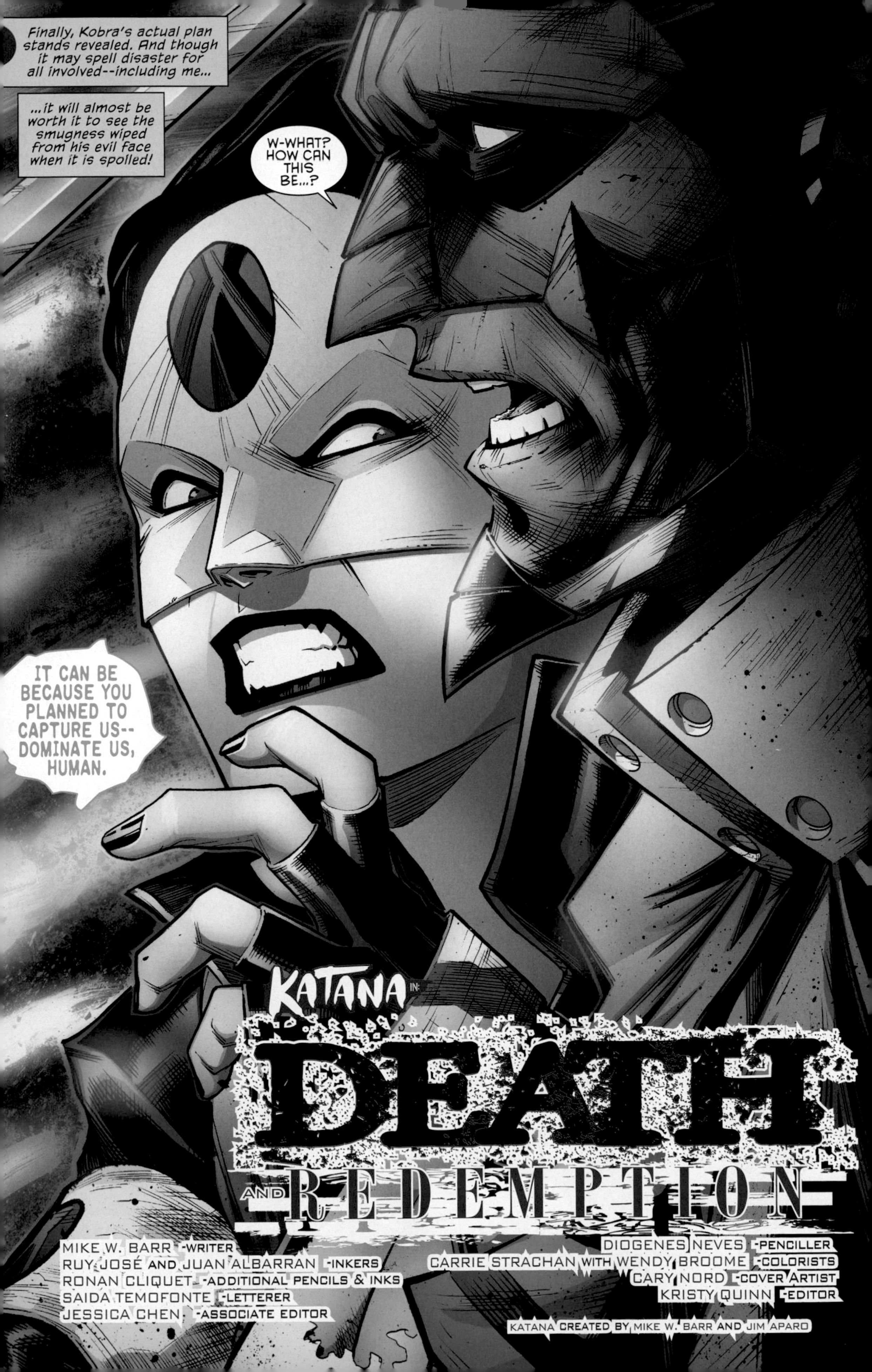

Finally, Kobra's actual plan stands revealed. And though it may spell disaster for all involved--including me...
...it will almost be worth it to see the smugness wiped from his evil face when it is spoiled!
W-WHAT? HOW CAN THIS BE...?
IT CAN BE BECAUSE YOU PLANNED TO CAPTURE US-- DOMINATE US, HUMAN.
KATANA IN:
DEATH AND REDEMPTION
MIKE W. BARR -WRITER
RUY JOSÉ AND JUAN ALBARRAN -INKERS
RONAN CLIQUET -ADDITIONAL PENCILS & INKS
SAIDA TEMOFONTE -LETTERER
JESSICA CHEN -ASSOCIATE EDITOR
DIOGENES NEVES -PENCILLER
CARRIE STRACHAN WITH WENDY BROOME -COLORISTS
CARY NORD -COVER ARTIST
KRISTY QUINN -EDITOR
KATANA CREATED BY MIKE W. BARR AND JIM APARO

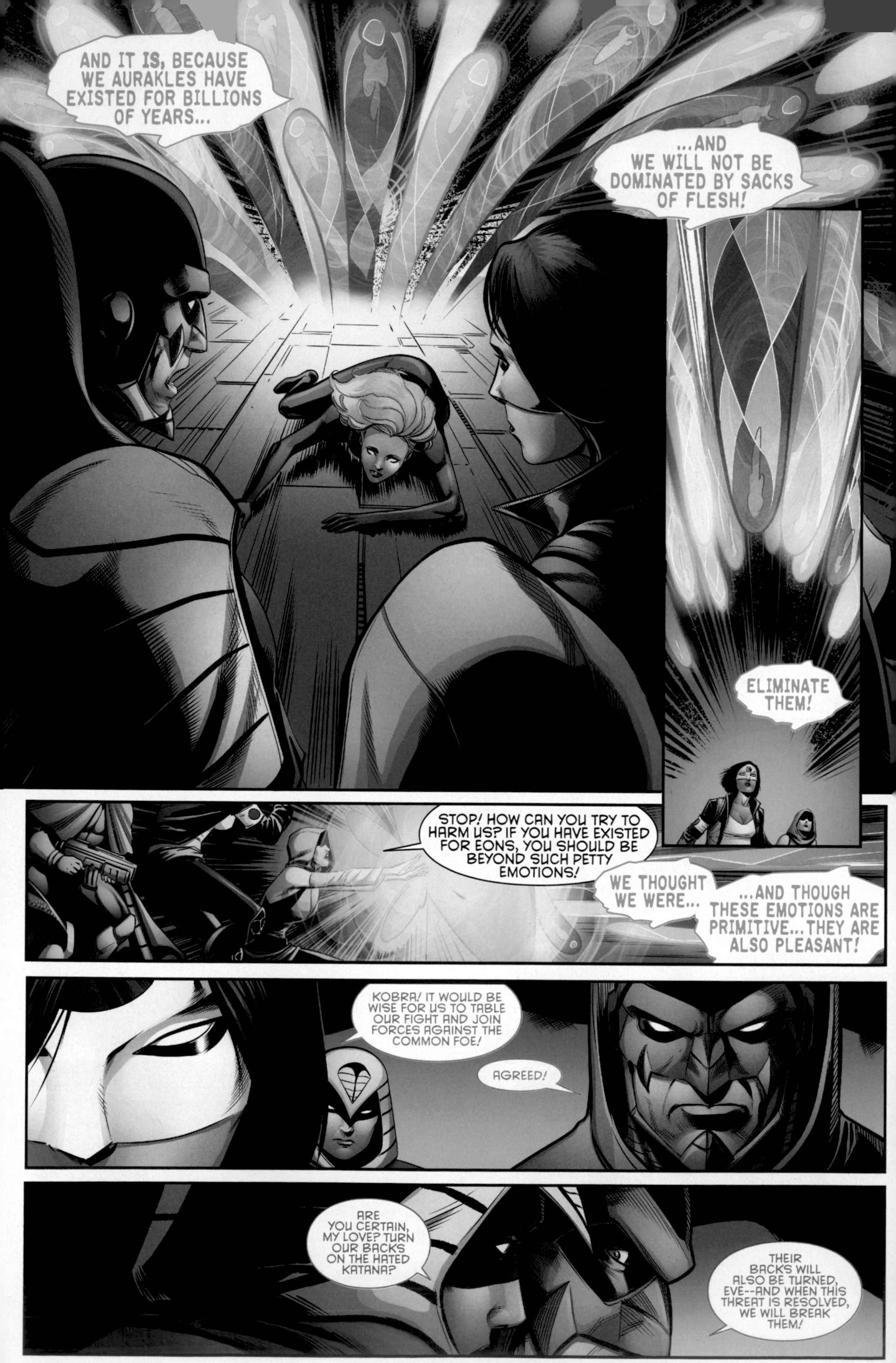
AND IT IS, BECAUSE WE AURAKLES HAVE EXISTED FOR BILLIONS OF YEARS...
...AND WE WILL NOT BE DOMINATED BY SACKS OF FLESH!
ELIMINATE THEM!
STOP! HOW CAN YOU TRY TO HARM US? IF YOU HAVE EXISTED FOR EONS, YOU SHOULD BE BEYOND SUCH PETTY EMOTIONS!
WE THOUGHT WE WERE...
...AND THOUGH THESE EMOTIONS ARE PRIMITIVE...THEY ARE ALSO PLEASANT!
KOBRA! IT WOULD BE WISE FOR US TO TABLE OUR FIGHT AND JOIN FORCES AGAINST THE COMMON FOE!
AGREED!
ARE YOU CERTAIN, MY LOVE? TURN OUR BACKS ON THE HATED KATANA?
THEIR BACKS WILL ALSO BE TURNED, EVE--AND WHEN THIS THREAT IS RESOLVED, WE WILL BREAK THEM!

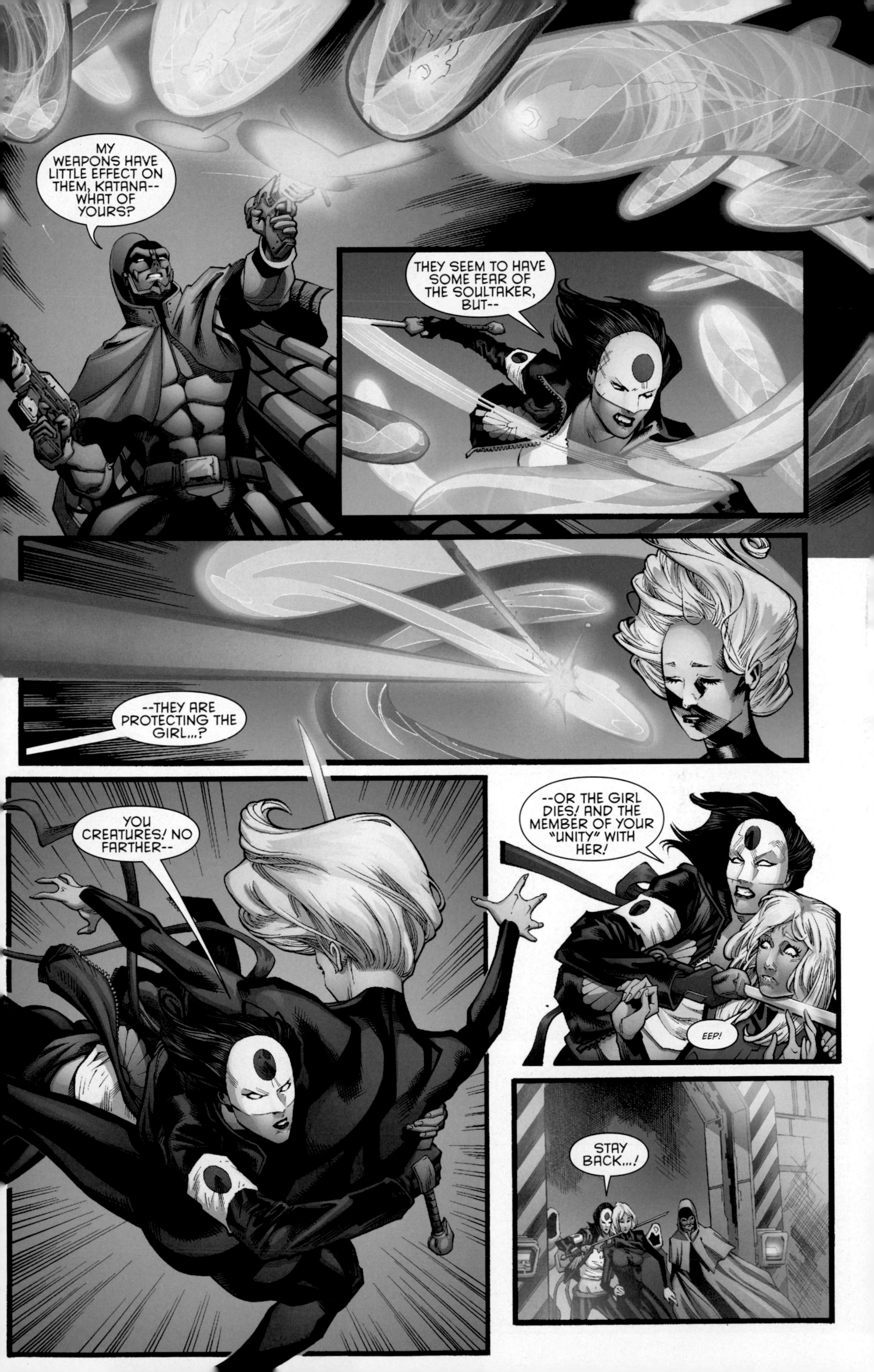
MY WEAPONS HAVE LITTLE EFFECT ON THEM, KATANA-- WHAT OF YOURS?
THEY SEEM TO HAVE SOME FEAR OF THE SOULTAKER, BUT--
--THEY ARE PROTECTING THE GIRL...?
YOU CREATURES! NO FARTHER--
--OR THE GIRL DIES! AND THE MEMBER OF YOUR "UNITY" WITH HER!
EEP!
STAY BACK...!

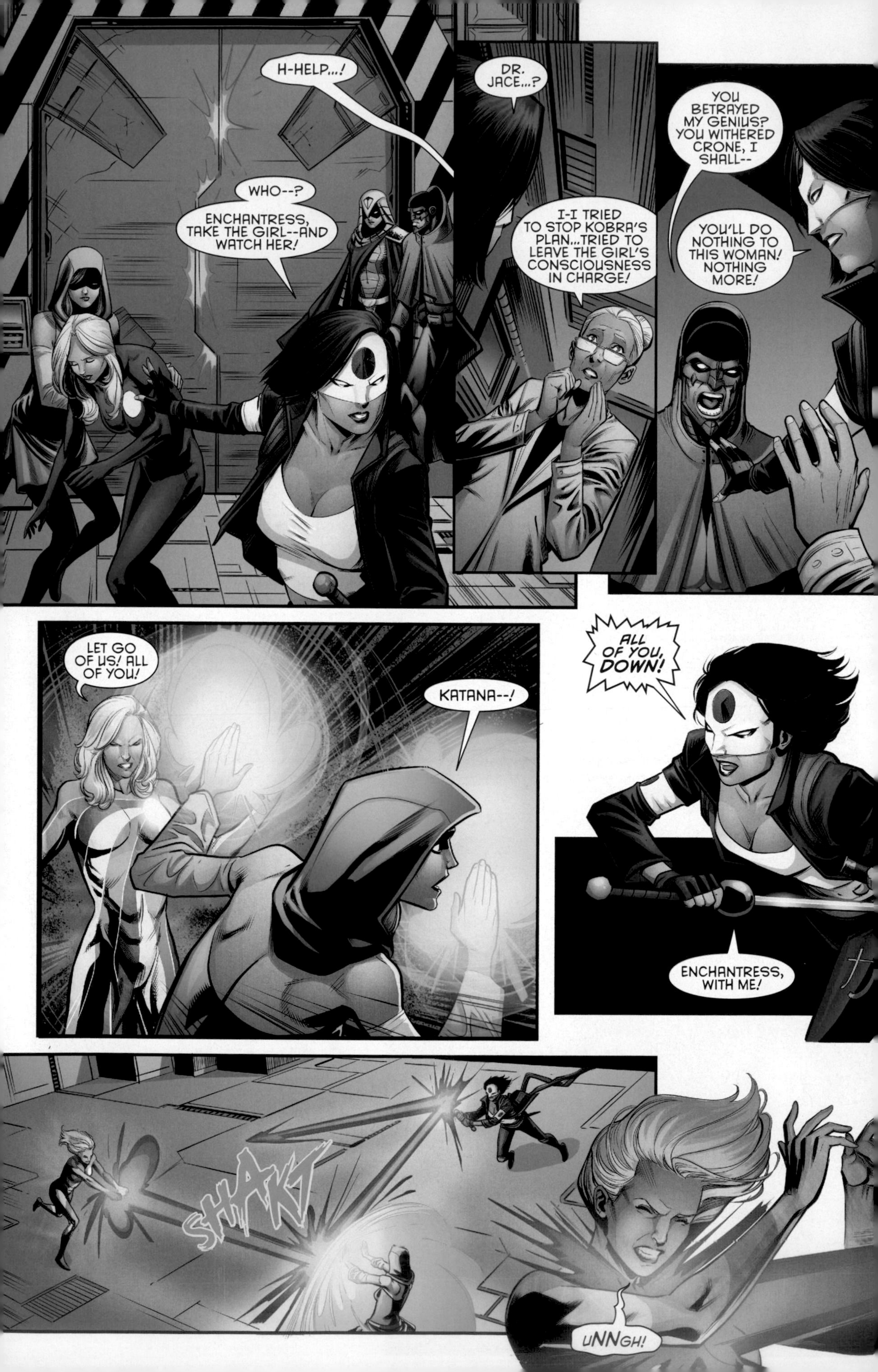
H-HELP...!
WHO--?
ENCHANTRESS, TAKE THE GIRL--AND WATCH HER!
DR. JACE...?
I-I TRIED TO STOP KOBRA'S PLAN...TRIED TO LEAVE THE GIRL'S CONSCIOUSNESS IN CHARGE!
YOU BETRAYED MY GENIUS? YOU WITHERED CRONE, I SHALL--
YOU'LL DO NOTHING TO THIS WOMAN! NOTHING MORE!
LET GO OF US! ALL OF YOU!
KATANA--!
ALL OF YOU, DOWN!
ENCHANTRESS, WITH ME!
SHAKT
UNNGH!

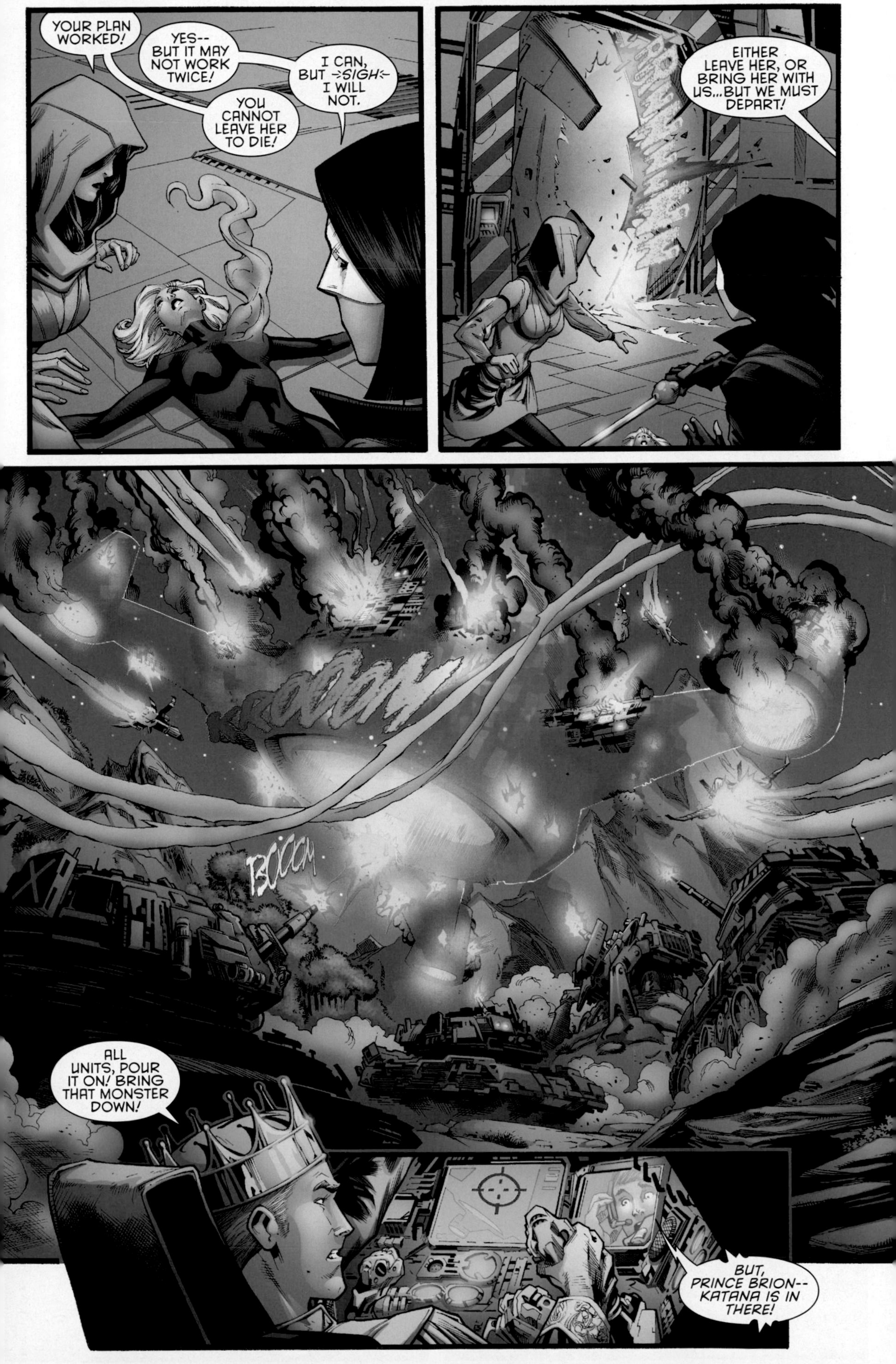

YOUR PLAN WORKED!
YES-- BUT IT MAY NOT WORK TWICE!
YOU CANNOT LEAVE HER TO DIE!
I CAN, BUT -SIGH- I WILL NOT.
EITHER LEAVE HER, OR BRING HER WITH US...BUT WE MUST DEPART!
KROOOM
BOOOM
ALL UNITS, POUR IT ON! BRING THAT MONSTER DOWN!
BUT, PRINCE BRION-- KATANA IS IN THERE!

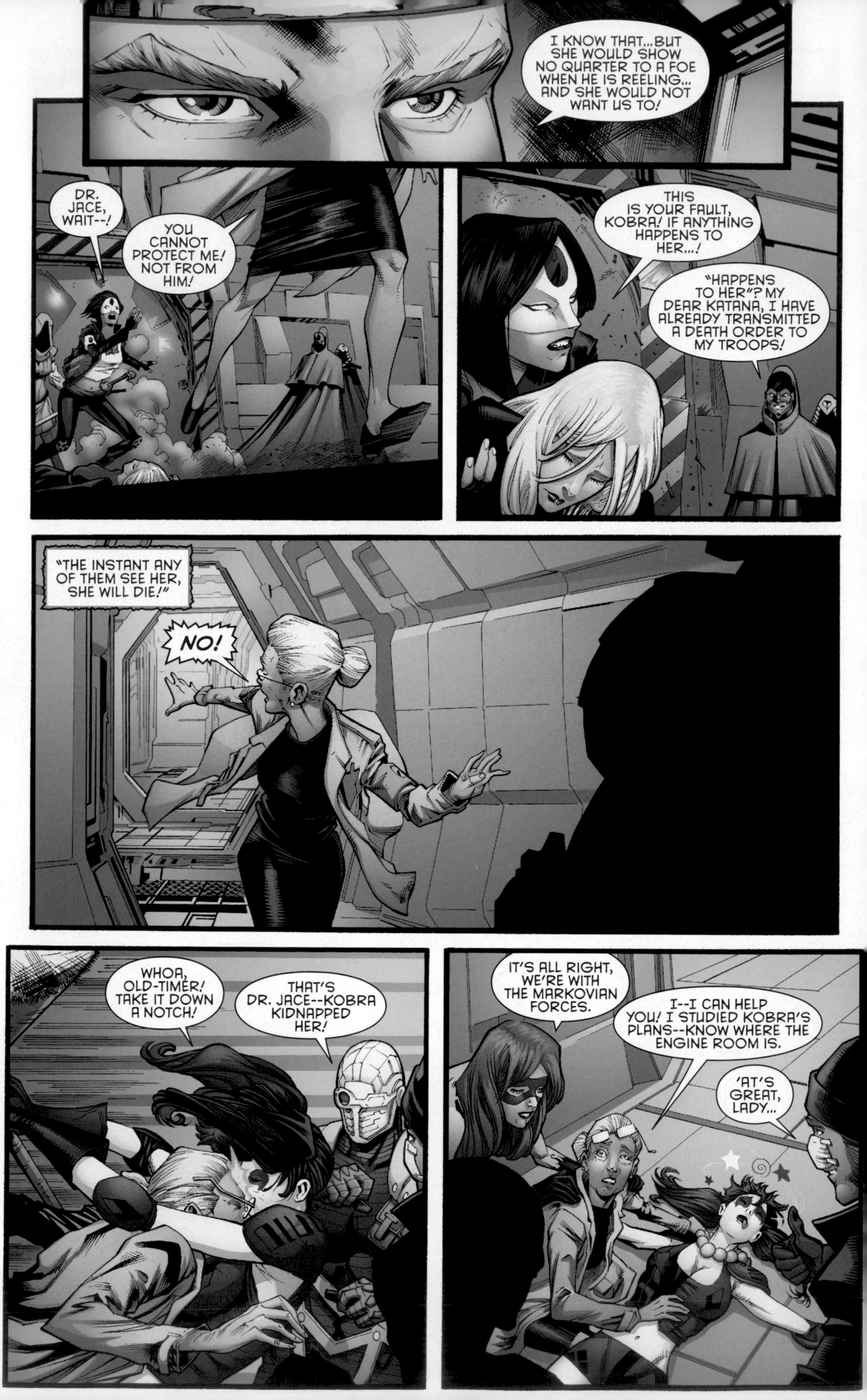

I KNOW THAT...BUT SHE WOULD SHOW NO QUARTER TO A FOE WHEN HE IS REELING... AND SHE WOULD NOT WANT US TO!
DR. JACE, WAIT--!
YOU CANNOT PROTECT ME! NOT FROM HIM!
THIS IS YOUR FAULT, KOBRA! IF ANYTHING HAPPENS TO HER...!
"HAPPENS TO HER"? MY DEAR KATANA, I HAVE ALREADY TRANSMITTED A DEATH ORDER TO MY TROOPS!
"THE INSTANT ANY OF THEM SEE HER, SHE WILL DIE!"
NO!
WHOA, OLD-TIMER! TAKE IT DOWN A NOTCH!
THAT'S DR. JACE--KOBRA KIDNAPPED HER!
IT'S ALL RIGHT, WE'RE WITH THE MARKOVIAN FORCES.
I--I CAN HELP YOU! I STUDIED KOBRA'S PLANS--KNOW WHERE THE ENGINE ROOM IS.
'AT'S GREAT, LADY...

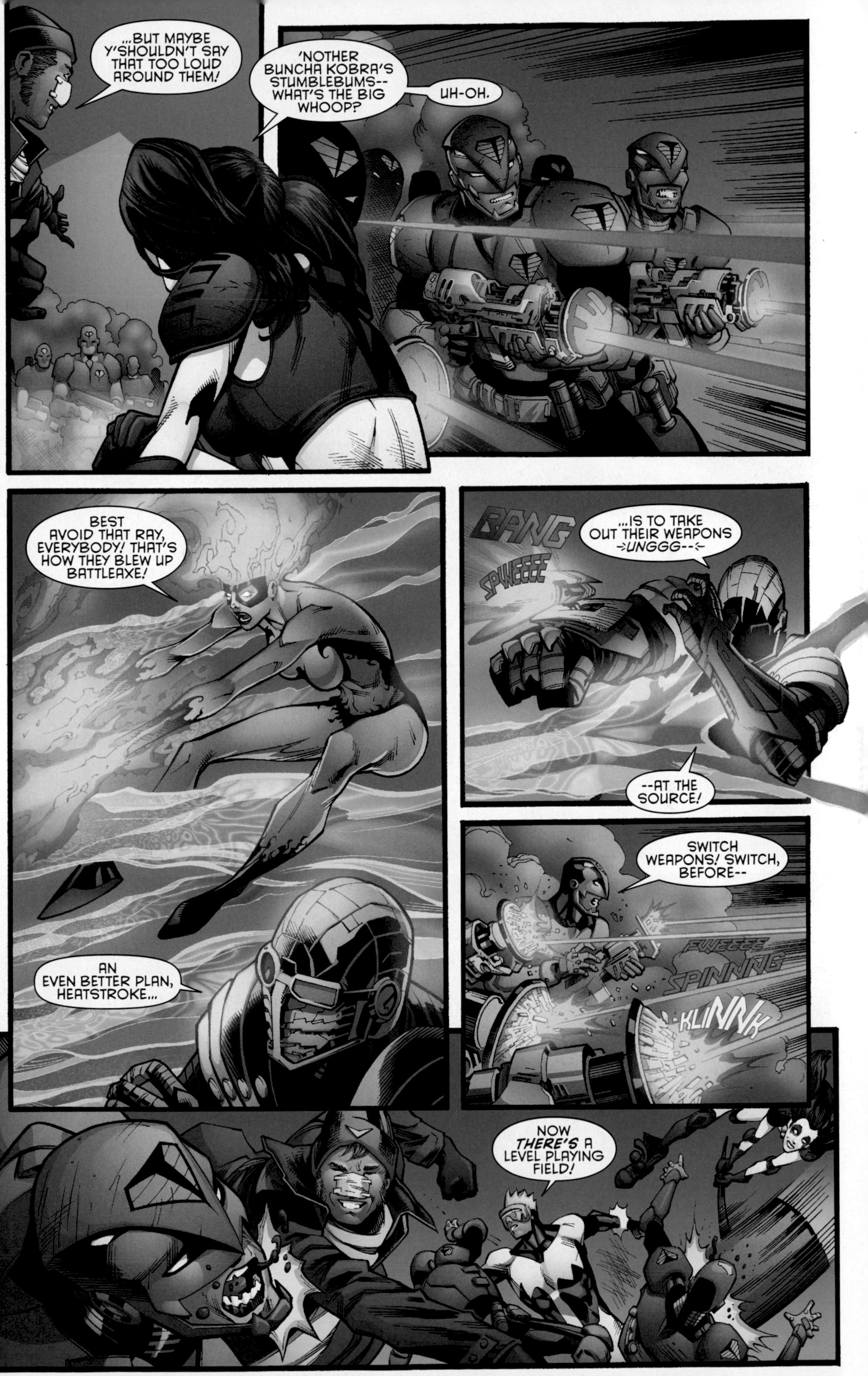
...BUT MAYBE Y'SHOULDN'T SAY THAT TOO LOUD AROUND THEM!
'NOTHER BUNCHA KOBRA'S STUMBLEBUMS-- WHAT'S THE BIG WHOOP?
UH-OH.
BEST AVOID THAT RAY, EVERYBODY! THAT'S HOW THEY BLEW UP BATTLEAXE!
AN EVEN BETTER PLAN, HEATSTROKE...
BANG
SPWEEEE
...IS TO TAKE OUT THEIR WEAPONS -UNGGG--
--AT THE SOURCE!
SWITCH WEAPONS! SWITCH, BEFORE--
FWEEEE
SPINNNG
KLINNNK
NOW THERE'S A LEVEL PLAYING FIELD!

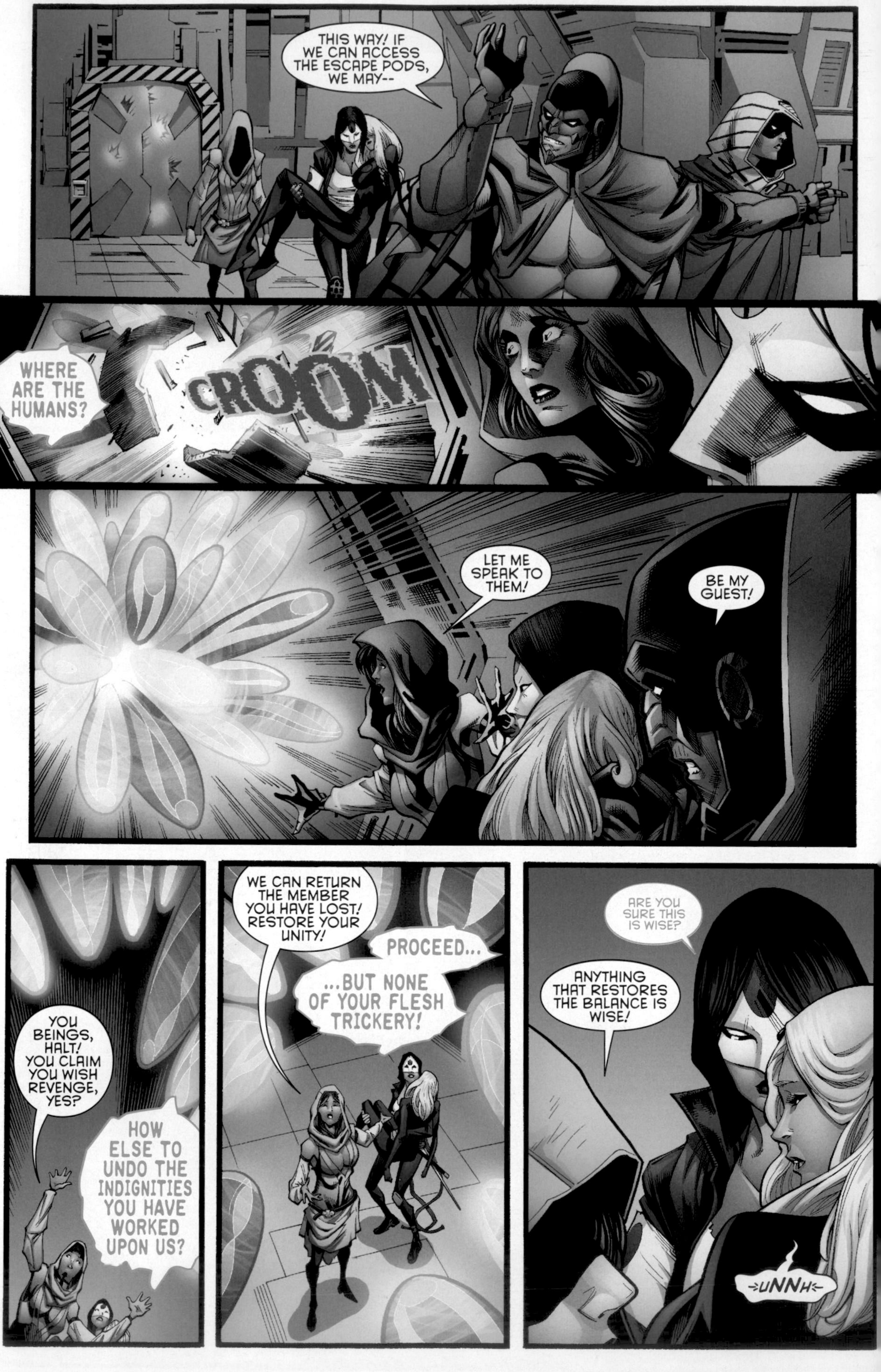
THIS WAY! IF WE CAN ACCESS THE ESCAPE PODS, WE MAY--
WHERE ARE THE HUMANS?
CROOOM
LET ME SPEAK TO THEM!
BE MY GUEST!
YOU BEINGS, HALT! YOU CLAIM YOU WISH REVENGE, YES?
HOW ELSE TO UNDO THE INDIGNITIES YOU HAVE WORKED UPON US?
WE CAN RETURN THE MEMBER YOU HAVE LOST! RESTORE YOUR UNITY!
PROCEED...
...BUT NONE OF YOUR FLESH TRICKERY!
ARE YOU SURE THIS IS WISE?
ANYTHING THAT RESTORES THE BALANCE IS WISE!
UNNH

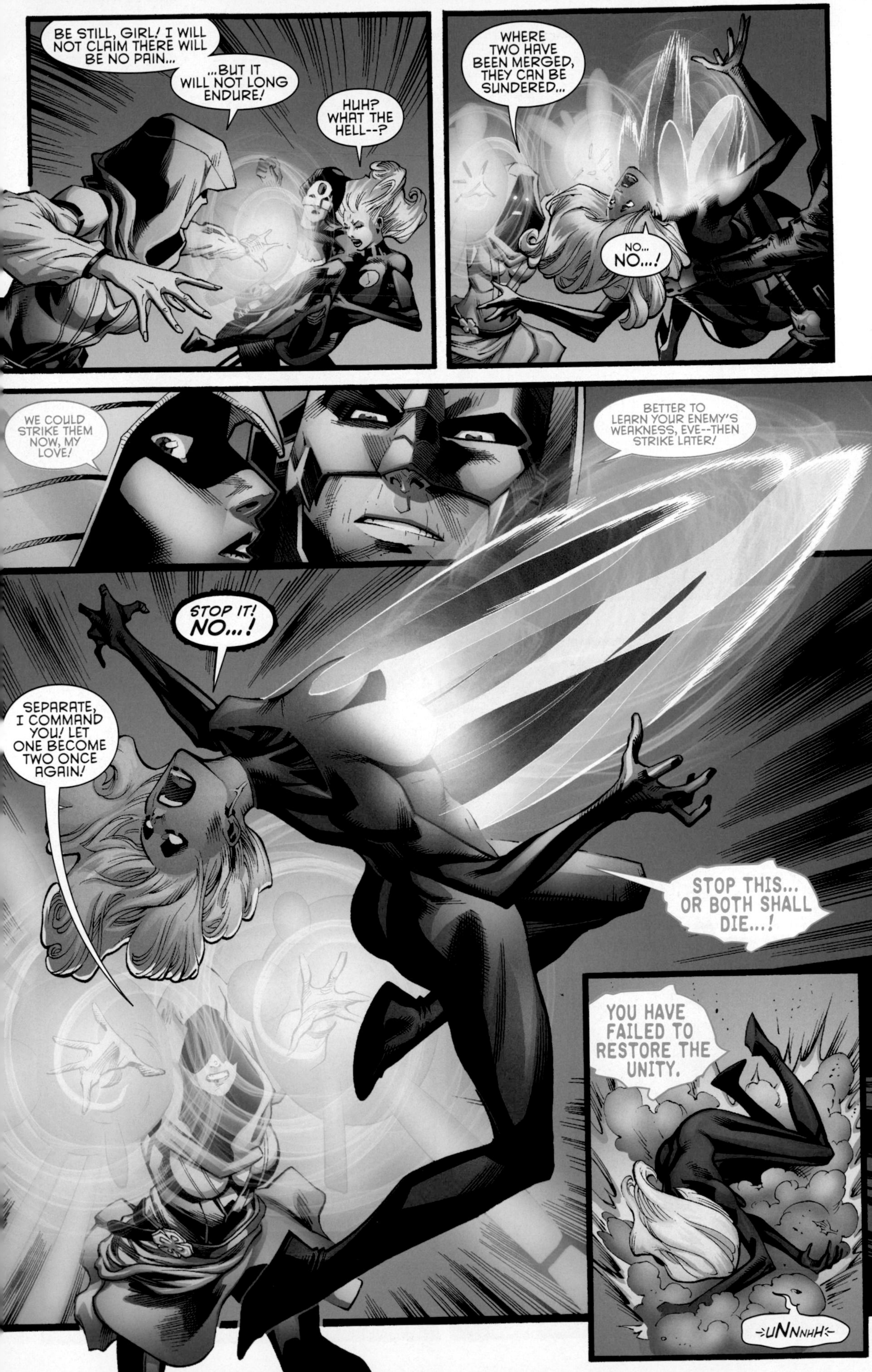
BE STILL, GIRL! I WILL NOT CLAIM THERE WILL BE NO PAIN...
...BUT IT WILL NOT LONG ENDURE!
HUH? WHAT THE HELL--?
WHERE TWO HAVE BEEN MERGED, THEY CAN BE SUNDERED...
NO... NO...!
WE COULD STRIKE THEM NOW, MY LOVE!
BETTER TO LEARN YOUR ENEMY'S WEAKNESS, EVE--THEN STRIKE LATER!
STOP IT! NO...!
SEPARATE, I COMMAND YOU! LET ONE BECOME TWO ONCE AGAIN!
STOP THIS... OR BOTH SHALL DIE...!
YOU HAVE FAILED TO RESTORE THE UNITY.
UNNNHH

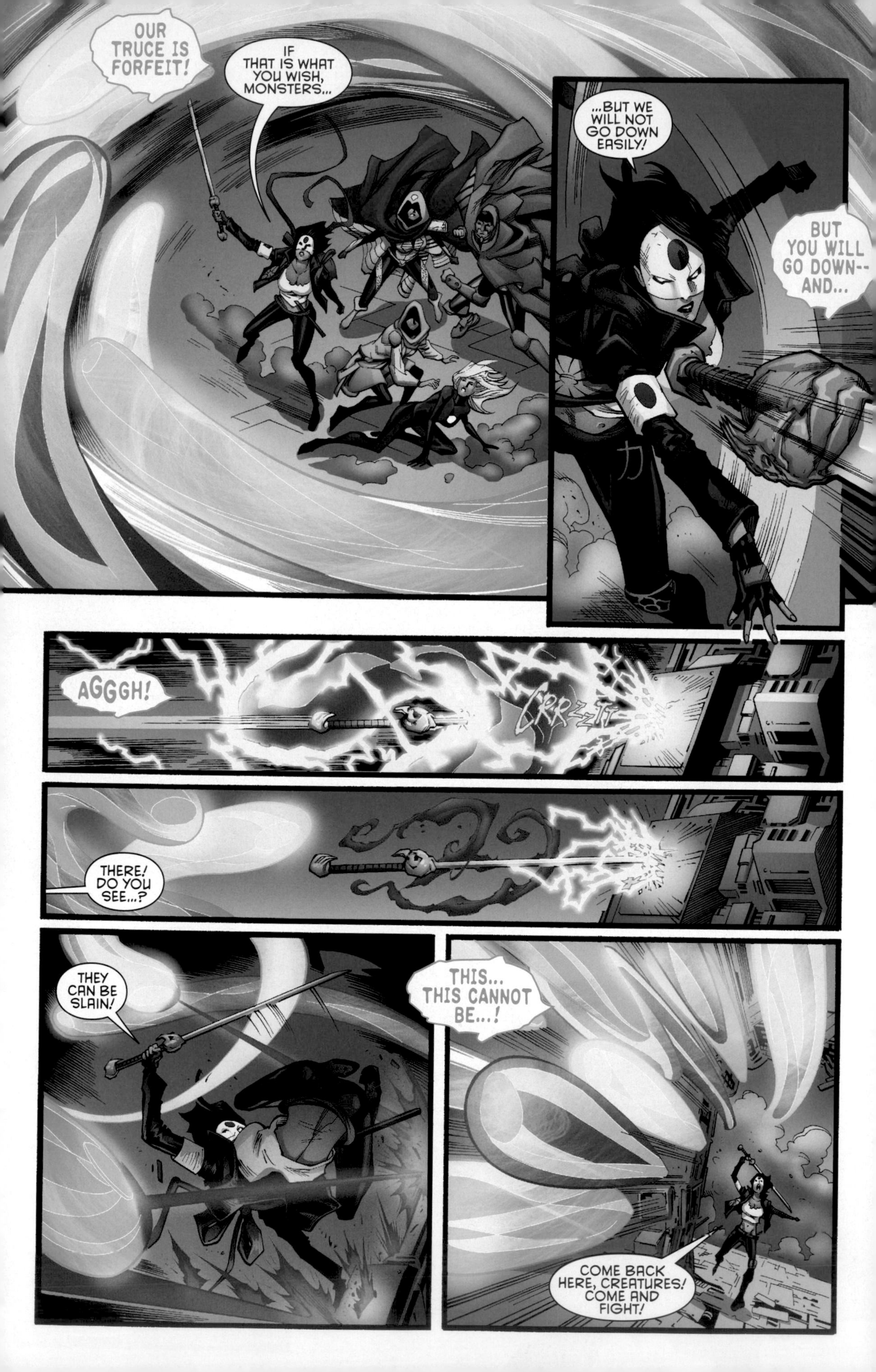
OUR TRUCE IS FORFEIT!
IF THAT IS WHAT YOU WISH, MONSTERS...
...BUT WE WILL NOT GO DOWN EASILY!
BUT YOU WILL GO DOWN-- AND...
AGGGH!
CRRZZIT
THERE! DO YOU SEE...?
THEY CAN BE SLAIN!
THIS... THIS CANNOT BE...!
COME BACK HERE, CREATURES! COME AND FIGHT!

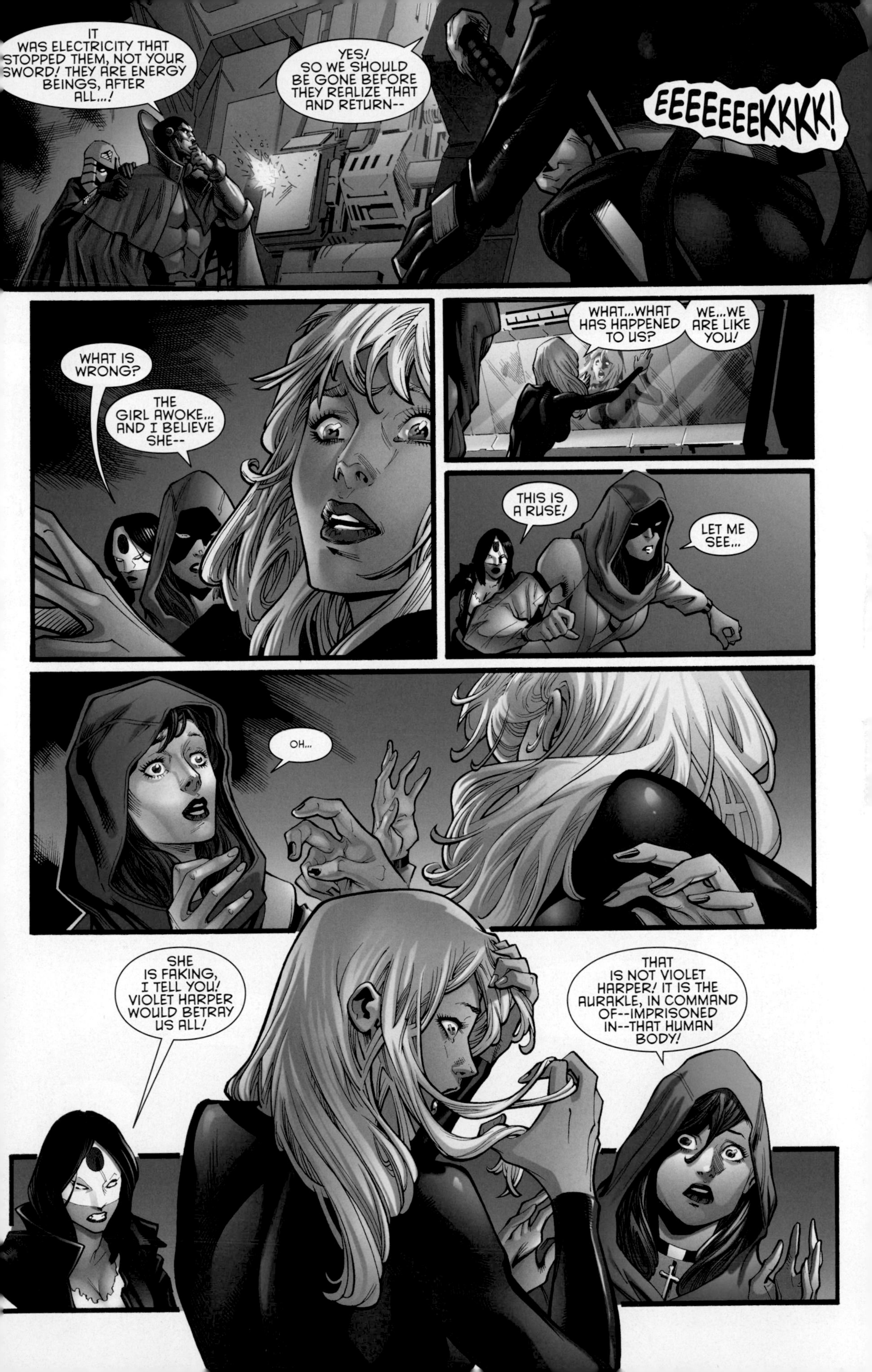
IT WAS ELECTRICITY THAT STOPPED THEM, NOT YOUR SWORD! THEY ARE ENERGY BEINGS, AFTER ALL...!
YES! SO WE SHOULD BE GONE BEFORE THEY REALIZE THAT AND RETURN--
EEEEEEEKKKK!
WHAT IS WRONG?
THE GIRL AWOKE... AND I BELIEVE SHE--
WHAT...WHAT HAS HAPPENED TO US?
WE...WE ARE LIKE YOU!
THIS IS A RUSE!
LET ME SEE...
OH...
SHE IS FAKING, I TELL YOU! VIOLET HARPER WOULD BETRAY US ALL!
THAT IS NOT VIOLET HARPER! IT IS THE AURAKLE, IN COMMAND OF--IMPRISONED IN--THAT HUMAN BODY!

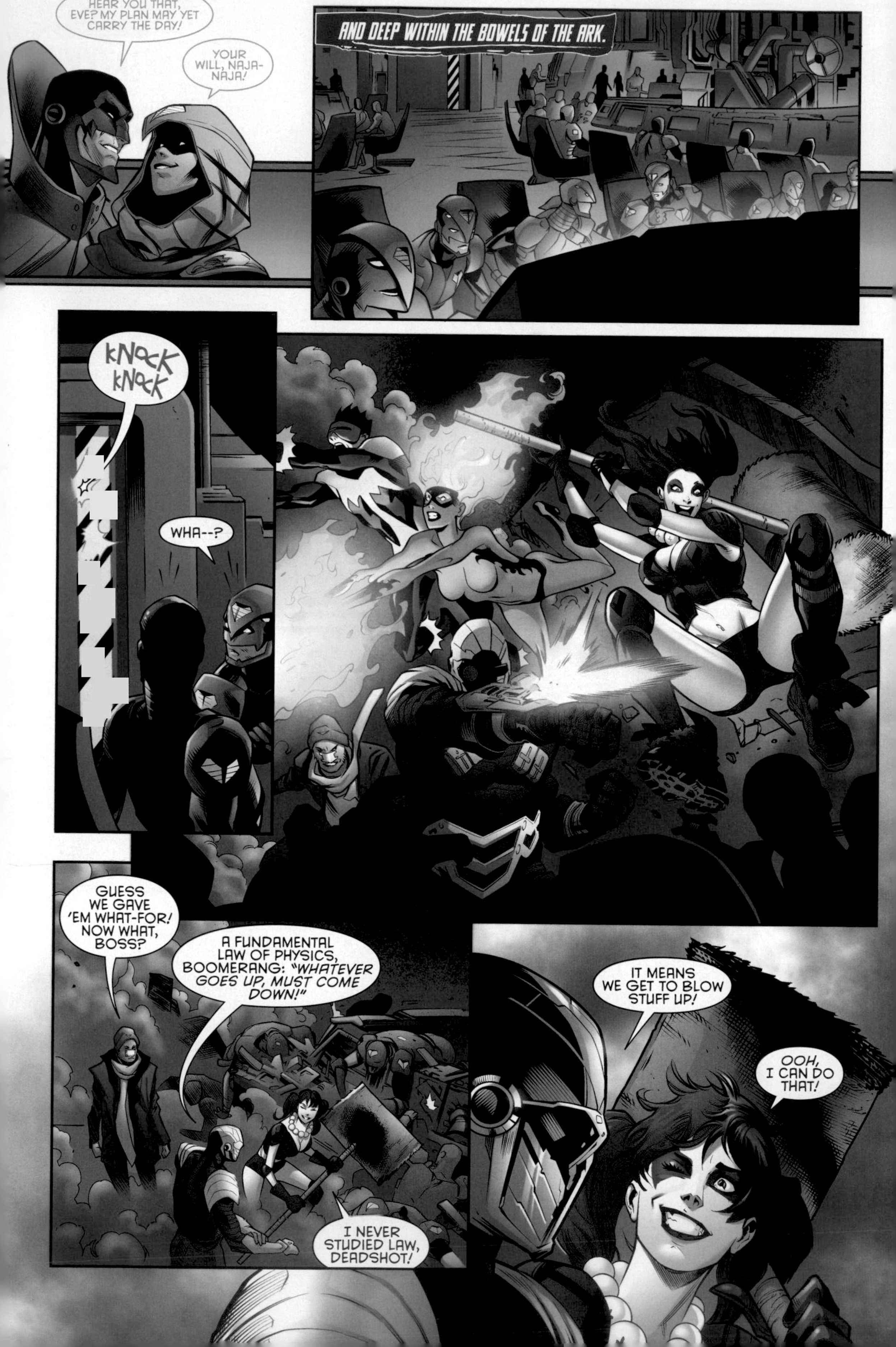
HEAR YOU THAT, EVE? MY PLAN MAY YET CARRY THE DAY!
YOUR WILL, NAJA-NAJA!
AND DEEP WITHIN THE BOWELS OF THE ARK.
KNOCK KNOCK
WHA--?
GUESS WE GAVE 'EM WHAT-FOR! NOW WHAT, BOSS?
A FUNDAMENTAL LAW OF PHYSICS, BOOMERANG: "WHATEVER GOES UP, MUST COME DOWN!"
I NEVER STUDIED LAW, DEADSHOT!
IT MEANS WE GET TO BLOW STUFF UP!
OOH, I CAN DO THAT!

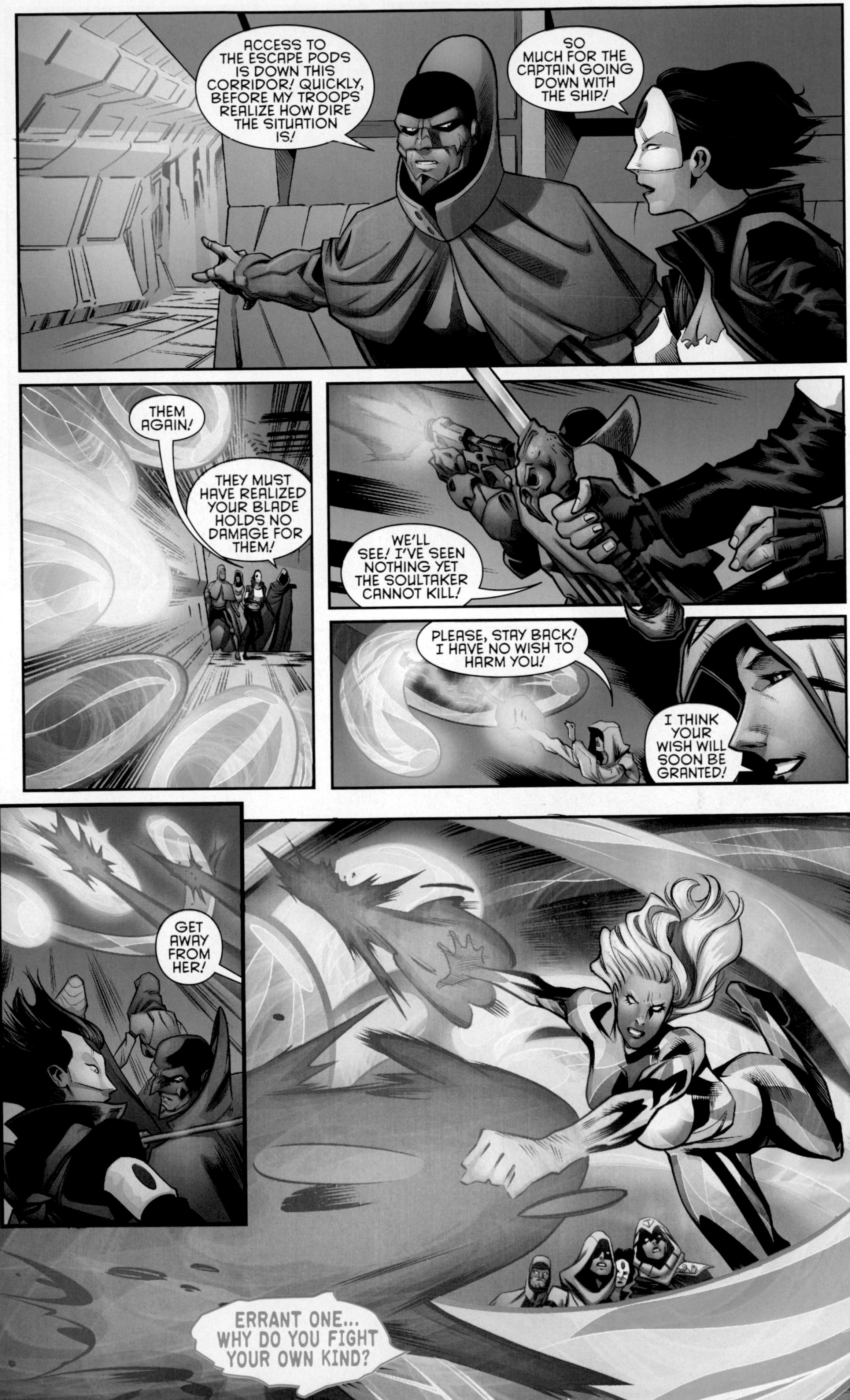
ACCESS TO THE ESCAPE PODS IS DOWN THIS CORRIDOR! QUICKLY, BEFORE MY TROOPS REALIZE HOW DIRE THE SITUATION IS!
SO MUCH FOR THE CAPTAIN GOING DOWN WITH THE SHIP!
THEM AGAIN!
THEY MUST HAVE REALIZED YOUR BLADE HOLDS NO DAMAGE FOR THEM!
WE'LL SEE! I'VE SEEN NOTHING YET THE SOULTAKER CANNOT KILL!
PLEASE, STAY BACK! I HAVE NO WISH TO HARM YOU!
I THINK YOUR WISH WILL SOON BE GRANTED!
GET AWAY FROM HER!
ERRANT ONE... WHY DO YOU FIGHT YOUR OWN KIND?

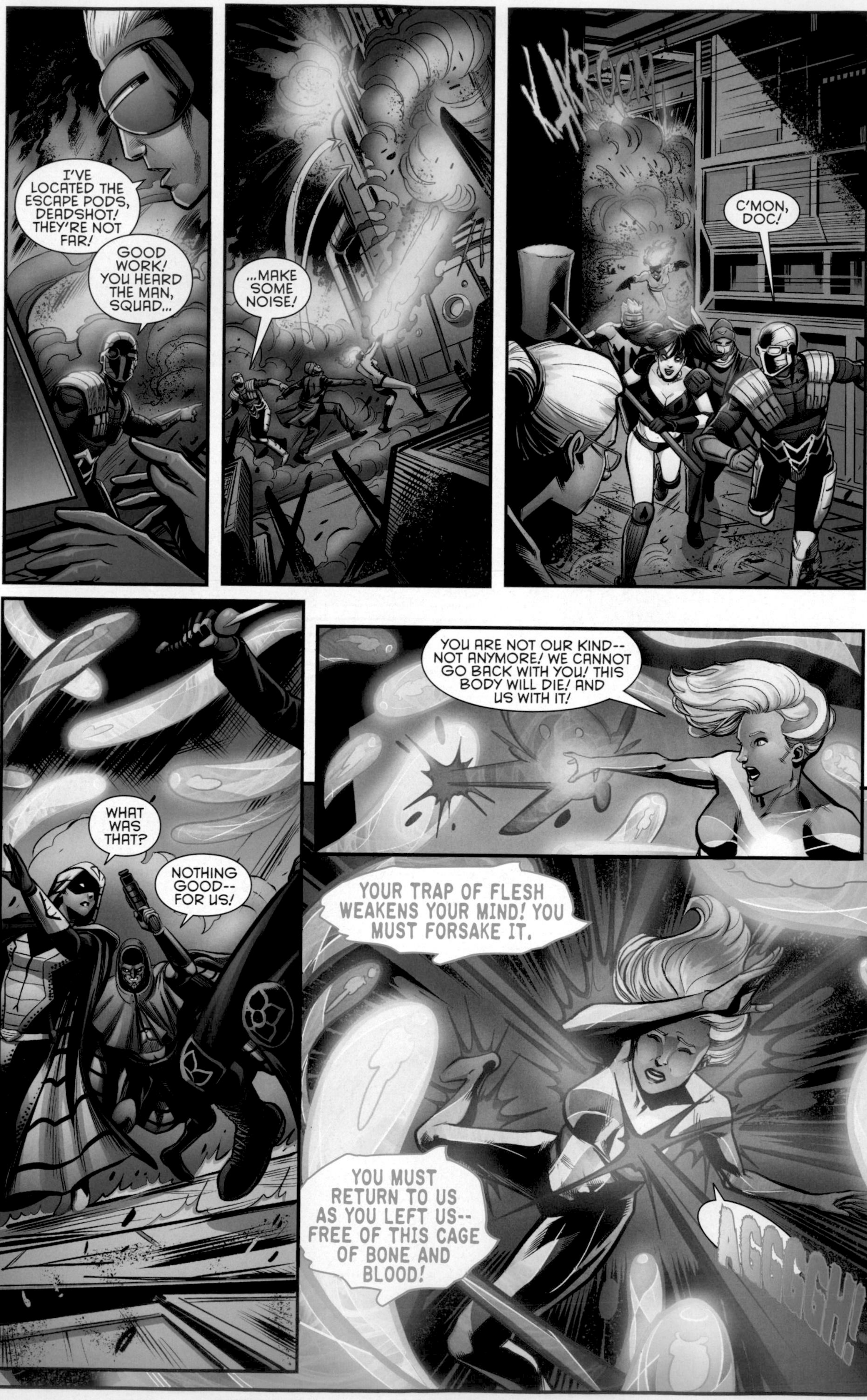
I'VE LOCATED THE ESCAPE PODS, DEADSHOT! THEY'RE NOT FAR!
GOOD WORK! YOU HEARD THE MAN, SQUAD...
...MAKE SOME NOISE!
KA-KROOM
C'MON, DOC!
YOU ARE NOT OUR KIND-- NOT ANYMORE! WE CANNOT GO BACK WITH YOU! THIS BODY WILL DIE! AND US WITH IT!
WHAT WAS THAT?
NOTHING GOOD-- FOR US!
YOUR TRAP OF FLESH WEAKENS YOUR MIND! YOU MUST FORSAKE IT.
YOU MUST RETURN TO US AS YOU LEFT US-- FREE OF THIS CAGE OF BONE AND BLOOD!
AGGGH!

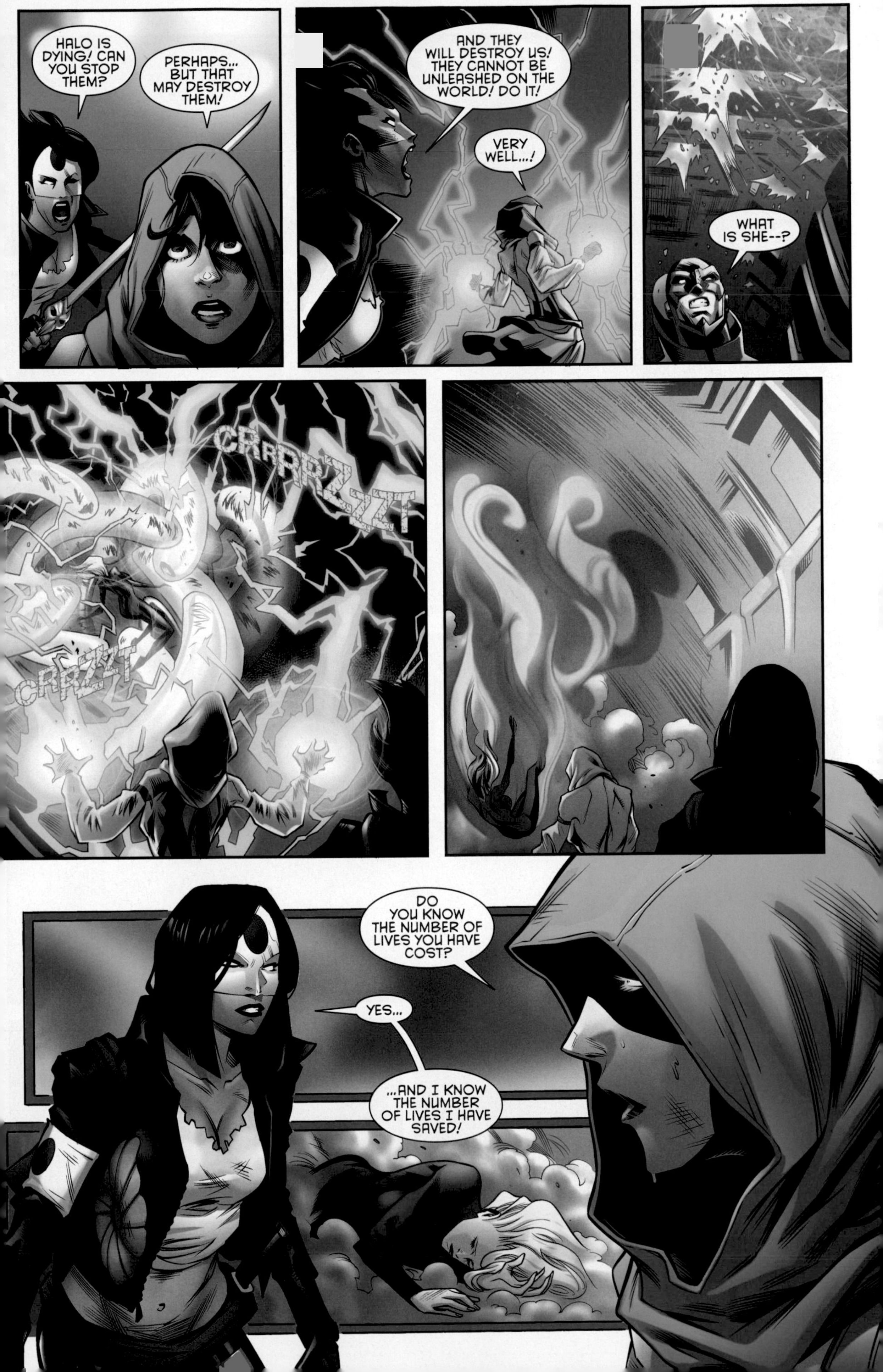
HALO IS DYING! CAN YOU STOP THEM?
PERHAPS... BUT THAT MAY DESTROY THEM!
AND THEY WILL DESTROY US! THEY CANNOT BE UNLEASHED ON THE WORLD! DO IT!
VERY WELL...!
WHAT IS SHE--?
CRRRRZZZT
CRRZZZT
DO YOU KNOW THE NUMBER OF LIVES YOU HAVE COST?
YES...
...AND I KNOW THE NUMBER OF LIVES I HAVE SAVED!

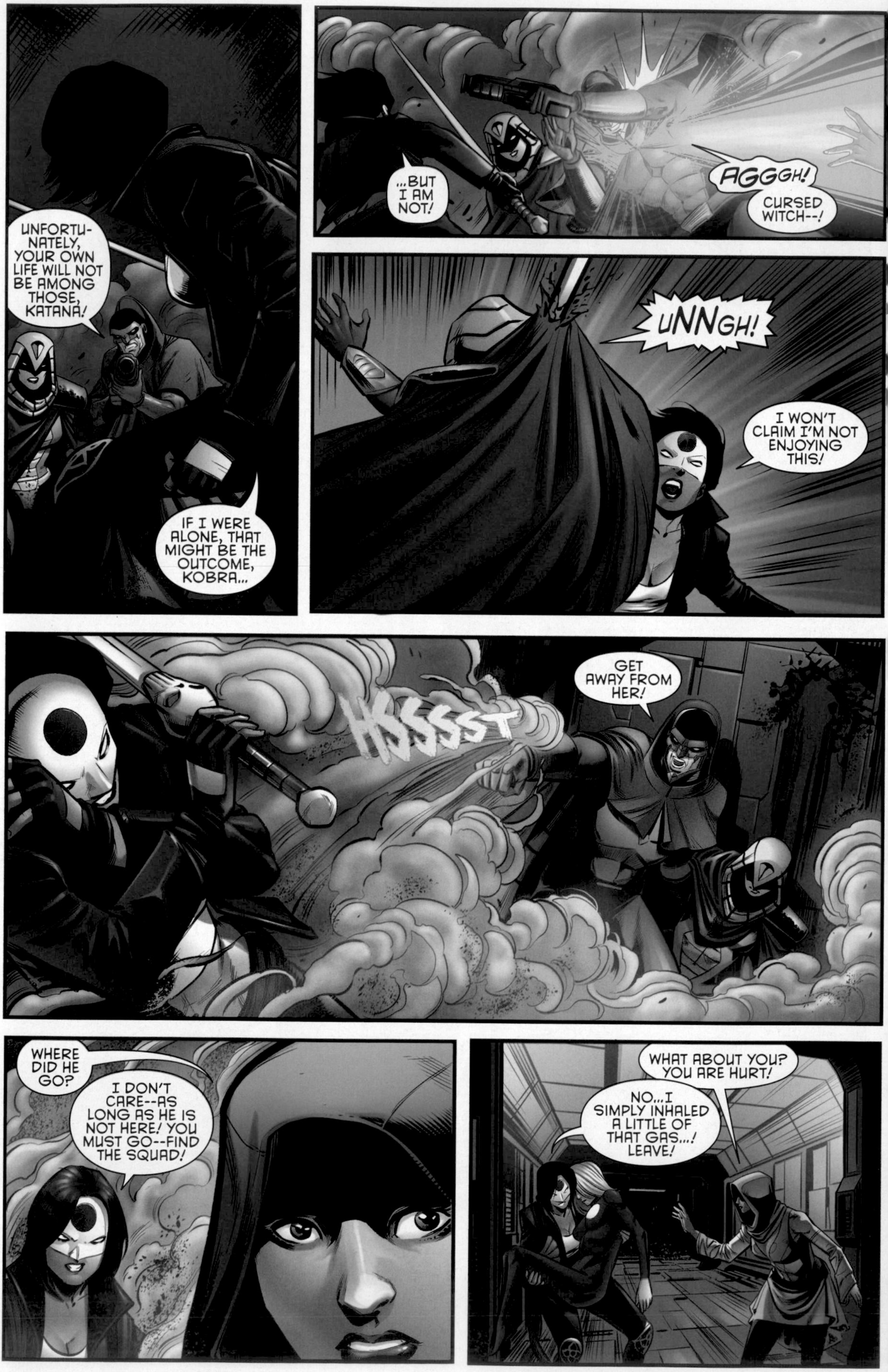
UNFORTU-NATELY, YOUR OWN LIFE WILL NOT BE AMONG THOSE, KATANA!
IF I WERE ALONE, THAT MIGHT BE THE OUTCOME, KOBRA...
...BUT I AM NOT!
AGGGH!
CURSED WITCH--!
UNNGH!
I WON'T CLAIM I'M NOT ENJOYING THIS!
GET AWAY FROM HER!
HSSSST
WHERE DID HE GO?
I DON'T CARE--AS LONG AS HE IS NOT HERE! YOU MUST GO--FIND THE SQUAD!
WHAT ABOUT YOU? YOU ARE HURT!
NO...I SIMPLY INHALED A LITTLE OF THAT GAS...! LEAVE!

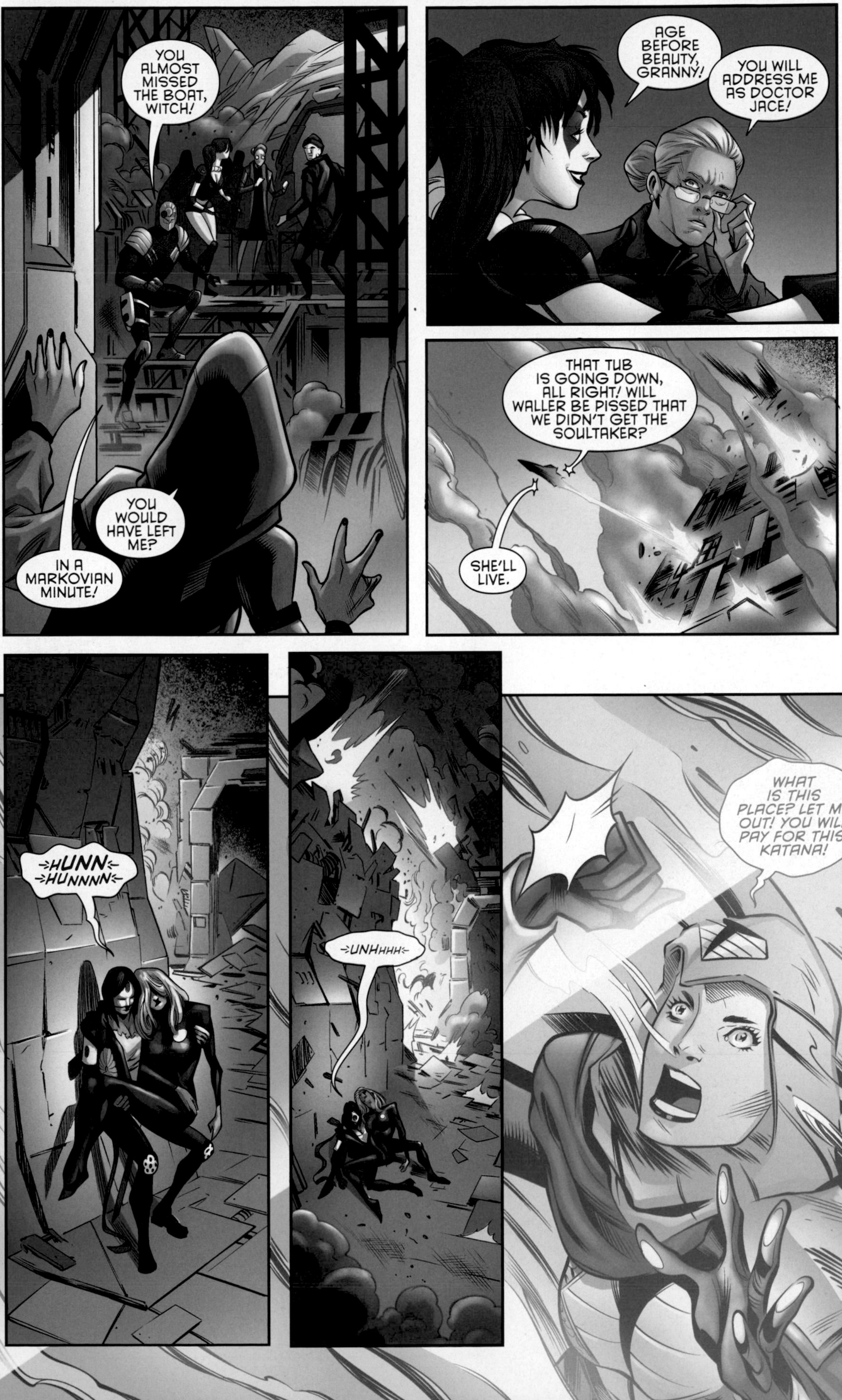
YOU ALMOST MISSED THE BOAT, WITCH!
YOU WOULD HAVE LEFT ME?
IN A MARKOVIAN MINUTE!
AGE BEFORE BEAUTY, GRANNY!
YOU WILL ADDRESS ME AS DOCTOR JACE!
THAT TUB IS GOING DOWN, ALL RIGHT! WILL WALLER BE PISSED THAT WE DIDN'T GET THE SOULTAKER?
SHE'LL LIVE.
HUNN HUNNNN
UNHHHH
WHAT IS THIS PLACE? LET ME OUT! YOU WILL PAY FOR THIS, KATANA!

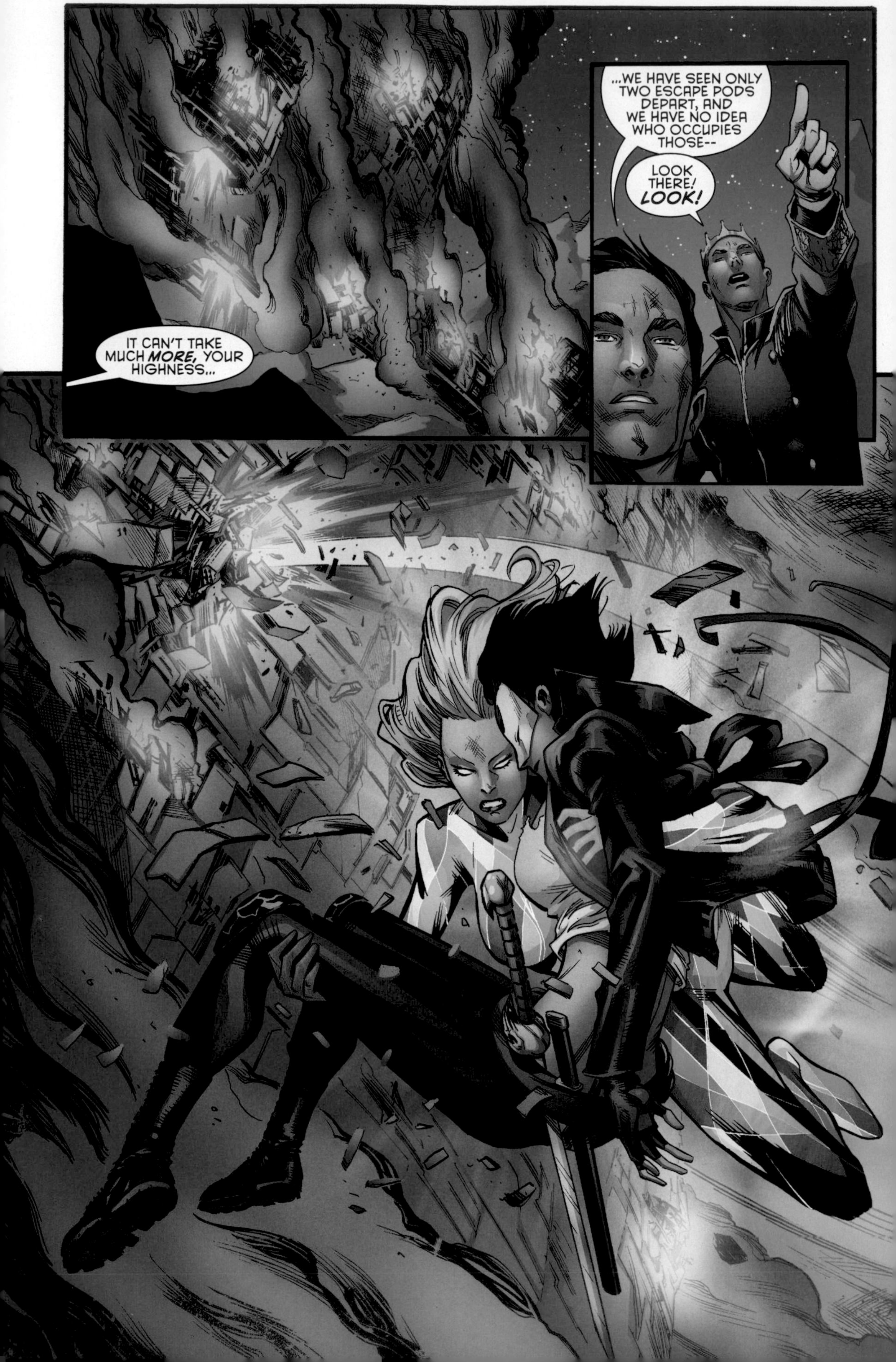
IT CAN'T TAKE MUCH MORE, YOUR HIGHNESS...
...WE HAVE SEEN ONLY TWO ESCAPE PODS DEPART, AND WE HAVE NO IDEA WHO OCCUPIES THOSE--
LOOK THERE! LOOK!

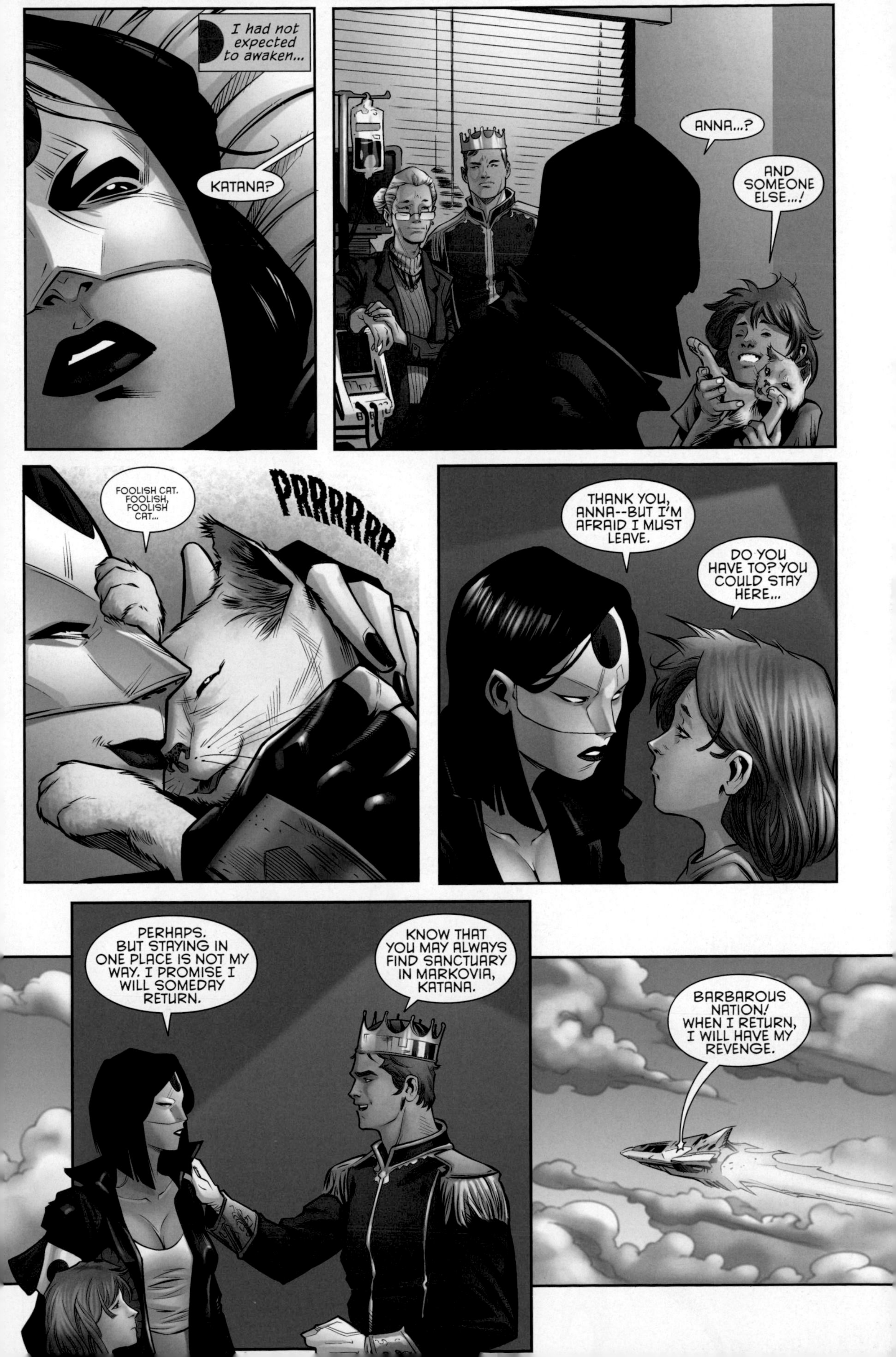
I had not expected to awaken...
KATANA?
ANNA...?
AND SOMEONE ELSE...!
FOOLISH CAT. FOOLISH, FOOLISH CAT...
PRRRRRRR
THANK YOU, ANNA--BUT I'M AFRAID I MUST LEAVE.
DO YOU HAVE TO? YOU COULD STAY HERE...
PERHAPS. BUT STAYING IN ONE PLACE IS NOT MY WAY. I PROMISE I WILL SOMEDAY RETURN.
KNOW THAT YOU MAY ALWAYS FIND SANCTUARY IN MARKOVIA, KATANA.
BARBAROUS NATION! WHEN I RETURN, I WILL HAVE MY REVENGE.

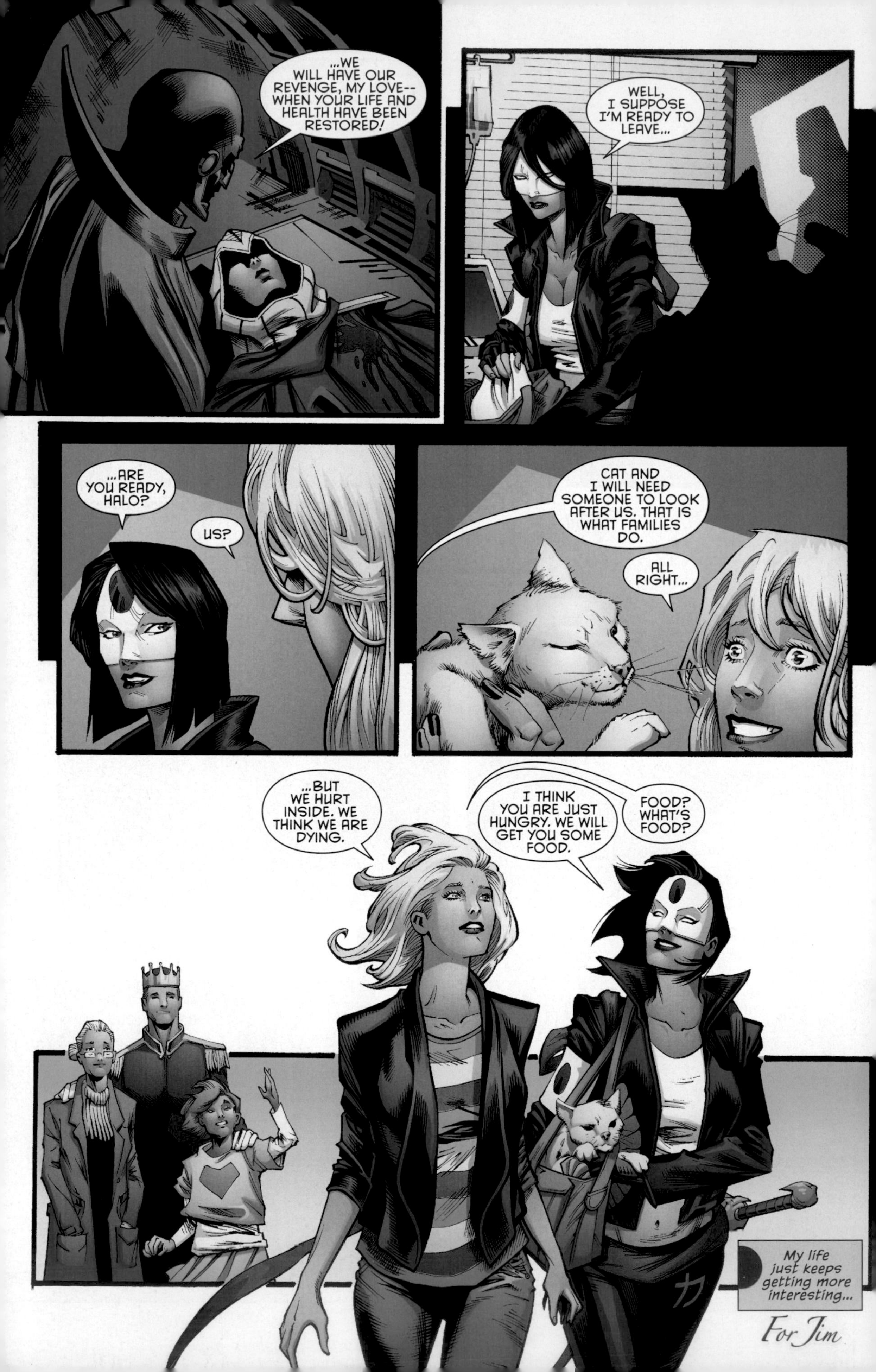
...WE WILL HAVE OUR REVENGE, MY LOVE-- WHEN YOUR LIFE AND HEALTH HAVE BEEN RESTORED!
WELL, I SUPPOSE I'M READY TO LEAVE...
...ARE YOU READY, HALO?
US?
CAT AND I WILL NEED SOMEONE TO LOOK AFTER US. THAT IS WHAT FAMILIES DO.
ALL RIGHT...
...BUT WE HURT INSIDE. WE THINK WE ARE DYING.
I THINK YOU ARE JUST HUNGRY. WE WILL GET YOU SOME FOOD.
FOOD? WHAT'S FOOD?
My life just keeps getting more interesting...
For Jim

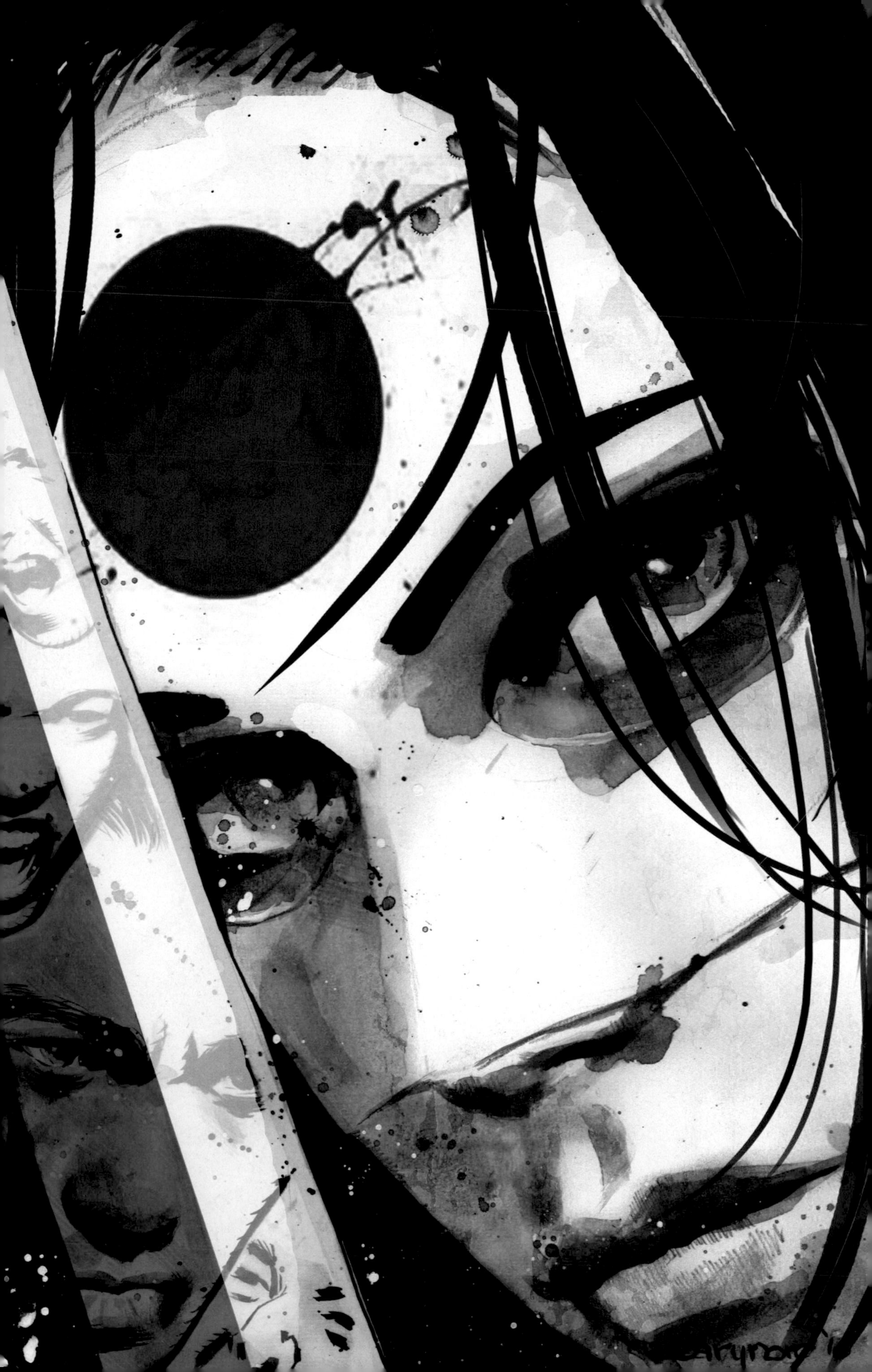

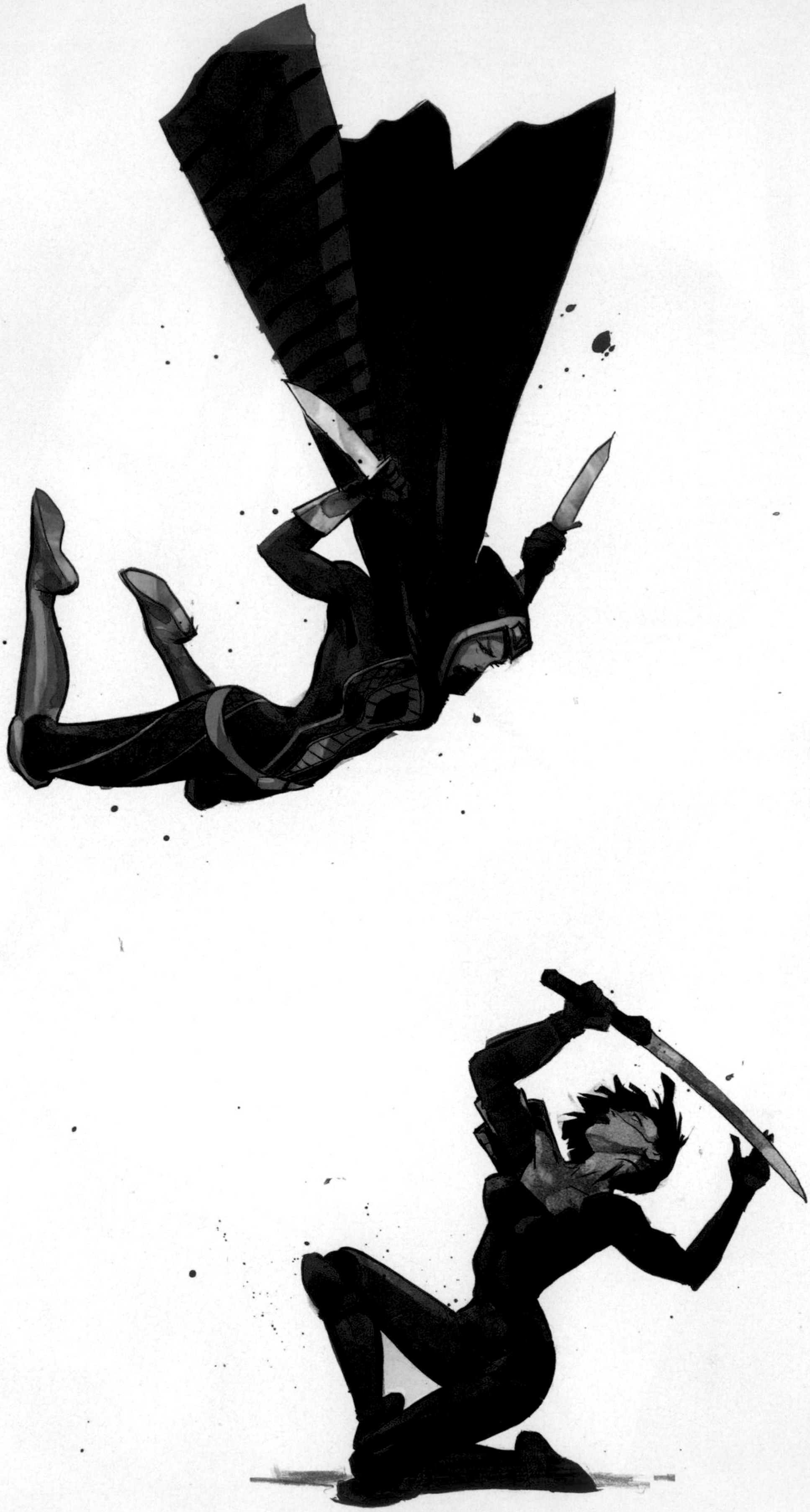
carynord

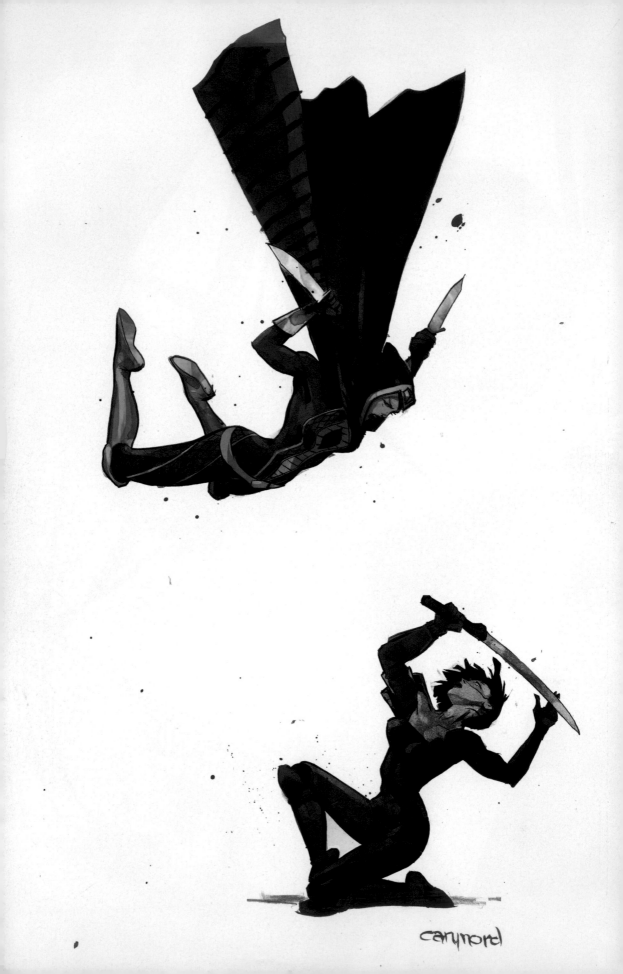

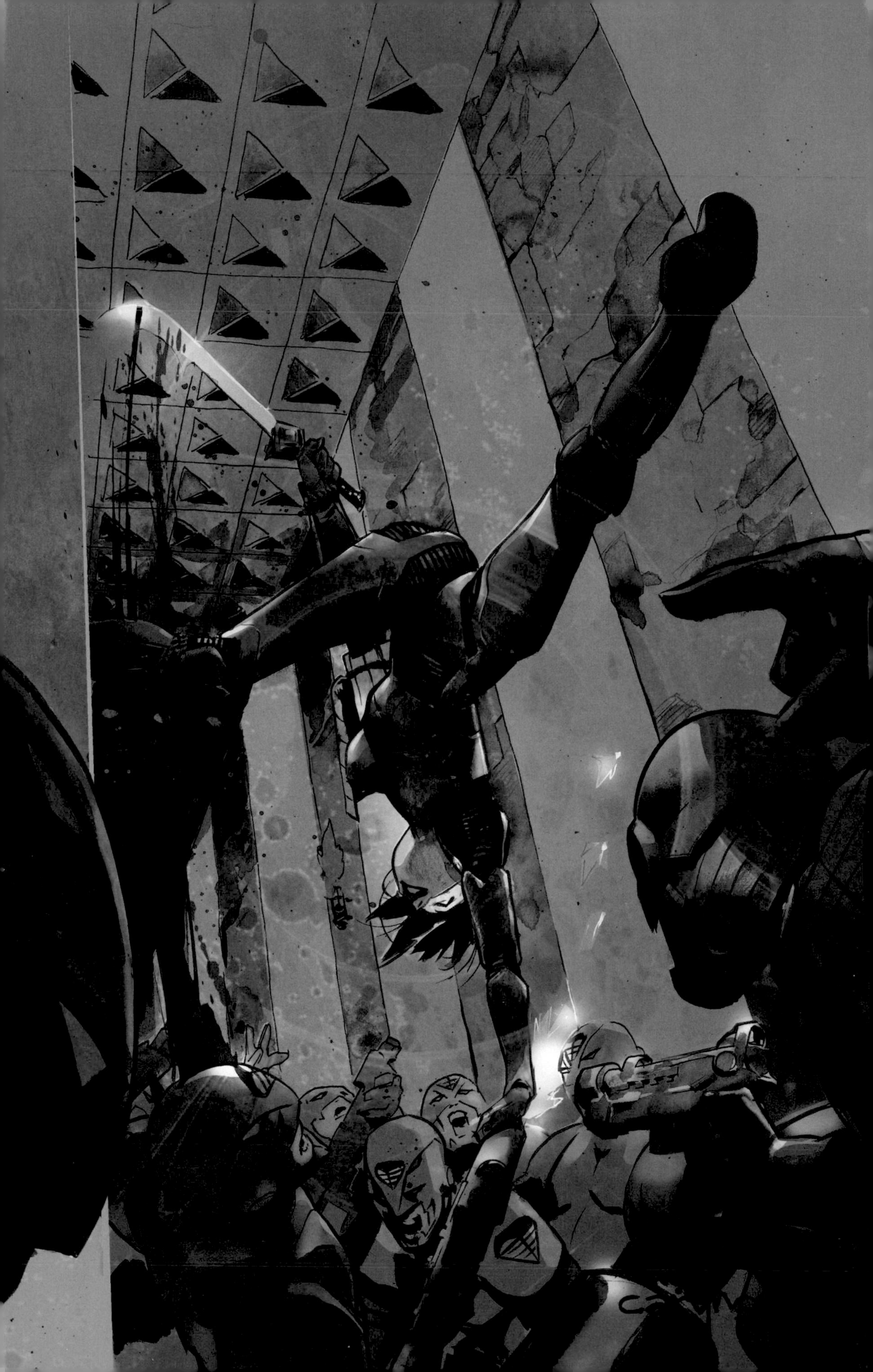

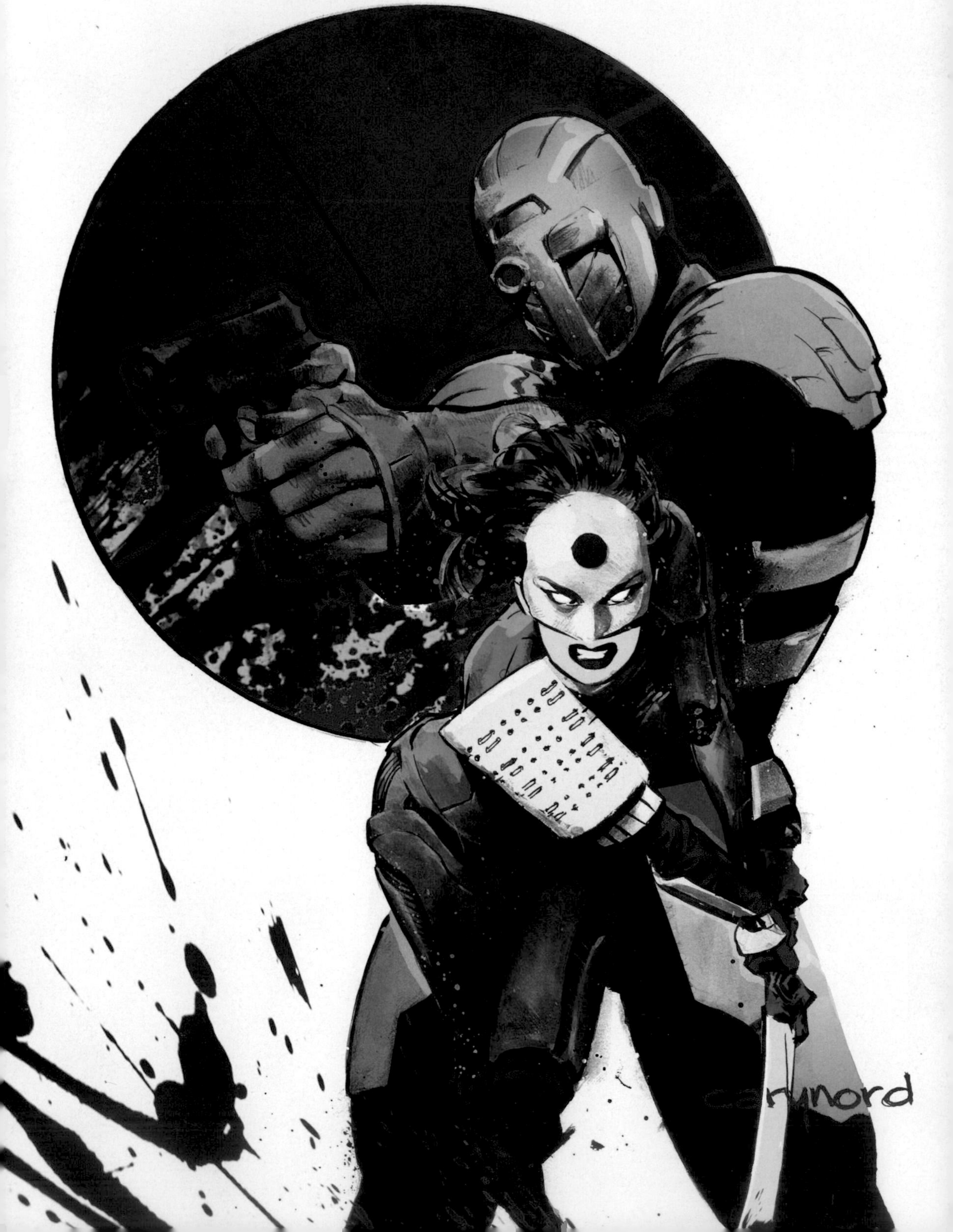